THE GOODNESS OF GOD

Peter A. Bertocci

PREFACE

THE GOODNESS OF GOD

In this book the attempt is to understand what
it means to call God good. Whether or not God exists,
there is both significance and justification, I believe, in the life good to live for all persons.
The life good to live guides us to belief in God,
and it takes on even more meaning by virtue of the
relation discovered between man and God. I am
mindful that for great believers and unbelievers
throughout history, and in the present, such a contention is untenable. Both have said so much that
is worth saying; the argument of this book will
assess especially important aspects of their spirit
and insights.

My first concern, however, is not to bring about
a meeting of minds between sincere humanists and
earnest religious thinkers, much as that is to be
desired in a world where, generally speaking, the
lines between high-minded naturalists and great-
spirited supernaturalists seem to be easier to draw.
My first concern is to understand the nature of persons, the roots in them and in their ambient for "the
things that matter most," and to draw reasonable consequences of this exploration for belief in God and
His goodness.

Readers who wish logical proof only may not wish
to read further. I proceed, as I think we all actually do in our daily reasoning, by what Bishop Butler
called the nonstatistical "probability" that is "the
guide of life." In a later context I shall call this
approach "reason grown courageous," but not until we
are clear about what is involved in the search for
truth and the warrant for our claims to truth.

Even in a slender volume on the relation of the
human good to the meaning of God in human experience,
we must begin by probing, in minimal terms at least,
the relation of man to the physical and the biological order. What it means to be a person--this issue

is as controversial as it is critical for understanding
what the nature and scope of man's central values are,
and what it means to affirm or deny that God is a
person.

My intent is to be as untechnical as I can as
I lay the groundwork in chapter after chapter for the
conclusions about persons, values, Nature, and God
that are most reasonably warranted. I shall forgo
ethical, theological, and metaphysical polemics, but
I shall be conscious of the invisible audience of
acute thinkers whose writings have been part of the
ongoing debate within myself. Yet, I am hopeful that
the serious reader will be kept abreast of the decisions I am laying before him as the evidence for
them is set forth and placed in increasingly larger
context.

At this point, however, I owe my reader a glimpse
of what animates this work. In the last forty years,
the "inner circle" of persons who have made "the"
difference to my life has been a variety of staunch
and undaunted religious believers and unbelievers.
They were all deeply devoted to the good for man, and
would argue that where a man's heart is, there will
his treasure be. However, it became increasingly
apparent to me that what they thought about man and
the good was reflected in, if not largely determined
by, what they thought about God and how "His will"
and goodness could be known. But it also became
clear that the values persons live by are paramount--
even if conscientious objectors often forget that
there are conscientious believers! Of course, many
believers are convinced that persons will not find
the inspiration and power to realize "the saving
good" without God. They thus deny their opponents'
faith in what human beings can do for human beings,
especially if they will turn all of their efforts to
creating a society that will save persons by fully
"humanizing" them.

Nevertheless, for reasons similar and dissimilar,
both believers and unbelievers often converge in
enough of their convictions about the good that they
work out social and political compromises even while

engaged in a tepid or cold war. At the same time,
purposeful cruelty and war take over when both
believers and unbelievers are convinced that they
alone know the truth and go on, in the name of
Humanity or God, to censor freedom of speech and
worship, and to so weaken the opposition that it
cannot go on poisoning the value-atmosphere by
which men live. Clearly, some minimal conception
of <u>the good for persons in this world</u> guides conscientious believers and unbelievers of every class
and creed. But, underlying this whole situation,
it seems increasingly clear to me, a philosophy of
the person undergirds much of the conception of the
good and of the strategies for its realization.

However, a curious fact seems to accompany the
controversy between believer and unbeliever as to
whether central human values are rooted in God.
This fact has become more apparent in the last fifty
years. Both believers and unbelievers seem to be
agreed that <u>only a certain kind of God is worthy of
worship</u>. As we shall see, what has so often controlled
the argument on both sides is the notion that only
(a certain view of) perfection can be affirmed of God.
In this book I shall set out the groundwork for a
related but different conception of what perfection
is, and for a conception of God the nature of whose
creativity calls forth worship even though a certain
"tragic" quality inheres in it.

I shall argue that while God is the self-sufficient Ground of all there is, His nature and His
attributes, insofar as we can define them, stand to
be related to the evidence available to us in the
history of Nature, living organisms, and persons.
Among other telling consequences of this approach is
the determination to resist being halted in our
tracks the moment it seems likely that God and His
attributes do not conform to the "received" conception of perfection. Permeating my argument is
the conviction that, in the name of some imperi-
al(istic) highway to God or to Truth, we have wit-
tingly and unwittingly subjected the interpretation
of our data (or what should even be allowed as data)

to a preconceived notion of what God, or Perfection, should be.

I shall attempt to show that experiential data--including religious experience--can be brought into an open-ended, systematic view that is a more adequate alternative than that of traditional theism and of humanistic naturalism. If, as I contend, these data adequately indicate that the good involves blessedness (not "happiness"), that I shall call "creative insecurity," then there is no good ground for being daunted by the classical contention of Perfection. Far from finding an unchanging One or Mind complete in every respect, I arrive at a Creator-Person whose continuing creativity is reasonably inferred from the history of the world, including man and the values that sustain his creativity at its best. The human pilgrimage is not, as a whole, reasonably intelligible in a nonhuman Realm indifferent and impervious to human existence and ideals. The grounds for this conclusion are set forth as I try to weave the relevant data into what I shall call the cosmo-teleological-ethical argument for God.

I submit that it is the relentless care of the Creator-Person Who, unflinchingly facing resistance with His own being, creates and participates in the risky co-creativity of persons in every dimension of their lives--it is this kind of Creator-Person Who brings us to our knees in awesome reverence.

Bibliographical references do not begin to express my indebtedness to many contemporaries, especially in the areas of metaphysics, theology, ethics, and psychology. But I would be proud if the spirit particularly of my first teacher and then colleague, Edgar S. Brightman, is evident in these pages, along with that of A. N. Whitehead, Frederick R. Tennant, W. R. Sorley, Brand Blanshard, Edwin A. Burtt, H. D. Lewis, and Gordon W. Allport. The invitation of Professor Andrew Reck to give three lectures on this topic at Tulane in 1976, under the auspices of the Matchette Foundation, is gladly acknowledged. But the conspicuous and friendly

generosity and cooperation of my colleagues at Boston
University, and of the Graduate School in Boston
University, leave me with a constant, grateful warmth.
To all this must be added the appreciation for varied
services given so cheerfully by Mrs. Paul (Judith)
Wilkis, Mrs. Robert (Angela) Trotta, Professor and
Mrs. Galen Johnson, Miss Marla Baron, The Reverend
Ronald Carter, and Mrs. Arthur (Ruth) Morrison.
There are few ideas in this and in other writings
that have not been improved in conception and ex-
pression by my brother, Angelo P. Bertocci, Professor
of English and Comparative English, Emeritus, Iowa
University. And my wife, family, and the students
who have been so much of my life over the years
have entered into dimensions of "creative insecurity"
that make for blessedness.

Peter A. Bertocci
Borden Parker Bowne
Professor of Philosophy,
Emeritus

Boston University, 1981

TABLE OF CONTENTS

ix

xii

Chapter One

KNOWING NATURE AND KNOWING GOD

1. Belief in God Is Belief in God's Goodness

(a) "God is good. If God is not good, he is not
God." So believers in God affirm. Unfortunately,
however, believers do not agree on the meaning of
'good.' Hence, they do not, in fact, believe in the
same God. In contrast, disbelievers in God justify
their disbelief by pointing to evils that, in their
view, show that God is not good. But disbelievers
also do not agree on the meaning of goodness. The
'God' they disbelieve in is for them also different.
What must come first, then, as basic to both belief
and disbelief, is a consideration of issues relating
to the nature of goodness. To such issues I shall
devote this book. But they involve the nature of
truth, of man in relation to Nature, and finally a
full discussion of the quality of goodness that can
be attributed to (a certain kind of) God. For, in
actuality, the question is never: Do I believe in
God; but, in what kind of God do I believe (or
disbelieve)?

(b) I hear believers protest that I have separated what cannot be separated in their experience.
"Our experience of God is our experience of God's
goodness--whatever else! To be sure, we believers,
like disbelievers, go about our business of living
with each other and with other living creatures in
Nature, but, owing to our experience with the
Divine, we see each other and everything in the
world within the perspective of divine Goodness.
Hence, what we consider good in our interaction
with other beings in this world is never our
complete estimate of what goodness really is."

In the history of the human quest for goodness and truth, this testimony is expressed in
myriad ways by the schooled and the unschooled.
Their belief in God's goodness ultimately springs,

1

they insist, from a non-sensory, awesome awareness of God, an awareness as "direct" as is their awareness of stones, starfish, and stars. Once they are aware of God's presence, they see everything in their lives in the context of that supremely magnetizing Goodness. The import of this claim we shall have to keep in mind to the last page of the book.

(c) Most persons, for all of their occasional doubts and hesitations about this or that experience of the world, cannot disbelieve that the external world is there to be known; nor can they disbelieve that they themselves are fit to know it and respond to it with a modicum of success. Similarly, believers in God, for all their occasional doubts, persist that there is a good God who is there, affecting their lives in more ways than they know, and capable of affecting them even more if they will prepare themselves for more thoroughgoing response to Him. Accordingly, most believers in the "natural Environment" and most believers in the "divine Environment" are willing to leave niceties about the nature of their awareness of their Environments to specialized scholars in the theory of natural and religious knowledge. But all detailed precision of theory, they both insist, must not obscure the central fact: at root, knowledge of natural, human, and divine Environment is grounded in direct awareness.

Our first order of business, then, is to examine this claim that religious knowledge and natural knowledge consist in direct awareness. I shall restrict myself to considerations essential to our thinking about persons, Nature, and God. Since believers and disbelievers, whatever their final view of Nature, agree that a realm common to them exists independently of their own existence and knowledge, I shall begin by examining the claim that persons know Nature directly.

Unless the context indicates otherwise, by "natural world" and "Nature" I shall refer to all that exists in space and time, usually referred to

2

as the physical world and the subhuman biological realms. For reasons to be given later, I do not include persons fully in Nature in this sense.

2. Do We Know the Natural World Directly?

(a) As I write these lines I hear a series of rings. "That's my telephone," I say, and I hasten to another room to answer it. There is no doubt in my mind that I hear that ringing, or that my telephone is ringing. However, I cannot be wrong about the ringing as I may be wrong about "my telephone" ringing. Indeed, if I do not hear ringing, there is nothing to be wrong or right about. So I distinguish between the ringings as given (data) and "my telephone" as my interpretation (that is, the data as taken by me), that may be mistaken.

This distinction between given and taken is vital to any view of knowing. "My telephone" that I was sure was ringing there turns out to be, say, ringings I cannot deny, given in a way that my 'immediate' taking or interpretation is not. Even if it had turned out that the ringings were an hallucination, I still could not deny them as experienced. Human knowledge of the telephone "begins" with experiencing data, always directly and immediately. But to know what is ringing, we bring to aid other factors that, taken together, support our belief that the telephone is ringing, and that both the ringing and the telephone are ringing there, whether we are aware of it or not.

On this account of the human knowledge-situation, no matter how direct and immediate knowing of x may seem, we must at least be on guard about claims to direct or immediate knowledge of x. Acute scholars have so warned, but still argued, that if we are to claim knowledge of x we must, in some way in knowing, be one with x. I think there is no adequate explaining of error on such views. So, with an exception to be discussed later, I shall

distinguish 'immediately,' 'directly,' <u>exper-
iencing</u> an "object" and 'mediately,' 'inferentially,'
<u>knowing</u> an "object."

Hence, I say, I know <u>what</u> is ringing mediately,
that is by inference from immediate experiences supported by other relevant considerations. I did not
allow, when I heard "telephone ringing," that "telephone" was my interpretation for, or explanation of,
certain, undeniable patterns of sound-data. Usually,
when I hear that pattern and quality of ringing, I
assume that my telephone is ringing;I am surprised
when I discover it is not the telephone--it is
(perhaps) the doorbell. If I were now to describe
the knowing, I would say,"It is more likely that my
telephone is ringing, given these sounds, than that
the doorbell is ringing." And I invariably hold to
this interpretation until I have grounds for changing
it.

To generalize, when I say I know <u>what</u> is <u>there</u>,
independent of my experiencing, I should correct myself. Hence, I do not literally know my natural
environment, if 'know' means know it directly or
immediately. I know it indirectly on the basis of
other experiences--in this instance, I go to the
telephone, pick up the receiver and if I hear the
telephone-voice of a friend that "settles" the truth
of my interpretation.

Even in this over-simplified rendering of an
example of natural knowledge, caution demands our
making note of two poles. For we move from the
"initial" pole of "ringing" (in which there is a
minimal interpretation), to the "terminal" pole
(that is, the telephone-voice of a friend, in which
there is much more to confirm the interpretation we
'immediately' gave). In short, we, in selecting the
ringing-data from all the rest of what we were experiencing, were involved in interpreting <u>these</u>
sensory, successive data.

(b) We must not assume that without further inquiry
this analysis of sense-initiated knowledge applies

to non-sensory dimensions of experience, such as the moral and the religious. But since this view of the human knowing-situation, for all of my simplifying it, basically applies to the natural environment that we (presumably) know initially by way of sensory experience, I shall state this view more formally so that we can later see whether this way of knowing can be extended to knowledge-claims in the spheres of moral and religious experience.

First, when we say we are experiencing x, we are stressing what we are (in some degree) consciously undergoing rather than consciously inferring. 'Experience' is a weasel word whose meaning in any thinker needs scrutiny lest an unwittingly assumed meaning settles what actually needs further discussion in the context. If, so far, I seem to have been stressing the interpretive aspect of our "experiencing object," it has been to prepare the ground for my present statement. When I talk about experiencing whatever it is that is being experienced, I wish to minimize the (indirect) inferential and interpretive aspect of my knowing-situation and to maximize the fact that I am undergoing "something" (directly). In any case, as I see it, we cannot expunge from the word "experience" either the direct 'undergoing' aspect, or the indirect 'knowing' aspect (inference and interpretation).

Second, despite our rough and ready usage, it is less misleading to say that we do not (directly) know any object in the natural world of which our initial experience has come through the senses. The fact that we say (when we hear "the telephone ringing"), "I couldn't help believing that it was the telephone," and then come to find out that it was the doorbell-- this constant possibility of error needs special noting.

It will be necessary, therefore, to bear in mind the distinctions between psychological certitude, logical certainty, and epistemic reliability. We usually live by our psychological certitudes, that is, convictions that x is so and so ("the telephone is ringing"), on the assumption that further ex-

perience and inference will not dislodge this conviction. Practically necessary as these psychological certitudes are--and, fortunately, we can depend
on most of them--they cannot be assumed to be logically certain and epistemically reliable. Again, in
terms of our illustration, I cannot affirm a particular conclusion about "what is there" simply because
I am undergoing x and experience the psychological
certitude, "x is the telephone ringing." It may in
fact turn out to be so, but I cannot assume that what
I experience as there is either logically certain or
epistemically reliable.

A word about logical certainty is in order. If
I say "A is larger than B, B is larger than C," then,
assuming that the meaning of the terms does not change,
I must conclude that A is larger than C. This logical
conclusion is certain in the same sense that only this
conclusion can be drawn by anybody who knows what all
the terms mean. So we say that the conclusion, A is
larger than C, is logically necessary (or logically
valid, or logically certain), because it is implied
by these premises.

I wish I could do more than give examples to
explain to my reader what I mean by 'logically necessary,' 'logically valid,' or 'logically implied,'
but I can no more do that than I can explain what
I mean by the sound of ringing. I shall have to leave
it to my reader to inspect what takes place in him
when he undergoes ringing-sound and when he undergoes
logical (or consistent) thinking. Only in that way
can he become aware of the difference between sense-
experience and thinking-experience.

(c) Let us reconsider our progress regarding "what's
there" in the light of these two distinctions. From
our hearing the ringing-sound with psychological
certitude, there is no logical certainty that the
telephone is ringing. At the same time, from any
sheer logical certainty, such as the conclusion that
A is larger than C, I cannot infer what A or B or C
is, or may be, in terms of specifiable experience.
To take the next step, when we speak of 'knowing
directly,' we must bear in mind that we may be

6

fusing (conflating) 'experiencing x' and being
logically certain' that what is experienced exists
independently of our experience.

If experiencing x does not logically imply
knowing what it is, then what can be our rock-
bottom affirmation about the natural object (telephone) we 'know'? No more than this: on hearing
certain ringing-sounds, we can affirm, on the basis
of them and other considerations, that it is more
likely, more probable, that it is the telephone that
is ringing than that the doorbell is ringing, or
that there is a "ringing in our ears." We thus attain
to epistemic reliability, which presupposes that we
have not made mistakes in logical inferemce and have
"sufficient" supporting evidence. Nevertheless, our
epistemic reliability that the telephone is ringing
is not logical certainty, even though we are "on all
sides" justified in believing that the telephone,
there, is ringing.

I draw the conclusion that is critical for all
of our future discussion. We must realize that the
psychological certitudes we live by need to be supported by other considerations before we can know,
not with logical certainty but with epistemic reliability, that what we are "so sure" is there, is
actually there.

(d) Perhaps another illustration will be helpful
in clarifying further the situation we human beings
are in when we declare that we know x is so, or there.
I have often drawn on the blackboard a horizontal,
white line a bit above the midpoint of a vertical,
white line, and have abruptly asked different persons:
"What do you see?" I mention here only a few of the
answers: a plus sign, a cross, two lines bisecting
each other, four right angles, the sign of death, a
sword, the ribs of a model plane (reported a fourteen
year old who, it turned out, was building toy planes
at home). No one said it was a bird--a remarkable
fact. Invariably, each respondent was surprised initially that another did not see what he saw. However, everybody agreed that if this had been a class

7

in arithmetic no one would have "seen" anything but a plus sign. Thus each knower, despite his own psychological certitude that he had seen "what is there," was soon willing to grant that the other reports could also be made. What had become evident was that "whatever is there" made it possible for each experient, given his psychological 'set' in that situation, to respond with confidence (not logical certainty) that he was seeing "what is there." But let us note again that somehow "what is there" did not call forth a view that it was a circle or a bird--or some such report. Only a plus, a cross, two bisecting lines, four right angles seemed to be "not too farfetched."

We need not pursue other aspects of this situation here. But it did not take long for each 'knower' to concede that, despite his own psychological certainty, what he "saw" was not logically necessary, although each report had different degrees of probability or likelihood (epistemic reliability). Each person was bringing to what he was experiencing much that he was already convinced was there.

(e) Could all agree on anything? Yes, eventually. All agreed that two white lines cross each other on a black background. To keep the illustration simplified: it was this configuration that was given, that withstood, in each case, the taken. What would have been the situation if the knowers had not been able to reach this refractory pattern of sensory experiences, this common denominator that was intractable to their private wants? They would have had no grounds to defend their conviction that "something's there, common to us."

(f) How, then, decide which of their "bringings" or "takens" about what is there is true? Or, how decide which hypothesis is more reliable than others, or epistemically warranted? So far the stress has been laid on distinguishing the experiencing x from the interpretation of x (the hypothesis about x) that would be logically consistent and bring together what the experients undergo. Do we,

8

after all, have more than reliable interpretations
of what we experience? Let us see.

3. Do We Know the Real World as It is?

(a) Knowing, at least in the sensory realm, is not,
as we have seen, merely a matter of psychological
certitude, or of being logically certain that what
we are experiencing is there as experienced. Our
mistakes bar the way to such a conclusion; we realize
that our own selective activities in knowing (like
wanting, remembering, imagining, anticipating) should
keep us from thinking of knowing as a "reading off"
of what is true about what is there.

     Accordingly, I shall hold that the relation of
our environment to Environment is never one of identity.
What is there, independent of our wanting-knowing activities and our psychological sets, I shall call
"Environment" (capitalizing the first letter, or
(later) the Realm of Eligibility, in contrast with
"environment" (no capital), that is our humanized
or anthropic environment. We do not know precisely
what the relation of our anthropic environment is to
Environment. Nevertheless, because our experiencing
of sensory data is controlled in quality and pattern
in forceful ways, because our actions have consequences we cannot control, and because we do succeed
in so many of our interpretations and anticipations,
we may say generally that our environment is relevant
to the Environment. (I am purposely avoiding the
term Reality, hoping that Environment and Realm of
Eligibility will connote all there is--related to
persons and yet lying essentially beyond their influence.)

     Again, since our environment seems to be the
receiving-and-taking that we, as wanting-knowers, are
limited to as we interact with and relate to the
Environment, there is no one-to-one correspondence
between what we interpret as the Environment that
holds us in check (even as it "guides" us). All

9

this does not mean that we know nothing, but only that in this sensory-related part of "our world" sensing alone, with interpreting being added, does not mean certainty in knowing.

'Knowing,' then, is neither immediate nor direct here. Between Environment and environment stand knowing-wanting agents with their kinds of sensitivity and responsiveness, their takings of what is given. Nevertheless, without Environment-al constraints and support there would be no foundation for our confidence that what we have taken to be our environment(s) are relevant to Environment.

(b) In the light of these considerations we should realize that Nature, our 'natural world' is rooted in our sensory-experiences and their relatively steady patterns and our more reliable interpretation of them. This does not mean that this natural world as our environment is a figment of our wishes or of our imagination, although at any given point wishes and imagination may enter into our interpretations more than we may realize. What we call "our natural environment," rooted in our sensory experiences, is the joint-product of Environment with its ways and of ourselves with our ways, as we express and adjust our needs and abilities to It. Increasingly we realize that in fact we never take camera-shots of the Environment. We infer Its interaction with us ← as persons--wanting, needing, hoping, organizing-- who learn that some of our ways do converge with, and some do not, meet Its ways. Hence, we are required to prune our needs and to discipline our abilities: we shape and reshape ourselves and our environment in response to what we infer to be the ways of Environment.

(c) In this context we may regard our natural scientists as persons who, puzzled by some conflicting interpretations within the commonsense, anthropic environment, learn ways of questioning and investigating, with concern especially for connections between being-events that can be publically checked and predictable. Many scientific interpretations of Environment go so far beyond our accepted environment

10

that we inexpert mortals cannot find our way back to our environment from 'the realm of Nature' that scientists hold to be there. Our mistake, and theirs too, however, is to forget that their most reliable interpretations of Nature (natural environment) are not identical with the Environment. For science in all its forms is the disciplined effort of persons who seek to discover, for a variety of purposes, the ways of Environment. Scientists deserve our trust insofar as they meet those standards of exploration (scientific method) that seem to be supported by their past efforts to know-act in relation to It.

(d) We are now ready to reflect more generally on the drift of our discussion so far. Knowledge, truth, in the area of natural knowledge at least, are what we knowing-wanting agents achieve as we seek to fulfill our desires, practical and theoretical, in the light of our experiences (with emphasis here on our sensory experiencing). The broader our experience is, the more experiences that scientific proposals, or hypotheses, embrace in mutually supportive or systematic relations, the more coherent they are, and the more we trust them. Put another way, we come to trust those knowledge-claims because they are reached by methods cautiously adapted to taking full account of observations and connections relevant to the problems at hand, and thus they encourage us to predict what will happen under given conditions. We need not stop to assess the reliability of scientific method in areas of human experience where strictly controlled experimenting is not possible. But such assessment would call for the same kind of comprehensive coherence that holds sway as the scientific method and interpretation is seen to be faulty and needing improvement by further observation under the best conditions available to the truth-seekers.

(e) Hence, I generalize: Any proposal, interpretation, hypothesis must be tested for its degree of reliability by its ability to guide thought and action, more comprehensively than any other available. Accordingly, I shall, unless we find good reason not to do so, defend the claim that our best test of

truth-claims or hypotheses is what I shall call
growing, experiential coherence. As just noted,
with regard to knowing the natural environment,
experiential coherence is best supported by the
disciplined procedures used by natural scientists
in their respective realms. But we may not substitute 'the natural world' for Environment even
though it may well be the environment known most
reliably or coherently by experts who apply scientific procedures in interpreting the data of sense.

4.   Do We Know 'God' Directly?

(a) Can the same line of reasoning apply to religious knowing? Believers through the ages insist
on two things: that God makes Himself known to them
by his presence 'in' or 'to' their experience; that
because of the unique quality of their religious
experience, all else they undergo and know takes on
new meaning. Religious persons of every persuasion
live, of course, in "the natural world" with their
"usual" selves; but their experience of the divine
Environment leaves them convinced that their lives,
if restricted to natural dimensions of existence, are
relatively impoverished. A Buddhist would radically
differ with a Christian's and a Hindu's interpretation
of the nature of the divine Environment. Yet, they
can agree that, once persons enter into the deepest
dimensions of their own being, what happens to them
is so illuminating that the other dimensions of
existence will never be fully satisfying.

(b) In the challenging form here presented, the
conviction of the believer--supported in essence by
the religious experts, the mystics--cannot be neglected
by those who seek the whole truth about human beings
and reality. For religious persons are bearing wit-
ness--so they insist--not to a figment of human
imagination but to a Reality (Environment, Realm),
which, when properly experienced and known, will set
everything else in a new perspective. I have not

12

used terms like "the experience of the holy" and
"worship," and other equivalent terms distinguishing
the religious response, since they are not required
for our purpose here. Also, until the context requires different use, I shall use the word "God" for
divine Environment without intending more than the
Being upon whom all existence and goodness depend,
a Being believed to care about the world and all in
it. The use of the masculine pronouns (He, His,
Him) is not to be taken strictly; nor is the implication that God is a person to be taken for granted
until after we have decided in what sense this term
is applicable to God.

Religious persons have and will differ about the
best way to understand and to respond to the divine
Environment. This should occasion no surprise. Even
the history of our scientific levels of understanding
is a tale of rough agreement along with serious disagreement. Why, then, not accept the claim of the
religious persons who, despite long debates that bring
out differences about the nature of God, still hold
fast to one contention: there is a divine Environment,
never reducible to persons and to their natural environment, that has and can make itself felt in such
ways as to make all things new?

(c) I do contend to begin with that every believer,
if he reflects upon the history of religious claims,
must confront the fact that other equally conscientious,
honest, and intelligent believers disagree with him
as to the impact and import of their religious experience. Such believers are aware that they, or others
like them, have soberly declared that God is to be
approached and appreciated in this rather than that
way, that this account and not that is more trustworthy. Yet they ask us to remember that their
supreme faith in a divine Environment, never a matter
of sensory experience alone, transcends the tests we
normally use at more readily accessible and commun-
icable levels. They confess that they are transgressors
against each other, and often in the name of God.
But in the end they refuse to betray what they regard

13

as crucial to their underlying vision. Theirs are
transforming experiences; and in and through them
they "receive" power that literally surpasses anything they have otherwise experienced. These experiences, they claim, are not products of their own
effort; their own wishes cannot break the grip of
the Divine; and, as the past experience of the race
shows, these experiences open new vistas of truth,
of value--of Reality.

(d) So impressive is this claim, coming as it does
in the variety of ways in which persons have responded
to the Environment, that it seems ludicrous to suggest
that our brief analysis of knowing the natural environment may be helpful in understanding the issues
involved in religious claims both for believers and
unbelievers. At least, if there is any important
and far-reaching contrast between sensory rooted
knowledge and non-sensory rooted knowledge, we should
be aware of it.

We saw that the bisecting lines in our illustration could be "seen" as a plus sign, a cross, and so
on, once the "sets" of the "seers" were kept in mind.
Persons who could hardly believe that classmates could
disagree with them as to what was on the blackboard
could, on reflection, come to realize that their
preparatory sets were involved in their taking what
was given. What they took to be 'objectively there,'
they had, at least, to admit was not disclosed in-
fallibly, or once and for all. Similarly, even believers who stand within the same religious tradition
sometimes may be in such disagreement about central
beliefs that they begin to wonder whether they do have
a common divine Environment after all.

Assuming for the moment that believers can grant
the kind of analogy I have been suggesting between
knowledge based on sensory givens and knowledge based
on non-sensory religious givens, we may nevertheless
expect a different plea from them, made in all humility.
They feel compelled to testify that what is distinctive
about their witness is not merely derived from their
individual preparation. 'Something' has broken into
their experience that, despite the acknowledged evils

14

of religious schisms, must nevertheless be preserved
and fostered. They must be steadfast in witness, in
the hope that those who have so far missed that Something will see it too, and be saved from error.

They will grant that some minor differences are
more the product of previous preparation than the
dissidents realize. Such differences are in the end
(if I may use a figure here) more like branches on a
tree; the branches must not blind us, they urge, to
root-and-trunk differences. It is these root-and-
trunk differences, from which, indeed, branches do
grow, that give vitality to the tree-of-life itself.
Loyalty to root-and-trunk differences makes for
divisions, they admit, that try their very souls.
Yet, believers insist on, and defend, these differences, often with their lives. For these "differences" are basic truths, without which their life is
death. "Arbitration" and "compromise" about religious
symbols and rituals may be possible though difficult.
For these seem inevitable, symbolic expressions of
all they have undergone and reached for. The root-
and-trunk, however, must be preserved, more carefully
cultivated, and propagated.

Drawing on my analogy, the disagreements that
such believers may give up, or suspend, are interpretations of the given bisected lines. The fact of the
bisected lines cannot be reasonably doubted. They
ground, they testify to Something there. Accordingly,
in crises, their differences of interpretation
suspended, believers stand together in witnessing to
the divine Environment. However inadequate their
root-and-trunk-saving-truths may be, they are grounded
in the divine Environment.

(e) It is at this juncture that those who believe
the Environment is indeed divine must challenge the
adequacy of views that hold to an Environment but
disbelieve that it is divine. Here let us marshal
against each other the strongest contentions of believers and disbelievers, and push to one side subordinate issues, however dramatic they are. One can,
for instance, point to horrendous evils perpetrated

by both believers and disbelievers, but such do not
seem to me decisive arguments for or against either
of the two parties. Let us honor both our believing
saints and the heroes of disbelief. Their sacrificial
commitments serve as beacon lights illuminating what
men can do with religious faith and what they can do
in denial of religious faith. The underlying issues
involve the trunk-and-root convictions of believer
and unbeliever. Let us consider these carefully without for a moment denying that they ought to make a
difference in the ways in which their exponents act.

I repeat: there is little if anything gained by
recalling that many witnesses "to God's will" have
brandished swords and even used them mercilessly in
order to halt movements of both believers and disbelievers who "served Him" not. One could wish that
the record of disbelievers had been better. In the
name of the State, in the name of a social or economic
class, they have cast contempt upon "visionaries,"
have been unspeakably cruel to minorities, and sometimes, in the name of "Humanity" or particular theories
about man's place in Nature, they have been insensitive
to the helpless, the weak, and the powerless. Hence,
in the deliberations that follow I shall not make
appeals to the actual influence of believers and disbelievers on the history of mankind. The record
within any culture, society, or political organization
is hardly such as to warrant conclusions that make
the underlying difference on the theoretical issues
we must face.

5.   On Arbitrating the Underlying Difference Between
     Believers and Disbelievers

(a) As is evident, the root-and-trunk differences
between believers and disbelievers (and in each camp
amongst them) have to do ultimately with epistemic
grounds forwarded in defense of their claims about
man, Nature, and their relation to the Environment.
That these root-and-trunk differences develop branches
that flower and bear ethical and political fruit is
inevitable. Nevertheless, I have just suggested that

it is too hazardous to attribute particular ethico-
political achievements to specific root-and-trunk
differences. This fact, however, must not keep us
from asking an important question. <u>Are there patterns of values, are there principles of human choice
and action that are more warranted than others as
determinative factors in deciding what the Environment
is?</u> Granted, both believers and unbelievers fail to
live up to the ethical principles they announce. Such
conduct, however, in no way justifies a moratorium on
underlying theoretical questions. We must still inquire whether the quality of living we find to be most
coherent provides a reliable clue to the Environment's
relation to us.

Accordingly, to affirm the essential root-and-
trunk convictions of believers and disbelievers is
to affirm not simply their differences as to the
nature of some abstract Environment. It is to invite
inquiry about the ultimate warrant for certain conceptions of the true and the good, and priorities
among human values. For example, those persons, convinced that the Environment cannot be known except
by elaborating on what is given by sense, engage
their thought and practice to their belief that they
must find the true and the good largely by relating
themselves to human and planetary laws relevant to
Environment that is itself neutral or indifferent to
all human purposes. In contrast, persons convinced
that their non-sensory religious experience introduces
them to a divine Environment will see themselves, their
environment, and their values in the light of their
conception of the divine. Their "roots are in heaven"
in the sense that "heaven" and "earth" are at one in
the finest flowering of their humanity.

(b) Please note: I am not suggesting that what is
at stake is simply the adding of a non-sensory environment to the sensory. What is at stake is the
horizon and quality of persons and of the content
and quality of truth and goodness presumably rooted
in the natural environment only. What may seem to
an adventurous humanist-naturalist as the best path
ahead for mankind may be followed, up to a point, by

17

the adventurous believer. But the believer's
loyalty will stem from, or include, a different
inspiration. His "adventure" will not be bound
by the limits of the naturalist's horizon. The
naturalist, whatever surprises his adventure leads
to, will find a place for them within a naturalistic
context. But the believer's 'invincible surmise,'
enlarging and reconceiving the naturalistic conception, opens vistas and responsibilities related
to the structure of the divine Environment.

I take some liberties with a famous biblical
story to illustrate a vital aspect to the fundamental issue that understandably divides believers
from disbelievers. Abraham was willing to sacrifice
an innocent son, Isaac, in accordance with his
experience of God's will. Suppose that Abraham's
wife Sarah had protested: "Surely a good God would
not demand the death of an innocent child! Surely
God did not command you to perform an act that we
would find morally hideous if any human being demanded
it!" The story suggests that Abraham, nevertheless,
proceeded to carry out God's will with a heavy heart.
But notice the determinative consideration: the goodness that God commanded cannot be judged by human
standards! This verdict and its implication are not
changed by the fact that God's angel saved Isaac's
life at the last moment. Assuming then that Abraham,
Sarah, and the reasonable humanistic judgment of
persons cannot approve the killing of the innocent,
could this judgment be invalidated in the name of
the divine Environment?

(c) It is this question that haunts believers themselves. Let us assume that they can have confidence
in convictions about the existence of the divine
Environment on the basis of their non-sensory religious
experience alone. Even so, the logical necessity of
justifying their primary (root-and-trunk) value-
judgments upon the basis of religious experience alone
brings the problem of the truth-claims of religious
experience home to them. The question they can no
longer escape is: Can our religious experience, in
independence of the other dimensions of experience,

be trusted as the final point of reference for judgments about what is good? In the name of religious experience, independently of what we learn about man and Nature, can we at critical points say: God's ways annul our ways?

Theological systems are built around the primary assumption that the saving-truths about the divine Environment can, and should, be interpreted and systematized in a way that resolves tensions within the religious community organized around root-and-trunk commitments. To be sure, similarities and differences of the saving-truths and the root-and-trunk values of other traditions should be carefully examined, but the theological assumption is that the primary experiential, (direct) witness is not to be dislodged by evidence inconsistent with the 'experience' vouchsafed uniquely to that community of believers. Thus, the "open-minded" Christian or Buddhist or Hindu or Moslem will consider "other paths" to the Divine, but he will personally not be troubled in the end by the fact that, in respects close to their root-and-trunk, these faiths do diverge. Again, in loyalty to contested root-and-trunk values, believers constituting a given community feel they must walk humbly but steadfastly, in the realization that the goodness of God's larger plan is not vouchsafed to them. But they except those moral insights that conflict with the witness of their religious experience. For the Christian, God's moral ways may be past finding out, but, of course, they cannot be the ways followed by the Buddhist.

(d) Must believers and disbelievers (be they atheists or agnostics or within the Christian communion) continue to pass each other by? Must the Buddhists also pass by each other because critical points of difference involve the independent, cognitive validity of their religious experience? Disbelievers, in the interests of truth and goodness, declare, with no self-righteous pride, that they cannot find a meeting of minds in the believers' terms. Believers, on the other hand, reject the disbelievers' premises. What is to be done?

This work aims to discover what can be said about

19

truth, goodness, and the Environment, if we declare
a moratorium on the question of the <u>independent,
cognitive finality</u> of <u>religious experience</u>. Since
we must, let us come back (chapters thirteen and
fourteen) to that conviction after we have examined
what can be said reasonably about man and his
natural and valuative environment. Without allowing
(presumably authentic) religious witness to settle
beforehand questions about man, his values, and Nature,
how far can we go toward believing in a divine Environment? How shall we characterize the divine goodness?

As I proceed, when there are conflicts between
"naturalistic" and "religious-theological" interpretations of man, his environment, and his values, I
shall try to resolve the conflict by refusing to
cordon off the dimensions of human experience from
each other. I shall refuse to let one dimension
dictate finally what the other must be taken to de-
liver, however tempting this may be in the light of
influential trends in our history. Though I have no
delusions about the difficulty of the task, I seek
for those links among human experiences that render
us more aware of the relation and interrelation of the
person's 'facts' with his 'values.' And this, whatever the final world-view may be. I have suggested
in this chapter that, in interpreting both the sensory
and the religious dimensions of experience, more is
claimed as <u>given</u> than is actually the case. But this
is a conclusion, and one that must be justified more
fully as we proceed.

6. Reflective Overview

Hence, the policy for the rest of this book:
Beware of fragmentizing our human experience! Allow
the different dimensions of our experience to speak
for themselves! At the same time, take it not for
granted that each dimension is equally trustworthy
or easy to interpret! Both matters of fact and
matters of value involve us as persons who, though
pulled hither and yon in the midst of complex demands,
cannot be satisfied by an easy truce.

20

We must reject solutions that sacrifice too readily the demand for as much harmony as possible. The best we can do when our psychological certitudes conflict with each other, be it within the sensory or within the non-sensory dimensions of our experience, is to organize them as coherently as possible with a view to eliminating inconsistency and developing as comprehensive a system as possible. When there is conflict between the systems, the only solution we can live by is neither that truth is impossible nor that every system is "as true" or "as good" as any other.

In our deliberative moments, we also realize that trustworthy conclusions are easier to come by in some areas than others. We must persist, however, in relating conclusions from one dimension of experience to another before deciding how trustworthy they actually are for us as active, knowing-wanting persons. This calls for facing conflicts between interpretations by re-examining their relations to our experiences as a whole and then accepting the interpretation that allows more of the relevant data to live in mutual support. This test, growing experiential coherence, gives us no more than probable conclusions for guiding further investigation and action. It does not, however, arbitrarily exclude any dimension of experience and any proposal. The task of reason, on this view, is, minimally, to increase consistency and, maximally, to weave together the different strands of experience so that as much systematic coherence as possible is achieved.

There is indeed an element of trust, if you will, in this approach. Persons in the human situation, characterized by fragmentary data at best, persons who nevertheless go on living and experiencing the different dimensions of their beings, will still seek more than they can fully grasp. But, if we adopt the policy of letting no one part of experience dictate arbitrarily to the other, we do not dictate once and for all what the truth-value of any part may be. We gradually learn to assess the contribution that different areas of investigation make to our search for truth and goodness. Reason's task (reasonableness) is to be sensitive to what is given and to what is taken in individual and social life; it is to follow the links and connections that are given and taken--with a view to placing before the person as broad and fulfilling an horizon as possible. In Professor Brand Blanshard's words: "The reasonableness we are talking about is, rather, a settled disposition of mind. It is a disposition to guide one's belief and conduct by evidence, a bent of the will to order one's thoughts by the relevant facts, and to order one's practice in the light of the values involved."[1] Reasonableness itself, it will be borne in upon us, can achieve its end as it expresses the concern of persons to be responsively-responsible in their relation to Environment.

Notes

A general bibliography is provided at the end of the book; the abbreviations (e.g., Burtt, MSD) will be clarified.

References especially relevant are: Bertocci, PGI, chapters 7,8; Blanshard, NOT, vol. 1; Brightman, POR, chapters 1-4; Burtt, MSD, SPU; Hartshorne, LOP; Hick, FAK; Hocking, MGH; James, VRE; C.I. Lewis, MWO; H.D. Lewis, OEG; Moore, TRE; Stace, MAP; Tennant, PT, vol. 1; Tillich, DOF.

[1] B. Blanshard, RAB, p. 564 (by permission of author).

Chapter Two

WHAT IS MAN WHO IS MINDFUL OF REALITY?

1. From the Environment of Man to Reality

We decided at the end of the first chapter to
suspend until later chapters a more adequate judgment
regarding the conflicting claims about God and His
goodness. To declare a moratorium on the evidential
value of religious experience renders all the more
important the investigation of the relation of persons
and of the values they deem most important in environment-Environment. I have already hinted broadly
that even the natural environment that we so readily
assume is independent of persons and their values is
the joint-product of Environment and persons who
coherently organize their "worlds." This approach
to the question of God and His goodness I shall call
the cosmo-teleological-ethical argument, and I shall
begin in this chapter to examine the constitution
of the person whose environment reflects his interaction with environment-Environment.[1]

By taking such an approach I subject myself to
a pointed question from many informed readers. Have
I learned nothing from great thinkers in the history
of philosophical theology and philosophy of religion?
Has not their verdict been that by such a route no
being worthy of worship has been reached? I believe
I am sufficiently aware of the dangers in the traditional cosmological, teleological, and the moral
arguments for God to pick my way through a heavily-
mined field. I shall leave it to my reader to
determine where I have disappeared, at least from
his view, in an explosion.

But, as will gradually appear, in my view
"weaknesses" in the traditional arguments spring from
questionable presuppositions as to what each argument should prove, or assumptions about what God must
be. The hyphenation in "cosmo-teleological-ethical"
suggests the possibility that, once we consider

circumspectly the nature of the person and of his
values and the way in which persons and the natural
environment are related, a more coherent interpretation is available as to the place of persons 'in'
Environment.

2. Man: A Little Higher Than the Animals?

(a) Man,[2] by scientific approximation, is a late
development on the tree of life that, so far as we
know now, has spread its roots and lifted its branches
only on planet Earth. A Spectator of all events on
the trillions of galaxies of stars would have observed
no living organisms. And, after our planet took shape
about three thousand million years ago, still more
millions of years were to elapse before our Spectator
would observe conditions conducive to the existence
of beings that can reproduce themselves on land and
sea. Before the human species (homo sapiens) appeared, myriads of species of plants and animals
appeared and perpetuated themselves according as
they were able to adapt themselves to each other in
the physico-chemical world.

     In the human body there are organizations of
cells not found among the highest animals; they are
conditions for many, at least, of man's characteristic activities. Nevertheless, remaining at
the bio-physical level of description-interpretation,
the fundamental conditions for survival and the similarity of so many structures and functions, especially in "higher" animals, is so great that homo
sapiens, in an essentially biological interpretation,
is readily conceived to be a higher animal. How
common it has become to speak of the animal origins
of man, and then to go on talking as if the clues to
the understanding of subhuman species would be the
clues as well to understanding the basic nature of
human life!

(b) Yet, we may wonder: Would our cautious Spectator, on the basis of his observation of the

wondrously fascinating developments of biological evolution from the "lower" to the "higher" forms of animal life, such as chimpanzees and seals--would he have possibly foreseen the quality of development of human beings' hidden <u>sapiens</u>? Those qualities, those activities are so unique that shifting the focus for description-interpretation to the word "person" is warranted.

It does not matter for our purposes here whether a hard and fast line can be drawn between subhuman "higher" animals and persons. No amount of exploring the twilight zones between these animals and persons should allow us, however, to assume that the understanding of the organic similarities we observe justifies the conclusion that[3] "in the end" human beings are complicated animals. In any case, our Spectator, having observed man's nearest neighbors, could hardly affirm, once he had contrasted the person as a whole and any animal as a whole, that the person is a complication of animal functions. It is the person as a whole, just as the ant or the seal as a whole, that must remain before us if we are to draw reliable comparisons and contrasts. And these comparisons and contrasts must, whatever else, presuppose appreciation of the person <u>as he consciously experiences himself as a whole</u> <u>and consciously communicates with other persons</u> <u>what he experiences himself to be.</u>[4] Certainly, if animals could communicate their conscious experience to persons, we should pay close attention to their reports.

(c) Accordingly, I begin with a skeletal definition in terms of activities that together distinguish the conscious-selfconscious person: sensing, remembering, imagining, perceiving, thinking, feeling, wanting (needing), emoting, willing, oughting, and aesthetic and religious appreciating. (There probably are distinguishable parapsychic capacities.) Many scholars I respect highly would not grant the specific interpretation I would give of these activities. However, except as my interpretation is critical for my argument (as in the case of willing and oughting), let

25

these activities serve to define the dimensions of
the person's conscious unity (as distinct from what
is further involved in and by these activities).

(d) I emphasize that these activities of consciousness are distinguishable dimensions of the person;
they cannot be ripped away from each other. A person
is an ongoing unity. He is not "made up" of these
activities as if they were separable "components"
that came together to constitute him as a person.
Each of us consciously experiences these activities
as his; they are what he is as he expresses himself
in and through them, as he responds to whatever is
not himself and yet within their reach. So, when we
speak, for convenience or emphasis, about sensing or
desiring, or emoting or thinking, as if they were
independent activities, we must remember that they
are phases of the unified agent-person and that each
in any phase has an "object" or "objective" that
does not exhaust its potential.

     My reader will, accordingly, note that when I
use hyphenated terms like "wanting-knowing-person,"
I do this to remind us that every activity distinguished is the activity of a complete unity (I).
Especially to be noted is my referring to the person
as agent-person, for, with William James, I shall
emphasize that the person is a "fighter for ends,"
indeed a conscious and self-conscious fighter for ends.
Yet, though to be a person at all is to be able to
experience in these ways, at any one moment in the
unified person, one pattern or complex of activities
is regnant. Moreover, an activity need not "act out"
its full potential; hence, in speaking of activities
I mean activities with their unrealized and latent
potential (activity-potentials).

(e) In focusing on these activities as conscious
I am not holding that person-al experiencing is
totally defined apart from any unconscious dimensions,
or from bodily processes. In a broader account, I
should wish to hypothesize a certain kind of uncon-
scious--telic mentality that must be related to what
occurs in the conscious and self-conscious unity.

26

But the activities are undeniably dimensions of the person, and I consider them essential. Without these interrelated activities the varied quality of personal existence cannot be accounted for, let alone the bases in their actual objects-objectives for legitimate inferences. (A terminological note: terms like 'self,' 'ego,' 'psyche,' 'spirit,' 'soul,' 'mind' are often used loosely as synonyms for 'person'; I shall use 'human being,' 'man,' 'person' and 'self,' without sexual denotation, but the words 'personal self,' 'subpersonal self,' 'divine Self' have in common unified consciousness, of quality to be defined.)

(f) I stress that the personal self is not only conscious but capable of self-consciousness, for without self-consciousness there are no 'free ideas' or symbols, and no planning and guiding of oneself by ideals. But these terms are relatively empty until we appreciate the quality of these activities as they exist in persons. For example, since sense-data are experienced by persons who can remember, imagine, think, and want as they do, sense-data of persons are not, as it were, detachable bricks from the walls of personal experience that, once the mortar has been scraped off, can be the raw material for other walls. We know very little about what happens in embryo and neonate. Yet we remind ourselves that what goes on there would be even harder to think of as an assembling process than as one in which there is a much more simple but still complex whole of experiencing. Which is to say that persons, as they grow from infancy onward, do not simply add to "animal" sensory-data. Even "raw" sensations are person-al initially. There is every reason to suppose that the same is true of feelings, emotions, and urges in person-al experience. (Hereafter I shall not hyphenate personal for the intention of this word is in my sense not 'private' or 'intimate' essentially.)

Too long have we talked about man as a thinking animal (or a symbol-using animal) without appreciating the distinctive difference it makes to experience ideas under the demands for logical consistency and

for the coherence I have already discussed. These
so-called "additions" to an "essentially animal
inheritance" of feelings and desires and emotions
change the whole quality of what goes on within
the person and of what meanings a person's experiences will have for him in relation to Environment.

In short, just as subpersonal selves, restricted
largely to sensory experiences and their own qualitative, psychic matrix, cannot be understood as persons
minus this or that quality of capacity, so the person
cannot be understood strictly as the "extension" of
even the highest subpersonal selves. We must not
exaggerate either similarities or differences. But
it simply will not do to suppose that the person is,
in the whole range of his experience, an animal, plus!
I must articulate this theme since critical parts of
the later argument depend on the conception of the
person.

3. The Person as Wanter-Knower

(a) Had I advanced this last contention simply by
saying that what distinguishes persons are their
connective, reason-capable activities, which result
in the free ideas and symbols that enable them to
communicate with each other and to transmit what
they have learned to their children, it would have
encountered little resistance. But I explicitly
challenge a tendency, often hidden, presumably consistent with evolutionary ways of thinking. The tendency is to think of symbolizing activities as
additions to a basically animal equipment--like
frontal lobes added to the central nervous system
similar to that of our nearer animal neighbors. The
task of these added activities--it is often more
assumed than argued--is to control and direct essentially animal appetites and emotions.

But I protest when, as often happens, basic
feelings, emotions, and the unlearned needs

28

or motives of persons are treated as man's "animal" ancestry that cannot be expected to harmonize with these later "rational" additions. I have no disposition to minimize the deep conflicts within personal experience, but are they indeed the conflicts owing to evolutionary additions to "animal residues"? Do they not, rather, occur within the qualitative level of personal experience? In persons neither emotions, nor urges, nor feelings actually function necessarily as opposing cognitive-rational functions.

In order to avoid this essentially additive, evolutionary approach, I purposely pointed in the definition of the person activities distinguishable as persons consciously experience their agency. Moreover, unless we can thus distinguish the activity-potentials that constitute the personal Gestalt, how shall we know the correlates and causes, let alone the consequences, of <u>personal qualities of experiencing</u>? Accordingly, if we do not distinguish the qualities of feelings, of primary emotions, and of unlearned needs (at least), as they are consciously experienced "in" the person, we resort to interpreting them in the light of what we presumably discover in sub-personal beings where conscious experience is not open to us. The consequence is that we try to discover the distinctive quality of human conscious experience by analogy with the physiology and behavior of animals.

(b) I must be more explicit on this whole matter, but I pause to emphasize the importance of examining and interpreting human <u>unlearned</u> needs (urges) and emotions without ever <u>losing the</u> distinctive quality of them within the personal conscious matrix. The fact that persons do have the cognitive capacities they manifest surely must enter into their very nature as the activities they are and can be. Surely, just as we do not expect to understand human cognitive activities by examining chimpanzees and seals at their best, so we should not expect to find the personal analogate to wonder, to respect (not fear), to tenderness, to sympathy, to sexual lust, or even to hunger and thirst in the lives of higher animals that as far as we know do not share human cognitive quality (<u>sapiens</u>). Hence, we must persistently ask:

Are not the qualities and differences in feelings, emotions, and needs of persons what they are experienced as being because persons—in their very nature as feeling, and needing, and emoting—are cognitive in and to the extent they are and exhibit? Conversely, is not the cognitive life of a person what it is because it is involved in the matrix of feelings, emotions, and needs that persons experience?

In sum, cognitive functions, including reason, are not simply directors of feelings, emotions, and needs. The cognitive functions are ingredient to what feelings, emotions, and needs are as they appear and function in persons. The life of meaning and of value open to a person is the life made possible by this level of interpenetrating feelings, emotions, and needs, as known and interpreted to be sure, but, nevertheless, as intrinsic activities in the unified matrix to which "cognitive" activity is not merely a later addition.

(c) I am aware that these statements run counter to some strong trends in psychology and ethology, and that difficult problems in very controversial realms of experience and behavior are involved, Nevertheless, I think that the time is more than ripe for regarding persons from within their own awareness of the qualitative dimensions of their own varied experience. Afterwards we can decide whether persons are imperfect images of God or developments of animals. The aim here is not to disparage animal capacities or accomplishments, but rather to achieve a better sense of what man's own problems in every dimension of being are. For, as we try to understand his cognitive and valuative aims, his struggles and accomplishments, our presuppositions are important. In our laudable attempts to discover the person's dependence on physico-chemical and physiological conditions, we cannot afford to neglect what he experiences himself as being.

Socrates, as we recall, said that the purpose of life is not to live, but to live well. But he defined "well" by saying that the unexamined life is not worth living. For Socrates there was no significant survival if he could not continue to examine and experience the feelings and emotions at his level of existence. When he took the poison, administered by an admiring jailer in the name of Athens, was he by "reason" humanizing an animal set of feelings, emotions, and needs? Or were his feelings, emotions, and needs of a quality no animal could experience? It was the quality of such activity-potentials and their development in his life that entered into the total meaning of survival for him. Socrates' love of truth, his loyalty to Athens, his concern for his sons' upbringing in a good social environment, his respect for those who sincerely disagreed with him, his conviction that no evil thing could befall a good man in this life or the next, and that not from money comes virtue but that from virtue comes money and all the other goods of man--these qualitative experiences could have been anticipated by no Spectator of the course of biological evolution who was observing only the feelings, emotions, needs, and cognitive reach of even higher animals.

I am urging, then, that the activities that I have distinguished within the unity of the person be seen for what they are within his Gestalt or form, whatever other relations we may discover between them and other nonhuman beings. Whenever persons appeared on the earthly scene, they came endowed with their activity-potentials and with their own capacities for response. It is they, as knower-agents, that are involved in their fulfillment and failure as they interact with the Environment. Thus, I shall particularly press the general point that, agreement on details aside, we shall not appreciate what a person's motivating predispositions are if we insist on conceiving of his experiences of feeling, emotion, and need as having their recognized qualities because of the "addition" of his unique cognitive (cortical) activities to affective-conative tendencies in his animal ancestors (perhaps to their hypothalamus).

The personal situation is personal, with all its strengths and weaknesses. And what stands out is the

telic or future-oriented dynamics of the personal
Gestalt. Later we must examine particularly the
person's agency as will and obligation, and as
aesthetic and religious outreach. But these, too
are unintelligible in the personal situation apart
from their relation to what I shall hereafter usually
refer to as the affective-emotive-conative (wholist-
ically, the conative) dimensions.

4. A Personalistic Approach to the Conative
    Dimensions of Persons

(a) In this section I enter into one of the most
controversial issues facing those who are seeking
insight into the unlearned demands that human
beings make upon themselves in any ambient. Indeed,
the very nature of the meaning of survival for
persons is at stake.

        I shall suggest briefly the main outlines of a
theory of human motivation. [5] Adequately defended it
would explicate the central theme that I have been
suggesting: First, that the person's responses be
inspected as they arise and develop at his level of
being; second, in respect now to what is so loosely
and vaguely called "his motivational life," that
we try hard to distinguish a person's predisposing
conative tendencies in human life in terms of the
qualitative differences they make in his experienced
orientation. We shall then realize, for example,
that the human panoply of conative tendencies can
hardly be seen as almost completely dependent on
transformations through social learning or cultural
pressures. [6] Indeed, if the person is not an "addition"
to the "basic" animal, neither is he a "mirror" of
culture. [7] What I set forth here will be relevant to
what I shall refer to later as the person's "being-
becoming" and to the quality of his values and disvalues.

(b) The conception of unlearned conative tendencies

(or predispositions) that I shall be suggesting will
find understandable resistance. Yet competent students
tend to agree that, without the maturing of their
unique cognitive activities, persons could not even
survive. For persons must learn to do much that
animals do by instinct alone. That is, persons must
adapt their total responses to situations where
animals need not (or cannot) adapt because their
responses to situations are inbuilt and relatively
invariable. Our Spectator of evolutionary development would note that the lower the species in the
biological scale, the less plasticity do they have,
because their unlearned needs and abilities are
so closely geared to each other that their responses
are all but rigid. The higher in the evolutionary
biological scale an animal species is, the more
likely it is to survive, because the same needs can
be gratified more flexibly by different abilities.
Moreover, once it learns new ways of adaptation, it
is better able to teach its progeny. More specifically, persons, by affective-conative and cognitive
endowment, are capable of becoming both increasingly
aware of goals that their abilities cannot auto-
matically fulfill, and also of becoming aware of the
scope of the abilities by which they learn the skills
required for gratifying their goals in varying environments. They are capable, we say, of learning
from their past experiences; they can also put their
considerable imaginative power to work in solving
new problems, and they are clearly unique in their
ability to communicate symbolically with each other
and to teach their children much of what they have
learned.

(c) Our Spectator, I am suggesting, would marvel at
what could occur on Mother Earth once self-conscious
persons appeared. To repeat, they could purposely
vary their abilities to meet their unlearned conative tendencies. The Spectator, I am also suggesting, could expect nothing like this from observing the kinds of interconnections in the physico-
chemical world, or even from the dramatic changes
in the adaptability of animals at the higher levels
of evolution. For, until persons appeared, what

could compare with creatures who developed their own cultures? What other creatures could stabilize this learned adaptation of unlearned, conative tendencies? Persons, as their (learned) cultures show, are neither at the complete mercy of the laws of the physical and biological world upon which they do depend nor of the conditions that constitute their own native equipment.

In short, the human children of Mother Earth develop themselves-in-their-cultures as they continue to gratify the kinds of feelings, emotions, and needs that define in large measure what the scope and quality of survival for them can include. Persons can at once take advantage of Environment and add their own forms of order, environment, to Environment. Their individual and cultural forms of "intelligent" adaptation and expression (environment) are impossible apart from their capacity for criticizing adaptations by norms of truth and of value. Their very definition of "survival" involves persons in examining themselves and the directions in which they can shape their destinies within the particular kinds of control that they keep discovering the Environment is exercising on them.

(d) The general meaning of survival for persons, I have now submitted, depends in good part on the nature of their activity-potentials as they interact with environment-Environment. I shall focus here on what they are predisposed to want as they interact with Environment with the aid of their varied abilities. For what survival can mean to persons depends on our answer to the question: What universal, cross-cultured motives (conative predisposition) do persons experience independently of any specific environment?

Here I cannot expound my own answer adequately, nor enter into the even more controversial question about whether some emotions are primary, or universal, motives (note: e-motives). But I should want in the end to do away with the distinction <u>and</u> the separation that is usually made between emotions and motives. If emotions are not at least motives in

34

our experience, what are they? Accordingly, I take
seriously the possibility that every primary (unlearned, universal) motive is a primary emotion.
And I decry the constant talk about "the importance
of emotions" to human action, while no one specifies
what emotions are being referred to. As if such
specification did not make a difference to an adequate theory of emotions and motivations! When
the words "emotion" and "emotional" are used in
omnibus fashion, they throw little light on the
actual motivating experience--beyond suggesting
some "excitement" and "irrationality"!

Hence, I propose that each primary, conative
tendency is a primary emotion (or an emotive-need
or predisposition), and that each primary emotion
be described by its own dynamics-in-context.
Avoiding also the omnibus use of "feeling," I suggest that we restrict the word "feeling" to the
experiences of pleasantness and unpleasantness
(hedonic and unhedonic tones) as each actually occurs in context. For pleasantness and unpleasantness do not exist apart from the experienced context; hedonic tone becomes unhedonic as contexts
change.

For example, normally the primary emotion
'anger' has its unpleasant tone, but anger, as in
"righteous indignation," may well have its own
hedonic quality. Hence, to speak of "the affective-
conative life" is to speak of a personal motivational matrix--emotive predispositions and the hedonic
or unhedonic tones accompanying each as each seeks
gratification in various contexts. Fortunately,
agreement with this identification of primary emotion
with "unlearned motives" need not stand in the way
of our pursuing related issues regarding the constitutive motives of persons. (See (f) below.)

(e) In (b) and (c) above I suggested that the higher
we come toward homo sapiens in the realm of biological
evolution, the less closely geared are the primary
motives to the organism's capacities for gratifying
their goals. (Contrast, for example, the nest-making

of birds with the house-making of human beings.)
I also contended that the very presence of cognitive
abilities in persons that are not present even in
higher animals should keep us from using animal
primary motives as the prototype for the human. For
example, the same infant who finds himself predisposed
to gratify a primary motive before he knows which
"objects" and "means" will gratify it best will soon
be able to learn other means also for gratifying
that motive. How many ways of gratifying hunger
develop as the infant grows! Open cookbooks and
marvel at the variety of recipes that human beings
pass on to each other as they learn about "edible
objects." And for persons food and drink take on
symbolic meanings that extend far beyond physiological gratification. This simple contrast can be
carried over to the gratifying of other "comparable"
primary motives of animals and persons.

However, so varied are the ways of gratifying
the motives of persons, and so varied are the
motives themselves in different environmental situations, that psychologists and other social scientists
have come to differ widely as to the criteria of universal motives. The list of primary motives (and
emotions) has dwindled down to those that can be
localized in the body and also resemble those of
higher animals especially. This reduction, in the
name of scientific "objectivity," has resulted in
restricting the range of primary motives in persons
to those that can be physiologically localized. My
suggestion, on the contrary, is that we should not
assume that the necessary physiological conditions
of primary motives (when specifiable) are the sufficient condition for their definition at the human
level. We must define the primary motives of persons
in the context of their own psycho-physiological
thrust and meaning.[8] For example, sex, in persons,
has physiological conditions, but the attempt to
restrict its primary psychological function in persons
to the expression or release of a physiological urge,
or to procreation, simply neglects the meanings and
symbolism in the sexual expression of persons.

To generalize: It is a mistake, with far-reaching consequences, to define human motives as primary solely on condition that we can define their physiological correlates. If the human mind has distinctive activities, why should we not expect to find primary psychic (or mental) motives that can be defined in terms of experienced objectives of their own, and be guided by these conscious e-motives in searching for physiological correlates?

(f) If this suggestion is taken seriously, we shall not assume, as is the fashion in some psychological quarters, that, with the exception of primary motives like hunger, sex, fear, and anger (for which we can indicate physiological correlates), all other human motives like sympathy, respect, tenderness, creativity, wonder, are secondary--that is, derived from the primary by social learning. Indeed, I ask: Can social learning in fact transform physiologically rooted 'survival' motives--say, fear, for example--into secondary motives that are so unlike in their objectives, and as <u>experienced</u>? In principle, I must protest the assumption that the experienced quality of <u>fear</u> (and the escape-submissive behavior that usually accompanies it) can be transformed by social learning into the experienced quality of <u>respect</u> (and the accompanying behavior, deference).

Not for a moment do I deny that primary affective-conative predispositions are subject to learning. Indeed, as I have emphasized, since persons are flexible, they do organize their knowing-wanting natures in cultural ways that become ingredients of their response to environment-Environment. Nevertheless, we need to be very clear about what we mean when we say that learning "transforms" motives. Again, it is easier said than done to show that the inner motive to help a being (understood to be suffering) can be taught, granted that learning and teaching are required to gratify that urge effectively. To say that we can teach persons to experience <u>wonder</u>, or to experience <u>tenderness</u>, when by assumption all we have to begin with is, say,

hunger, sex, fear, anger, is to burden learning
with more than it can bear.

I realize that a whole theory of learning
and of the roots of society itself is at issue here.
Yet, some acquaintance with pertinent ethological
and psychological literature leaves me astounded
at the miracles that are performed in the name of
social learning or social pressure. For, while I
myself insist that a person can be taught the more
specific ways of dealing with the (primary) tenderness that all but impels him to help the being
perceived as helpless, I seriously question whether
he can learn or be taught to experience tenderness!
And I continue to ask: Are wonder and creativity,
as experienced, teachable--whatever the physiological correlates--and is either only the means of
gratifying other primary needs?

It will not help to reply that the "urge to
survive" will suffice to induce the drastic trans-
formation in motives and emotions I am referring
to. For, once more, it is the very meaning of
survival-for-persons that we are trying to define.
If the directions in which I am pointing are correct, survival involves also keeping alive the
primary "mental" motives that are so significant
in activating the person.

(g) Having pressed for this more fulsome conception
of primary motivation, I must insist equally--in-
deed more--that any list of "higher" primary motives
may lead to every quality of evil as well as good.
This is so because the person, plastic within limits,
with cognitive (and other capacities to be described
later) can express them and adjust them in myriad
ways.

We must not succumb to the temptation to
base an ethical theory on a particular one (or

set) of primary motives.* Were primary motives not important to forming a theory of the good, or a theory of knowledge, or generally of environment "within" Environment, I should have gladly omitted this thorny approach to the dynamics of personal life.

However, to have omitted even this thin discussion would have meant to pass over the considerable difference it makes to many ethical and political issues when we attribute primary motives to persons that, for whatever reason, seem so alien to our inspection of personal experience from within. For example, a society built on fear as the dominant primary emotion will not have as a possible psychic bond what respect creates. And it is a long, long way from anger-pugnacity to sympathy-succor and the variety of bonds that it may create. I am simply pressing for a more intelligible base for the vast panorama of values that are rooted in persons who, for better and worse, are the kind of affective-conative beings who make primary demands, demands that may indeed be expressed in different ways and are not readily suppressed or repressed.

(h) Another subject for caution is the appeal to "survival value" as the irrepressible foundation of personal motivation. For in persons this expression

---

*The primary emotions or motives I should defend are: hunger (and physiological survival needs), fear-escape, anger-pugnacity, lust-sex, tenderness-parental, sympathy-succor, respect-deference, zest-competence, wonder-curiosity, creativity-enlivenment. But each requires careful definition. Our usage is loose; one cannot be too sure that his description captures the telic matrix of each. On this view, the 'lived' nucleus motivating behavior is the e-motion; it activates the thought and behavior that characterizes each. Assuming that such a spectrum of primary motives is plausible, this topography of personal needs should be seen to tend toward benign behavior, not assure it.

hides an evaluation, a contrast between survival and quality of survival. The person as wanter-knower seeks to know what is better according to some criterion. It is the person, as active evaluator of the value of his existence, who lives and dies. From his infancy onward, so much of the person's perceiving, conceiving, and judgment take place in the process of his discovering how to gratify his "survival wants," that some thinkers succumb to the temptation of thinking that the reasoning of a person is ultimately a rationalization of his strongest want(s)--a conclusion with far-reaching consequences if taken seriously, for example, in scholarly work.

Hence, I return to a persistent, underlying theme. Since man's unique cognitive powers from their dim beginnings are factors within the matrix of his unique affective-conative life, we cannot allow ourselves to say, even at the "survival level," that man is a complicated animal. For he cannot be an animal at all. However uncertain his steps, the person is a wanting-evaluating agent from his earliest days. The quality of the person's selectivity depends both on the range of his plasticity at each stage of the maturing process and on the environment actually available to him. Even if persons were limited only to sheer survival needs, they would, as they mature and learn, be blaming, praising, welcoming, and rejecting certain forms of adjustment and expression in the light of the new goals and the ideas they learn as they reflect on the interrelations among their primary motives and the means available for gratifying them.

5. Can "Pleasure" Be the Dominant Motive in Persons?

(a) With these cautions in mind we can more readily ask whether the general conception of primary motives being advanced can withstand the contention that survival with as much pleasantness as possible is the dominant motive of personal thought and action.

I have already submitted that it is an egregious mistake to talk as if pleasantness and unpleasantness exist as such, or that they somehow become goals by themselves. For pleasantness and unpleasantness (or hedonic and unhedonic tone) never exist by themselves; they qualify experiences and contexts of experience. To say that a person lives for as much pleasantness and as little unpleasantness as possible tells us nothing until we know _what_ experiences, yielding their own quality of pleasantness and unpleasantness, he is pursuing. For example, there is the quality of chocolate-ice-cream-pleasure, and there is the quality of vanilla-ice-cream-pleasure. Say that we prefer one to the other in a given context of experience. The pleasure gratifying the one cannot be substituted for the other, since it is the hedonic tone of _that_ experience we prefer.

Again, to suggest that one pleasure is only greater in a quantitative sense than the other simply misreads experience. For it follows that, if pleasantness is not some experience by itself, one cannot select more or less "pleasure" apart from the experiences that yield one quality of pleasure rather than another.

Accordingly, "pleasure" by itself does not govern choice. Hedonic and unhedonic tones "live" in myriad ways in all kinds of sensory-experience-in-contexts and all varieties of gratification-of-motives-in-context. Just as the infant does not eat initially "for pleasure," but gets the quality of pleasure from eating _that_ particular food in _that_ way, so throughout a person's life "pleasures" arise from the gratification of wants in relation to _what_ gratifies those wants. Some pleasures spring from the sheer release of tension, others from a peculiarly gratifying "object." Human experiences in their variety and complexity carry their own hedonic or unhedonic tones with them; and, so often, as the context changes so does what is ordinarily pleasant become unpleasant: "Too much is too much!" we say.

(b) We may conclude that the task of persons seeking

41

the good is to decide at least which hedonically-toned experiences and contexts are more worthy of pursuit than others; and to this task we shall soon turn. Personal existence without pleasant-unpleasant tones as determining factors--indeed, existence itself without the lush variety of qualitative hedonic-unhedonic experiences--is simply unthinkable. The problem for moral-ethical choice in any case is: Which pleasures?

6. Reflective Overview

(a) We have reflected on some considerations basic to a theory of the person both as knower and as actor. What shall I say to a critic who, aware of the difficulties we have barely touched, makes the practical rejoinder to "my" conception of primary affective-conative tendencies? "After all," he asks, "does it really make a practical difference whether wonder, tenderness, and sympathy (for example) are learned rather than unlearned? If they are learned motives, they can become 'second nature,' and, as such, become as powerful as the constitutive wants from which they derive." I grant the very important point that 'second nature' motives are powerful ingredients in a person's life; after all, we want much of a person's 'moral character' to become second nature. But I must persist--since good practice must square with adequate theory: If you do not grant the importance of these "non-physiological" motives, how will you explain how the want to explore, the wonder, can be taught to a person lacking it constitutionally?

(b) Having posited more vertebrae in the human backbone of conative dispositions, I must finally warn that, despite my listing them separately, they are not to be conceived as coiled up in separate jack-in-the-box compartments, jumping into action when the catch is released. These tendencies are distinctions, not walled-off faculties, as are all activity potentials within the matrix of the person's unity. All the more, then, a person's problem throughout life is to note

42

the interpenetration of activity-potentials even as
he learns the distinctive orientation each takes at
various times in various ways. For example, the
lust-sex in persons may be expressed in many ways,
and the quality of its contribution depends on the
way it is related to other primary tendencies and to
the acquired motives and values the person lives by.
In the end I hope to show that while this larger
Gestalt of qualitatively different primary tendencies does not prejudice an ethic in favor of some
objectives rather than others, the life good to live
must be defined in relation to these ranging motives
of persons and to the possibilities for value and
disvalue they bring into being.

(c) But before turning to that central theme we
must link the theme of this chapter with that of
the last, thus providing a more adequate basis for
considerations already advanced concerning the way
in which the anthropic environment is related to the
Environment.

     In the last chapter we saw that the knowing
person cannot do much about the quality and order
or pattern of his sensory experiences (bisected
white lines), and that he cannot alter the principles of consistency (logic) that are the minimum
necessity for his relating ideas to each other.
In this chapter we have taken seriously the fact
that human cognitive capacities are part of a total
affective-conative Gestalt that are constitutive
ingredients in the quality of personal outreach.
Accordingly, a person's conscious and self-conscious
existence is never one in which, as it were, his
sensory experiences and his logico-coherent activities
face each other across an empty psychic field, the
former needing organization, the latter demanding it.
For both occur within the personal Gestalt animated
by feelings, emotions, and predispositions that
contribute their own pushes and pulls, that are not
to be separated even in infancy. The person never
begins with "a blooming, buzzing confusion" (to
use James's terms), since the affective-conative
predispositions themselves involve sensory patterns
and relatively simple cognitive organization.

I shall later insist, with Wilhelm Stern, that
kein Gestalt ohne Gestalter is the crucial fact
about the person, but such a view would mean little
did persons not undergo initial, varied affective-
conative attachments. Certain sounds unpleasantly
startle, others are pleasant; certain impulses and
desires move smoothly to gratifications, others meet
frustrating obstacles. That is, there is plasticity
within the telic Gestalter.

What becomes increasingly evident is that the
task of "reasoning about life" involves neither the
superimposing of some pattern on sheer confusion
nor the necessary subservience to the initial
preferences and pressures. From the beginning of
self-consciousness (at least), there is the inspection and assigning of priorities that take into
account the different, more or less dominant, streams
in the flow of psychic traffic.

This is hardly the place to work out in any detail what goes on as the infant develops into childhood, the child into adolescence, the adolescent
into adulthood. The main concern here is to give
further content to the theme that between Environment
and persons are their environments--that these are,
in part, the joint-product of persons' affective-
conative involvement with the Environment. From the
momentary, episodic, and wavering self-awareness of
sensory, affective-conative, and cognitive experiencing to the development of more fully self-conscious, comprehensive, and unifying purposes, the
telic impulses of persons stir them into sorting
and weaving together the more or less plastic patterns
in their endowment and their interactions. But it
is persons, actively oriented constantly by both
primary and secondary motives, who interpret, who
propose and hypothesize as they reflect on what is
and what is not good in their interactions with each
other in their environments-Environment. Let us
examine more closely, then, the knower-evaluator.

Notes

1   Paul Weiss, NAM; Peter A. Bertocci, IPOR, PSI.

2   Sir Charles Sherrington, *Man on His Nature*, Doubleday, 1953.

3   Henry Bergson, *Creative Evolution*, trans. A. Mitchell (Holt, 1911), Random House, 1944; Teilhard de Chardin, *Phenomenon of Man*, trans. B. Wall, Harper and Row, 1959.

4   Marjorie Grene, ed., *Interpretations of Life and Mind*, Humanities Press, 1971.   See also my "The Essence of the Person," *The Monist*, January 1978.

5   See Peter A. Bertocci and R.M. Millard, Jr., PATG, especially chapter 7.

6   See William McDougall, *Energies of Man*, C. Scribner's Sons, 1933.

8   Magda Arnold, *Emotion and Personality*, 2 volumes, Columbia University Press, 1960.   See also the Loyola Symposium *Feelings and Emotions*, ed., Magda Arnold, Academic Press, 1970.

9   John C. Eccles, *Facing Reality*, Springer Verlag, 1970.

Chapter Three

THE ENVIRONMENT: ARE PERSONS THE MEASURE?

1. Knowing as Anthropic

In this chapter we enlarge on distinctions we
have already referred to as environment(s)-En-
vironment. We shall be bypassing steps in the total
knowing-process that a more complete presentation
could not do. In my judgment, however, what has
been considered and what I shall set forth would not
be contravened in a fuller account. I shall expand
three related themes.

First, while, as we have seen, persons are very
recent newcomers on this planet and dependent for
sheer physiological survival on physico-chemical-
biological musts, the clue to their cognitive success is not any capacity to produce ready-made
copies of that something they call 'Nature.' What
is meant by 'Nature' is far from clear-cut. For
"ordinary folk" Nature actually is 'environment'
insofar as they come to rough and ready agreement as
to what they may expect from whatever is 'ultimately
there'--for them as more or less disciplined wanting-
knowing agents. Even for natural scientists Nature
is not 'all the universe,' but the orderly realm that
these learning and learned persons, following more
explicit norms of investigation, have helped the
rest of us at least to understand and use. Their
'Nature' (and ours) is not finished, if for no other
reason than that there are data beyond themselves
and within themselves still to be understood. Nature
is not "what they want it to be," but it is what
they take Environment to be within the parameters
of what they discover they can cope with, at best
in quantitatively predictable terms. In this
sense Nature, technically speaking, is their product,
their scientific environment.

Second, the values of persons (basically involving, as we shall see, their primary conative

47

tendencies), are engaged in guiding their interaction with the Environment. Hence, 'Nature' as
conceived by our natural scientists, as persons
with _their_ dominant values, may be presented to us
as there, independent of human effort, but actually
it is "the realm of order" that in part is theirs as
taken and in part not theirs as _given_. There is no
neat, discernible line between "theirs" and "not
theirs," environment and Environment.

The third theme is a general thesis related to
the first two. In seeking to discover and act in
any realm not of their own making, persons perceive
it and conceive it as they act to gratify their own
developing natures as affective-conative and cognitive
agents. Thus, we may say that persons _interact_ with
the Environment but _take_ it in the context of the
sensory, affective-conative responses that they as
reason-capable persons can make. They are always
challenging some views of themselves-in-relation-
to-Environment and considering others that seem
more coherent at the time. We must put more flesh
on this contention that (even) knowledge of Nature
is anthropic.

2. Nature as Joint-Product of Persons and
    Environment

(a) What appears in our total sensory experience
does not carry labels authorizing _this_ rather than
that view of _what_ the Environment _is_. Hence, Environment delivers no commanding message about its
nature that we can know with logical certainty.
Moreover, since sensory, memorial, and reasoning
activities cannot be ripped away from each other,
and since they develop at different rates and also
have different limits, persons must always check
their own responses and interpretations against
those of others. Persons are constantly proposing
and defending, when they raise questions consciously,
those interpretations of their experiences which

are 'concurrent' with Environment, or 'relevant.'
Thus, while Nature is no man-made product, neither
is it a copy or final version of Environment.
Nature is Environment <u>for and of persons</u> seeking to
fulfill themselves, uncritically and critically, as
they learn to cope with themselves via environments
'in' Environment.

Speaking broadly, then, we may say that persons,
in interpreting their sensory experience, find
themselves involved in moving back and forth from
private to commonsense and to scientific conceptions.
To illustrate: persons all over the world could
readily agree that there are two shining objects in
the sky, the one always "rising" in the east and
"setting" in the west (the sun), the other (the moon)
having regular phases of light and being more visible
during the darkness than the stars. The steady ways
in which these two visible 'objects' enter human experience, in relation to human needs and abilities,
led to their becoming signal objects in the sky by
day and by night; they became the common denominator
for all people, around which other experiences could
be interpretatively organized.

As I have hinted, these perceived objects appear
in so dependable and in so orderly a fashion that
they were considered to be the causes of the light
persons were actually experiencing--as if the light
they were seeing was not the joint-product of
'something out there' and their own preparedness as
knowing-wanting persons.[1] These assumed independent
existents, sun and moon, as commonsense viewed them,
were the points of departure for further responses
and interpretations by poets, astrologists, geome-
tricians, astronomers, philosophers, theologians
(and others).

However, when such questions as the relation of
the earth and other celestial bodies to the sun and
moon arose, it became necessary to examine and evaluate the contexts of interpretation with a view to
deciding which one could be most reasonably accepted
for both practical and theoretical purposes. Today
the contexts of interpretation provided by the com-

munity of astronomers and other physical scientists
are accepted as the foundation for understanding
what happens--and can be assumed to happen--in the
realm of (physical) Nature. Interestingly, even
though our scientifically reasoned conception of
the relation of the sun to its planets is our
critically approved view, most of us still say that
the sun rises in the east and sets in the west. And
who of us experiencing the "light of the sun" right
now is affected by his knowledge that the rays we
are experiencing is our experience of what "left"
the sun several minutes ago, according to our most
reasoned view.

    To summarize: Persons live in relation to En-
vironment in terms of interpretative perspectives
(environments) that express their own total natures,
constitutive and learned, at a given time in their
history. The Nature they construct is for all
practical purposes the Environment as known to them
especially by way of their sensory responses within
the context of their total preparedness. Since
persons can never know the Environment except in
relation to perspectives that they think they can
trust on the basis of their past response, their
knowing of the Environment is never the acceptance
of final messages simply 'delivered' or 'revealed'
to total human responsiveness.

(b) To put this conclusion in another way. Strictly
speaking, there are no statements of fact, that is,
of what is, that do not reflect human ways of dealing
with their own conative nature, conjoined as it is
with their cognitive capacities. The environment
'within' the Environment, the Nature 'within' the
Environment is not independent of the dimensions of
human experiences that are being gratified, frustrated,
or challenged. Nevertheless, as persons discover that
their environments fit the problems of their existence
within the constraints of Environment, they make the
theoretical and practical compromises--some more
comprehensive than others--that seem required and
that promise to serve them well. These more comprehensive agreements are neither impersonal nor nonpersonal. They are, to coin a word, omnipersonal;

for they are always personal responses and the more
reasonable interpretations of Environment²--until
there is significant challenge by new data.

(c) Man, accordingly, lives in environment(·s)-
within-Environment, and in the end his task is to
decide how to accommodate his environments so that
they will express both the dimensions of his own
complex nature and also enlighten him as to his
relation to the Environment. That relation
("within"?) is never one that makes it possible to
say with certainty where the one begins and the other
ends.

     All the more then, the test of the truth of
any proposed relation requires that the knowers aim
at a maximum comprehensiveness as they seek to
discover the clue(s) that will be most coherent with
all the dimensions of their experience. Whatever the
Environment is, man is victor or vanquished in accordance as he satisfies adequately, or fails to
satisfy, his own measure.

(d) I shall now adopt an analogy that will serve us
also in later phases of this study as we try to conceive of the total person's relation to Environment.
What has already been suggested is that the common
analogy for knowing (drawn from our vision of bisected lines, of sun and moon) encourages a pictorial
view, approximating camera-likeness. We might remind
ourselves that such could not be the picture encouraged by nonvisual senses (like hearing and smelling,
for example). The analogy I shall now suggest will,
of course, involve vision for sighted persons, but
auditory, tactual, and kinesthetic senses are the
point of departure.

     Let us liken the agent-knower to a pianist who
is seated at the keyboard of a piano and who knows
only that the keys he strikes are connected somehow
with something beyond his field of vision (the piano's
soundboard). The keyboard, we remind ourselves, is
itself the result of long, human experience; technicians
and musicians have succeeded in setting before the

51

pianist (with his anatomical structures, including five fingers on each hand), an organization of keys that are accommodated to him and connected eventually with the soundboard. Let us suppose that the pianist has learned from others' and from his own experience that the soundboard (Environment) does have a certain structure that can make a very wide range of sounds possible, but not all sounds. The Environment, thus, has an unknown but not unknowable range of possibilities in relation to the players, and we may well refer to it as the Realm of Eligibility (hereafter, usually, Realm).

The Realm in this instance, as the pianist is to discover, makes many sounds and many combinations of sounds possible by way of this anthropic keyboard. For the particular keyboard at which any pianist sits is the environment which he has inherited from others, the environment to which he must accommodate himself if he is to learn what can become actual thereby.

A pianist, as he learns what he can do with the keyboard, may not be especially interested in raising questions about what it is in the soundboard (Realm) that makes a certain range of sounds possible. He may accordingly treat the Realm as if it were not there, focusing on his keyboard (environment, Nature) as if it exhausted all there is. But he may think of other sounds he has heard elsewhere, and he may ask why they cannot be made by way of this keyboard and this piano. And, of course, he may never be fully aware of what in himself is stirred and soothed by the sounds 'his keyboard' makes. But when such questions grip him he must ask about himself, his keyboard, the Environment (Realm), and their relation to each other.

The pianist (the agent-knower), the keyboard ('world'-Nature), and the Realm of Eligibility-- these are the situational factors in the human piano-music-situation. The keyboard is the joint-product of pianists and Realm, even though many pianists may consider the keyboard as the sole cause of the music (just as we consider the common-sense sun to be the cause of the light we see).

That keyboard may also be accepted as the basis for further musical thought and expression. And, let us make no mistake about it, the keyboard is the Realm insofar as human responses, including those of persons especially prepared as artists and technicians, have been able to appreciate what is available to them 'in' the Realm. Pianists learn that while they are limited in their control of the quality and range of sounds as they play surprises await them in the previously unheard patterns that occur as they experiment with themselves in relation to a particular keyboard.

This suggests that the Realm, by way of the keyboard and what the pianist does, makes eligible for us more than we have ever dreamed. But there is no situation in which the pianist can leave his environment, the keyboard, and observe the Realm independently of the sounds and patterns he makes at the keyboard. He can only use the segments of musical patterns he has, change his keyboard in different ways, and live with the surprises and disappointments that result as he accepts the challenges from within himself and from the environment as already established. There are further possibilities within himself and beyond himself to be explored; there is no ready measure for the quality open to pianists and their keyboards.

(e) In this interaction between the total knowing-agent and Environment that makes itself effective in his experiencing, the model of knowing cannot be conceived of as direct knowing, as mirroring, as copying. The piano-sounds are neither 'in' the keyboard nor 'in' the soundboard; but they could not be what they are without the influence of keyboard (accepted environment) and Environment upon him. Or, beginning with the musician-piano-composer, the sounds and musical themes he has in mind may or may not be 'represented' in the keyboard or in the soundboard, although he hopes that he may find the interaction that makes his total musical experience one that connects their possibilities and their meaning for him more satisfactorily.

53

3. Anthropic Knowing and Mystery

(a) Our discussion does not support the view that
the Realm is an impenetrable Unknown, or the view
that since we can never know the Realm 'as it is'
we must remain skeptics. It does require that we
keep in mind that our alternatives are <u>not</u>: either
direct, experiential certainty, or logical certainty,
or skepticism. As long as our conative-cognitive
agency can find by mediation of their keyboards
(environment, Nature) support from the Realm, knowing
requires not one-to-one correspondence between our
human efforts and the Realm, but concurrence or
relevance, that is, support to be defined as carefully as we can as we reasonably respond in each
knowledge-situation in the different dimensions of
our experiencing as persons.

        There is indeed a prime mystery of Being itself,
and no investigation will fathom that mystery. But
the human task is to appreciate how our different
human proposals, moving from trial and error to more
disciplined experiment and comprehensive surmise,
in every area of our lives, may be better related
to each other. Which proposed discoveries will lead
to those developments of a keyboard (environment)
whose links are most adequately supported by the
Realm? We never know with certainty, <u>what</u> that
mysterious Realm is in relation to persons; that
relation remains an inference from the experiences
persons undergo and organize. Or, again, <u>what</u> the
Realm is in relation to persons remains an inference
from the keyboards they have thus far developed but
would not have developed if, <u>in expressing their
own natures</u>, <u>they found inadequate support in the
Realm</u>.

(b) Is the Realm itself, then, only an hypothesis?
Of course not! And it is time that this weary objection died of its own fright. For the hypothesis,
the human proposal of one person to himself and to
another, is that thus-and-so as experienced is sufficiently supported by the Realm that its mystery,
however abysmal, is not alien to disciplined personal
responses. To <u>think</u> reality is not to <u>be</u> Reality;

to act is not to be Reality acting. For it is the person, prepared for and by his culture and its constructs of Nature--it is this person who probes for further hints as he reaches for what he needs and what brings gratification and satisfaction. What the person is constantly doing is using the patterns of his performance at the keyboard, segmental as they always are, as guides to how the Realm of Eligibility may respond to his larger interests; that is, he understands his segments better by setting them into a larger setting than he earlier realized was eligible.

Accordingly, I articulate the principle underlying everything else I have had to say: any proposal we, as persons, make never rids us of the primal mystery of things. Our proposals are aimed at helping us understand and act in relation to the Realm without foreclosing unnecessarily the criticism and revision of our proposals when logic, evidence, and new concerns so indicate. Any proposal, therefore, is no more--yet, no less!--than the most coherent formulation of our experience with the Realm (Environment) to date. To return to our piano example, there are many actions and formulations that are allowed by the soundboard. The task for each of us and for groups, societies, and cultures is so to think and act that our guided responses bring out the (presumptive) best in human nature in relation to the (presumptive) structures allowed by the Realm.

(c) I shall suggest that the Realm is most coherently conceived as a Person, a person who purposely sustains the regularities that encourage us to discern Nature (keyboard) in relation to our activity-potentials. Included in His purpose is the enabling of persons to participate in the creation of a new order, new environments. This hypothesis will not be about what is itself an hypothesis; it directs our attention to our total interactive responses to what the Realm is insofar as we can follow the patterns of reasoned observations. For me to add: "The Realm is a Person-and-more," may be an appropriate way of indicating that "there is more than I can think."

But since such a 'more' is always understood in connection with any human hypotheses, it never can be used by reasonable proponents to justify any particular conclusion without adducing evidence for what the 'more' proposed is.

4. The Person--Willing to Know

I now introduce a factor in the nature of the person without which, I suggest, the whole conception of the person as knower and evaluator is idle talk. "Willing" is held in many quarters to be a derivative from other activities we already have presented. Let me reset the stage for this new actor.

(a) In our examination of the situation of the person as agent-knower, what is evident so far as the interrelatedness of the activity-potentials of sensing, remembering, imagining, affective-conative predispositions, and thinking (inclusive of logical and reasoning activity), is the process of solving some problem. Thinking without sensory experiences, memories, and affective-conative tendencies would be empty. The self-conscious person inspects his activity-potentials and their objects or objectives, and, as we have said, weaves them together into as coherent an hypothesis as possible. But among the steps, ranging from the varieties of sensory and of conative data to the organizing of a comprehensive, reasonable hypothesis, there is another phase that cannot be omitted, free willing.

(b) Let us now look at this process of organizing reasonable hypotheses as it often takes place when the person is engaged in sifting out only the factors that are relevant to the problem at hand. It now becomes critical to distinguish between the outcome of this total psychological process as such and the outcome whose purpose is truth-finding. It is one thing for a psychological process to move from one stage to another--say, to an ending that is the outcome of the regnant trends in the complex psychological situation. But it is another thing for a process to aim, and to arrive, at a true conclusion. The true conclusion, of course, is also a psychological process, but the end-goal cannot be simply an outcome of dominant factors psychologically. For the goal, the true conclusion, must fit the demands of logic and reasonableness, despite the factors in the psychological situation that might obstruct this achievement. This goal of truth-seeking often cannot be reached unless the person can will (as well as sense, remember, feel, want, and think).

What do we find if we take a closer look at the actual process by which we come to select the hypothesis that we deem to be true? We discover ourselves relating ideas, sifting out among them the more relevant from the irrelevant, though psychologically attractive, others--all this in accordance with our ideal of truth. To this ideal we will to hold even as we continue despite obstacles to achieve coherent relevance.

This experiencing, this effort or willing, is not desiring--much as some think of 'willing' as the 'strongest desire' making itself felt. But the effort to organize must often oppose the strongest desire in the psychic field. This conflict between desired conclusion and true conclusion often is, to put it simply, the conflict of weaker desires that we approve with stronger desires that we do not approve. It is now especially that we must initiate thinking, construct an hypothesis, and keep it before us as we organize the more relevant data in accordance with our ideal of truth. It is now that we "make the effort," that is, will to keep that hypothesis before us, despite the massive opposition of ideas linked with stronger but unapproved desires. Again, to resist the desired but unwarranted solution, to delay coming to a solution before other more relevant ideas and desires can make themselves felt, to persist in thinking when we would prefer to stop, and to keep that thinking conforming with our logical and coherent ideal--it is this will-full, purposeful process that is the person in action as truth-seeker.

(c) Our distinction between a conclusion that is a
rationalization of wishes and a conclusion that is
reasoned rests on the assurance that the reasoned
conclusion follows from the sorting and evaluation
of factors relevant to the problem to be solved; as
reasoned, it must not merely register the outcome
of conflicting power-factors in a given psychological
situation. Accordingly, the very factor that makes
all the difference between a mere outcome of psychological pressures and a conclusion that we consider
true depends on the person's activity of willing.
Such willing must be sufficiently free, within the
matrix of conflicting forces in a person's purposeful activity, to initiate activity toward the goal
approved. This free will can act (initiate, continue), even though it cannot always enact.

    The existence of such free will (or will-agency)
is subject to much dispute. But deny this personal
will-agency and the consequences are momentous. For
it means no less than the mere substitution of the
outcome of a psychological process for purposeful
truth-seeking. It means that we do not discover
truth, but that truth, so-called, is the outcome of
the stronger psychic forces alone. Hence, speaking
for myself, were there no further reasons for believing
in a person's free will-agency, I should postulate it.
Otherwise we cannot say we reach conclusions; we reach
only the eventual outcomes of the stronger factors
in a situation. How can we expect reasoning really
to enlighten us about a situation if there is no activity in us that can initiate and keep thinking
'moving' toward the goal of truth?

(d) The particular view of will-agency I am proposing
is so vital to the total discussion in this book that
I must expand on my conclusion that free will-agency
is a constitutive and not a derived activity of the
person.

    In the first place, persons experience such
effort or agency (or fiat, to use William James's
word). (Both determinists and libertarians usually
agree to this, the former interpreting it as a derivative that is itself the outcome of psychological

58

dynamics.) Did we, in experiencing will-agency, identify it _prima facie_ with, say, wanting, I should be given pause. But I hold to free will on its own appearance unless I find good reason to suppose that it either feels like or is the strongest want. In so holding I am doing what I do with my experience of blue, or of pleasant, or of anger, or of thinking. I resist any claim that I can reduce any of these to the other unless there is good reason to reject what appears to be distinct.

(e) Hence, when I am told, and when I sometimes tell myself, that such a conception of free-will conflicts with another equally basic and less debatable truth about our experience and the world, namely, that any given event or pattern is an effect of some deter-minable cause, I am indeed given pause. But then I ask why the particular truth-claim about 'causal law' should be held to be so universal as to rule out even the possibility that what I claim to experience as free will cannot be so interpreted. In the end I reflect that if _this deterministic interpretation_ of my experience of free will is true, it is true only if the proponent is free to assess the evidence, in-cluding his experience of will-agency. If any deter-minist's conclusion that there is no free will is drawn from evidence that does not include his experi-ence of freedom in drawing that conclusion, why should he trust that conclusion as truer than any other sheer outcome of his psychological processes?

(f) This line of reasoning is all the more important if we keep in mind the dynamic _Gestalt_ of personal activities. For, in that Gestalt, reasoning, as one dimension of my activity, does not simply enforce its logical and coherent norms on feelings, sensations, needs, emotions, and even willing. Reasoning itself must (often) be initiated and sustained as it weaves together the considerations that fit some one hypoth-esis better than others, or vice versa. In reasoning, I, as a person, am attempting to reach the systematic understanding of what is _in_ my experience and also what is possibly _related_ to it, with a view to dis-covering the most coherent way of conceiving myself. To be trustworthy my reasoning requires that, though

59

I must work within limits, I can really at this
critical point restrict, release, or inhibit factors
in my ongoing experience, so that my envisaged goal
will be reached despite the opposition. Of course,
I accomplish nothing unless in willing I can depend
on observable and inferred connections within my experience and beyond this situation. But I stand, at
the heart of problem-solving, choosing at least my
own attitude toward what is going on in me or hap-
pening to me.

(g) I have been urging that willing is one of my
activities whose aim is to actualize purposes that
in actuality may or may not be reasonable. In any
case my will and reasoning never occur in a psychological vacuum. I will to reason and keep reasoning even though I do not know in a specific situation whether I can actually make any headway in
overcoming obstacles. My will-agency, therefore,
does not have adequate power in relation to the obstacles that confront me at choice-point.

     It is important, therefore, to distinguish
between my will-agency and my will-power, that is,
the power of my will-agency. Will-power, accordingly, will vary from situation to situation depending on the dynamics of each situation. Obviously,
we cannot cut will-agency away from will-power
absolutely; but the situation is helpful theoretically
and practically. Theoretically, it points to the
actuality that 'free will' is never active in a psychological vacuum; will-agency is an activity of the
person dependent for its power to enact on the organization of factors within and beyond the person at
choice-point. Practically, it means that a person
himself cannot be certain that in willing he can
achieve the objective he has in mind to any one of
the degrees he had envisaged. Often when we say,
for example, "He has no will; he cannot stop smoking,"
we should say, "He has no will-power when it comes to
smoking." This person may be able to achieve what he
wills in other areas even more important to him.

(g) Incidentally, the actual dynamics of will-agency

and will-power should forestall the objection that
to grant will-agency is to open the life of a person
to any whim, that now he cannot depend on his training
to stand by in the face of 'arbitrary' will-agency.
Note: The actual situation is always a person who
is investing his activity-potentials in habits, attitudes, sentiments, traits (and other formations)
that presumably will help him to form the quality
of personality that will indeed influence his expression of himself. Thus, the person choosing is
willing neither in a vacuum nor in chaos as he seeks
self-actualization. Of this more when we consider
the choice and organization of values.

This view of persons as willing-agents does not,
therefore, minimize any of those factors in the total
person that influence, and often are conditions for,
both survival and quality. Indeed, in a fuller exposition, I would stress the physiological, physico-
chemical, and unconscious conditions involved in the
comparative plasticity of telic personal response,
as well as the interrelation, yet relative autonomy,
of cognitive factors. Here I stress that reasoning
cannot realize its objectives if it is simply the
servant of the matrix of sensory-conative data
and dispositions (unlearned and acquired). For, I
persist, the aim of weaving together relevant data
in the attempt consciously to resolve problems
requires the free effort to include what is relevant,
exclude what is alluring and even seductive but not
pertinent, and move to conclusions justifiable by
evidence and not by the psychological explosives
forever present in any serious purposeful activity.

(h) It is this volitional factor within the total
Gestalt of personal existence that enables us to
understand why men do hold themselves morally
responsible for so much in what they believe is
within their control. We shall need to take up (in
the next chapter) the nature of human obligation
(oughting). In this chapter I have been trying to
fill out what is involved in placing persons, among
the living beings of the world, as the truth-needing
and truth-seeking creatures. It is the person, as
wanting-willing-knowing-agent, who interacts with

Environment, who responds, within the scope of unlearned and learned orientations, and who develops
the environment that takes his measure in terms of
this _kind_ _of_ _Realm_.

5.   The Engagement of Persons to Reality

(a)   The time has come to draw together the considerations that are relevant to a question that we shall
pursue in a different context: Does the phenomenon
of man, the agent-knower, provide any clue at all to
the Realm? Whatever we finally decide about a cosmic
purpose or a cosmic Person, if I read the record
aright, we may say that were the environment simply
that presented in physico-chemical perspective we
would have no inkling of the living beings that,
in reproducing themselves and adjusting to the
physico-chemical orders, actually help to constitute
an environment _related_ to their responsive natures.
Add to this the total cultural environment(s) that
persons live in and by, and we have the largest
available context for interpreting what the Realm is.

     There is no parallel to this relationship between
the anthropic natural environment(s) and the Realm.
Physical and biological scientists tend to regard
persons as only another unusually fascinating development in accordance with principles "inherent in"
Nature. I argue for a very different view. Why?
Because persons, developing their methods of learning
in relation to their own needs and in response to
what was imposed upon them, do not "find" what is
"simply there in principles." Working within their
activity-potentials, persons have interacted with the
Realm even as they interpreted and organized the
plethora of given data into controllable, predictable,
and quantitatively measurable patterns. And the
joint-product is their environment, "the order of
Nature." Thus, we are not just products of Nature
with principles completely its own, ready for persons
to "find" them. Nature-with-persons is anthropic
from beginning to end. I hasten now to add that

anthropic Nature is no artificial product, not, indeed, if it is throughout the joint-product of persons related to each other in response to Environment (Realm). It is persons, thus situated in this anthropic-natural-environment, who realize that they can depend on a steady, inferred foundation, concurrent with, and relevant to, their interpretations of their interactions with each other "within" the Realm.

(b) Substitution of the anthropic keyboard for the soundboard, or of Nature as equivalent to, or identical with, the Realm of Eligibility is the target of the protest in this chapter. Necessary as Nature and the understanding of natural principles is, it is not in itself, we shall increasingly see, the cornerstone for a coherent Realm-view. What I have particularly stressed so far is that from physico-chemical principles of change there is no adequately warranted path to the will-agency, reason, and quality of conative action in persons. And I have added that it is because persons are free to become reasonable in thought and action that persons may reasonably trust their conclusions.

(c) What the most reasonable view of Nature-environment and of its relation to the Realm is must remain open for more comprehensive philosophical discussion. I have proceeded so far on the view that the method(s) guiding most scientists in organizing their physico-chemical-biological observations cannot be exemplars for understanding persons as a whole. While the matter is not critical to my argument in this book, perhaps I owe it to my reader to add that I stand on these metaphysical issues closer to those philosophers who are usually called pan-psychistic idealists. They hold that instead of understanding physico-chemical fields of energy as non-telic, and instead of explaining telic biological being-events and societies in terms of non-telic processes, we reconstruct the basic conception. They conceive both the physico-chemical and biological processes to be psychic and telic. But since the physico-chemical 'beings' are so regular, since they are relatively so constrained

63

in the order of their going and coming, their natures
are viewed as sufficiently limited in telic spontaneity and freedom that they can form the stable,
"physical" ground for the more spontaneous, telic,
organic beings we observe in our evolutionary scale.

I have some reservations about pan-psychic, telic
organicism that will be noted at a more pertinent
stage of our considerations. But, sidestepping further
metaphysical issues, I now set forth, on the more
limited grounds already advanced, what will, nevertheless, be foundation-stones for the personalistic
teleological theism to be expounded.

(d) Persons arrived on the cosmic scene. Their survival--more than that of any other creature--depended
on their ability to guide their actions by cautious
observation and creative response to their own given
constitutions and to conditions not of their own
making in the Realm. Persons did not simply arrive
fully prepared to add their own new quality of being,
related to prior levels, to the dimensions of being
already existent. The awakening of their critical
self-consciousness, their adaptability to vast ranges
of pain and unpleasantness, their sensitivity to many
varieties of satisfying experiences, found them
setting priorities within a larger context of collocations to which they did not assume they were alien.
If I seem to jump ahead of "hard evidence" to a comprehensive teleology, I do not apologize--as if the
burden of proof fell on the teleologist. For, granted
the impenetrable mystery that faces us all, we cannot
trust any of our own reasoning about any of that
mystery, if we assume that our natures, especially
as guided by our reasoned self-criticism, are incapable
of shedding any light on the Realm. To be sure,
reason may discover, even at the end of its imaginative
and magnificent scientific constructions, that Nature
and Life (naturalistically conceived) did indeed spawn
a creature whose range of sensitivity and yearnings
put on no more than a 'good show' while it lasted!

(e) But why court the unnecessary opaqueness that
thus enters our theorizing--with such a flourish to
boot! For it still remains that what 'just happens'

to persons is not like what happens to leaves being blown about by forces beyond them--or even to what happens to cells that multiply by the trillions wherever they can evade destructive forces. When we take a closer look at man's appearance, we cannot minimize the impressiveness of a kind of creature who, indeed, cannot survive without utilizing both nonliving and living orders, but who, nevertheless, comes significantly into his own as he builds on his understanding and appreciation of what they may contribute to his own existence.

I submit that we can do more. We may look for a teleological conception of the Realm because persons as agents are also persons who, in knowing selectively, organize their affective-conative, volitional, and cognitive experiences as the condition for fuller appreciation of what their ventures in wanting mean. It is this kind of telic being--no simple or complex sequence, or composite, of events--who self-consciously reaches for goals that require disciplined, imaginative appreciation of what is beyond him and yet related to his aspirations. It is this kind of being who has been so weak, dissolute, self-deceptive--and yet also able to transform his frustrations into challenges, to smile, to laugh as well as to cry, to manicure his life as he has his fields, to rebuild after he has himself destroyed or seen some of his best efforts destroyed. It is this kind of survivor, never content just to live but to live well, as Socrates put it, that asks whether in his experience as a whole there is a clue to the Realm.

What I have been suggesting will have been in vain if it is reduced to: "Well, a thinking-being will, of course, ask the question about the purpose of his life in relation to what is ultimate." For the splitting wedge is <u>what it means to think clearly and adequately and totally</u>. To change the figure, we may not, as we think comprehensively, find the linchpin for tying the human and the cosmic Whole together; we certainly may not deny that the person's search for knowledge often ends in utter defeat, and with frightful pain, anxiety, and misery. Yes, a light that stays on long enough to illuminate what "his" Nature is like makes the darkness for persons more than dark when it flickers out.

But our concern must still be to take the light and the darkness, and the whole they reveal in relation to each other. We cannot do this if we make assumptions, for whatever reasons, that arbitrarily put a stop to our search. I hold it to be a hopeful meliorism, not an easy optimism, that justifies the contention that persons, within the confines of conditions for survival, and for all their fumbling beginnings and stumbling progress, are gradually more capable of managing their own styles of survival in relation to other persons, and are becoming more aware of what the quality of such survival requires in this kind of Realm.

Again, we cannot begin to pretend that persons know all they need to know, or that any particular keyboard which persons have constructed is the best one possible for them on the soundboard. Nevertheless, no hypothesis about the Realm can neglect the quality of effort and the quality of achievement by persons so fragile and yet so powerful--yes, even, so often, in quiet desperation. We can only ask which hypothesis, short of logical certainty, most reasonably warrants the human trust that, once persons have learned to organize appropriate responses in relation to the Realm, they will not discover, like characters in Kafka, that the Realm itself is all illusion and malice. Such responses, we have the right to believe, are more likely to be "promissory notes" to "more of similar."

This is the pilgrimage of whole-some reason seeking faith, a faith supported every time a person lights a Bunsen burner with confident expectations, say, that the blue flame will be hotter than the yellow. Our teleological stance supports the scientists who enter their laboratories and go to work on the assumption that their intelligence will not be disappointed finally in a Realm that has supplied clues that both heroic and prosaic faith may live by.

(f) This is the time to ask in a preliminary way:
Must we not bear in mind that persons and the small
segment of the Realm they rightfully relate to themselves as their environment may well be an oasis in
a vast desert? This alternative is logically possible.
But it certainly is not the hypothesis that natural
scientists live by as they proceed from their segmental knowledge of the Realm to 'unknowns' that, as
they believe, will not defy the clues their disciplined
method has discovered in the segment.

In any case, we should recall that 'environment-
as-oasis-in-a-desert,' too, is a hypothetical construct. Furthermore, it is one that, consistently
applied, would discourage the growth of knowledge.
But let us pronounce knowledge vain only when, para-
doxically, our reason assures us that evil is pre-
dominant and failure certain. Meanwhile, let us now
move on, as the most reasonable course, to what is
far from blind faith. Why, I persist, purposely cut
the intellectual limb on which we are sitting from
the branches and the trunk of Reality? Of course,
our telic hypothesis, like all hypotheses, is anthropic: it reflects our cognitive, conative, willing
agency, but by now we should see that to be anthropic
is not an uncritical anthropomorphism. Our hypotheses, our keyboards, are not simply reflections of
our makeup; and they certainly, given our experience
with them, can be taken to be the reasonable measure
of ourselves as we interact with the soundboard Realm.
But let us not disqualify the measures we have because they are ours, or disown them because they
clearly are no final camera-shots of the Realm.[4]

6. Reflective Overview

(a) Looking back to the problems of knowing that
commanded our attention in the first chapter, we can
further confirm our suggestion that neither believer nor disbeliever may assume that his own fervent
beliefs directly capture the 'mystery of being,' and
this all the more because his feelings, his needs,

his emotions, his cognitive powers, and his will-
agency mediate his transactions with the Realm.
The Truth-value of the different dimensions of his
experience, the relevance of the world within his
grasp to the Realm of Eligibility must always stand
ready to be re-evaluated in the light of new data
that call for interpretation. While no one segment
of human experience or of the world may dictate
arbitrarily to the rest, neither can it be assumed
that every segment is equally important. There is
an ethics of belief. It grows out of the situation
I have been depicting: persons realize that at every
stage of their growth they must distinguish between
what is related to desires and wishes and what is
relative to them alone.

(b) Thus, influenced by William James's essay,
"The Will to Believe," I have been applying what
I take to be James's essential point, namely: a
person ought to interpret his evidence as a whole
in such a way that the thought and the action following from that interpretation will not foreclose
reasonable options still open to him, even if they
are not demonstratively certain. The options that
make considerable difference to our goals in living,
if we follow them, can never be logically inconsistent
among themselves nor logically demonstrative. There
will continue to be debate about evidence, old and
new. A person has no right to believe anything he
wishes, especially in the face of more challenging
evidence. Given no decisive, negative evidence, the
reasoned and reasonable lines of thought and action
(lines which, if taken, may themselves help to create
the human situation soberly and hopefully desired),
may be followed as trustworthy. James at one time
would have said that persons have the 'right to
believe' them. I affirm: they ought to believe;
as persons, they ought to act so that their belief
may be better appraised!

(c) But, at the end of this chapter, I must set in
relief the fact that our exemplar of knowledge must
move from eye-analogies--camera-shots and visual
mirroring--closer to auditory ones. Musical sounds

68

suggest interaction between persons and world for which eye-analogies are not illuminating. Musical sequences in the personal world reflect what musicians 'say' about themselves and their adjustments as expressions related to structures they do not create. Musicians and composers develop scores by which they guide their response to a Realm that itself need not be complete or completely expressed in those scores. We need not, and shall not, assume that only our knowledge is in the making; for aspects of the Realm, at least, may be in the making also. And whether these aspects are realized may depend upon the kind of thought and action a person takes toward himself and the known and knowable environment.

Do we, then, taking the evidence before us, have the right to believe either that man is made in the image of God or in the image of basic patterns of physical and biological forces? Surely, the preponderant evidence so far adduced justifies neither conclusion. I have in this chapter challenged the contention that man as agent-knower is an extraneous happenstance that can give no clue to the Realm. In contrast I have proposed, with the varied patterns of organic life before us, and with the scope of the human venture in truth-seeking (and its presuppositions) before us, the option of taking the interrelations between the physico-chemical, the organic, and the wanting-willing-knowing persons to be phases of a teleological trend. The cognitive outreach of persons cannot be ripped away from personal being as a whole, least of all from the person as an agent free within limits to ground his conclusions on evidence.

In sum, the Realm of which persons are mindful seems to come into their lives neither as brute power nor as imposing very narrow alternatives. In the chapter that follows I shall elaborate on the structures of value in persons, structures that underlie, and are supported by, the cognitive-conative ventures of persons. At the same time they, too, reveal what can happen when persons-with-persons cooperate with tendencies in themselves and in the Realm.

Notes

1 See Brightman, PAR; C.I. Lewis, MWO; and especially
Tennant, PT, vol. 1, for in depth developments of my
general thesis. Brand Blanshard, NOT, brilliantly
moves into an opposing position, against which Lovejoy,
RAD, is a worthy contender. But the presentation as
developed in this chapter is my responsibility.

2 I should express my indebtedness to much in
phenomenological and existential analyses throughout
these pages; however, at this point, I have in mind
the works of Martin Heidegger, Gabriel Marcel, and
Paul Ricoeur, although the treatment here has more
general scope. In such approaches the relation of
person to environment, not the least the epistemology,
leaves me still hesitant.

3 See William James's treatment of will in his famous
Psychology, 1896, and in WTB. See C.A. Campbell,
In Defense of Freedom, 1912; Gilbert Ryle, The Concept
of Mind, 1949; B.F. Skinner, Beyond Freedom and
Dignity, 1971, and G.W. Allport, PGP, present opposing
views. See Bertocci and Millard, PATC, for expansion
of the view presented here, and see in Howie and
Buford, CSPI, Robert M. Beck's critique, "Will."

4 See Bertocci, EAG, where historical background in
English thinkers of the 19th and early 20th centuries
is provided and evaluated. See also Robert C. Neville,
The Cosmology of Freedom, 1974.

Chapter Four

ROOTS OF THE LIFE GOOD TO LIVE: FOR PERSONS

1. The Natural Environment as Included in the Search for Values

In this chapter we begin the examination of what makes personal life good to live. Believers and unbelievers, as we have seen, come to broad agreement about their most common environment, Nature, but do not usually realize how much is presupposed in that agreement. The nature of man, as we have begun to realize, involves him in decisions about the scope of Nature within a larger anthropic environment, itself basically a joint-product of persons and Environment.

(a) Actually the stage is set for our deliberations about the good. For it is no mere insinuation that persons seeking the most dependable interpretation of their sensory data, persons disciplining their observations, theorizing, and practicing in order to ascertain their most common environment, are already engaged in the search for what matters most. In seeking a conception of Nature, persons, especially as natural scientists, make a value-judgment that gives priority to pursuit of the most predictable, public, and dependable orders of experience that, in turn, become a common base for their further discoveries in thought, practice, and ideals. From the beginning the search for Nature was, in fact, itself part of the more far-reaching search for enduring values.

Unfortunately, the best of scholars can forget what they earlier purposely neglected. The result of that neglect in this instance: a conception of Nature as the ultimate framework indifferent to values. Hence, the Realm of Eligibility for environments-for-persons became the Realm of Indifference to all living organisms, to persons and to their values.

The burden of much of our preceding discussion has been to challenge this view. I have argued that some anthropic environmental patterns in 'the natural world' encounter little conflict with Environment, and, thus provide dependable ground for human action and thought. This conclusion is assumed for the remainder of this book. But, again, we must not think of anthropic environments as veils that, once pulled aside, reveal the Realm independently of what conative-cognitive-willing persons are prepared to know.

(b) Accordingly, insofar as the 'natural environment' serves basic, common needs of persons, we begin to wonder whether the supposed 'Realm of Indifference' is not too limited a view of a Realm that, in fact, is omnipersonal. We remind ourselves that the natural-<u>istic</u> perspective, after all, did not establish itself. 'Nature' cannot be understood apart from its relation to conative-emotive interests involved in organizing human sensory dimensions and relevant data in accordance with norms of logic and experiential coherence. In this sense Nature manifests what persons can make of what the Realm makes eligible.

(c) Thus, not in a Realm of Indifference but in an ongoing self-discovery through self-discipline, knowing-wanting persons, aided by givens beyond their control, "construct" the order of Nature as part of their search for the things that matter most. As our attention now turns to value experiences ingredient to persons, we by no means turn away from desire, feeling, and emotion, nor from logic, coherence, and methods of accurate discovery. For persons to value is for persons actively to respond to their natural world in the context of their total sensitivity to that mysterious Realm that supports, frustrates, haunts, and inspires.

2. Can There Be Values or Ideals Independent of Persons?

(a) Let us suppose that Moses on Mt. Sinai discovered

tablets that had two commandments carved into them by God. The first commandment defined man's obligation to love God and to love one's neighbor "as thyself." The second commandment was the great mandate, Micah 6:8:"What doth the Lord require of thee, but to do justly, and to love mercy, and to walk humbly with thy God?"[Authorized (King James) Version]. Would Moses then actually have known the will of God for persons? Or, suppose, in our day, on a vast, celestial billboard were written across the skies for all to see a confirmation of Micah's insight: "The purpose governing all activities of the Realm is love, justice, and mercy." Would we then, at last, know the will of God for persons?

Would not the human viewers be like children who can see but not read, persons who cannot comprehend what the difference is between the injunctions to do justice and to love mercy, let alone to walk humbly with their God? Let these same statements be written on the tablets of our minds, let it be evident that God wrote them, how would persons make the connection between them and their daily thought and practice?

My own answer begins with another question: Even if we could begin our search for the good with an indubitable awareness of the Good, or God's will, would we not still have to inquire in terms of what persons are capable of: what the deeds, thoughts, habits, attitudes, sentiments, traits, and other dispositions are that express both the concrete content and the spirit of justice and love?

I am not denying that we can acquire dependable knowledge of the good. I am raising the question that it seems to me is the permanent obstacle to the view that persons can know what is good for them as a structure of values or goods wholly independent of them. Can such a structure in a Mind, or a Platonic Realm, reveal to them <u>what</u> they ought to do, or whether their own natures can possibly actualize these ideals?

(b) I am aware that a hidden premise in such views

73

is that man, after all, is created by God in His image, or that man has inner kinship with this objective pattern of ideal values. But if so, my main point is conceded: persons in knowing values cannot know what is simply independent of their own natures. The good is the good _of_ or _for_ a particular kind of being in a certain kind of situation.

To put my point directly: Even if we could know the Good (as God, or as Ideals independent of the cosmic Mind) directly as somehow valid for persons' guidance, we should still have to discover the links between that wholly objective or independent order of values and what can be reasonably demanded of persons, given their constitutions and their situations. To say this is not to reject once and for all the ways in which what are frequently called "moral intutitions" may influence our conclusions about the good. But it justifies hesitancy about direct and immediate knowledge of the good held to be independent of the human potential. For we are still left with the problem of linking such a good to the concrete human potential. I shall, therefore, begin the search for the life good to live for persons (the anthropic _summum_ _bonum_) at the point of interaction and transaction between the Gestalt of dispositional wants and abilities in persons and the nurturant, challenging, threatening environments-Environment to which the becoming of persons is related.

3. What Does: "No Persons, No Values!" Mean?

(a) If persons wanted nothing, if they found nothing that evoked their affective-conative natures and gratified them, there would be no values. A _value_, then, is primarily _any_ _experience_ _wanted_ _by_ _a_ _conscious_ _person_, be it at the unlearned or the derived level of conative experience. A _disvalue_ is an unwanted experience. For example, an apple or a pear gratifies hunger; and each has its own hedonic tone in a given context. As _wanted_, the apple or the pear is a value.

74

But note: Neither the apple nor the pear in itself is either a value or a disvalue. Hence, it is
better to speak of the pear and of the apple as
having value-possibilities (or disvalue possibilities)
that, in relation to the person who wants them, will
yield value-experience or disvalue-experience. What
is here proposed is: not the value-possibilities of
apples and pears but the experiences as wanted, as
unwanted, by persons, that are the actual values
and disvalues which go into persons' forming their
ideal of the life good to live--at least initially.

(b) It may seem inevitable that we are already locked
into a 'subjective' relativistic, theory of value,
since I seem to say: No wants, then no values. But
even at this initial stage, this conclusion does not
follow. For value- or disvalue-experiences (hereafter
"experiences" will be understood) are joint-products
of wanting-knowing persons, their own potential for
gratification, and of the value-possibilities of the
gratifying objects. The apple, the pear, are not
values in themselves, although we come to call them
"values." So, I persist, there are no values without
conscious, wanting persons; no persons, no values.
But persons find that they want experiences that
do not depend upon their wanting them alone; they
cannot manufacture values and disvalues "at want" or
"upon demand."

(c) If the variety of primary motives (or primary
emotions) I have suggested be granted, then we can
say that the scope of human values is related to these
kinds of needs and their learned variations. The
scope of these conative activity-potentials enters
into the formation of horizons of the good-in-relation-
to-environment-Environment. But equally important,
owing to our failure or success in achieving values,
are the value-possibilities in what is wanted as
available in the actual and possible environment.
For example, friendship-values do not exist independently of persons who, after all, depend on factors
in each other to support the particular quality of
that friendship within the social-physical environment.

(d) Several comments may clarify the situation we
face as we move from values and disvalues to the
good. First, in everyday speech we talk about being
mistaken about our values (and disvalues). That is,
what we took to be a value, or a 'real' value, turned
out to be mistaken. Hence, a change in terminology
would serve to warn us when we claim certain experiences to be values (or disvalues). Let us say that
prima facie, a given wanted experience is a value-
claim; an unwanted experience, a disvalue-claim.
To revert to our illustration, initially the experience, apple taste, is wanted: the experience, pear-
taste, is wanted. They are both value-claims. No
amount of thinking can change that initial, prima
facie experience with its hedonic tone--any more than
thinking can change the sensory experience of red
into blue. Realizing that this wanted experience is
subject to further exploration, we say more cautiously
that "this apple-value" is a value-claim. Nothing
we add will annul this initial experience. Nevertheless, one taste can turn the tables on our psychological certitude that "it's what I really want."

     But, even in the case of seemingly trustworthy
value and disvalue-claims, we need a further evaluation. Which of them are more trustworthy, and
which, if gratified, will obstruct the actualization
of other value-claims? We need, therefore, to reflect
on each value-situation, comparing and contrasting
it with others, considering its relation to conceivable
value-possibilities and other factors relevant to the
situations--and this in view of some guiding ideal.

     I pause to stress that the ideal is not the value-
experience; it is a conceptual construct, possibly a
plan for realizing value-claims in an approved order
of priorities. Ideals that are not built on value-
experiences are empty or deceiving. Hence, my warning
against looking for values beyond the lived-in-and-
reflected-upon-values that are our wanted experiences.
The ideal of justice (or mercy, or...) is critical for
human guidance, but only if it is guided by factors
in our experienced and presumably experiencable values.

     When, for example, I decide, after tasting apple-

76

value and pear-value, that I want the quality of the
first more than the second, I am already engaged
in evaluating value-qualities in terms of what they
are in actual experience, and what they promise for
other values I also want. If I judge that the difference between the quality of the apple-value and
of the pear-value is slight, and if the purchase of
apple-value leaves me less money for the procurement
of other values, then I take the pears rather than
the apples. I call the pears more valuable (as if
they, in themselves, had value; in reality they have
value now only in relation to the ideal good. But
the good is not 'ideal' independent of human experiencing; it is the conception drawn from our more
comprehensive lived-value-experiences.

(e) Accordingly, a person's progress in deciding
what the good is will continue to involve his inspection of qualities in his own experience that
he finds himself wanting or not wanting, even as
he reflects upon them in relation to each other.
This means that, while we must begin with ourselves,
as wanting or not wanting this or that experience at
a pre-reflective level, e-valuating our value-claims
calls for a reasoned discrimination. We must note
our critical and uncriticized preferences and decide
on such other matters as how far, for example, our
preferences are at the mercy of forces beyond out-
selves.

Hence, the search for the best value-complex,
for the (ideal) good, concerns itself with what value-
experiences (and what value-possibilities), if consciously chosen and actualized, would conserve as
much value as possible and decrease as much disvalue
as possible, keeping in mind both quality of values
and range of values. For example, the person, as he
becomes increasingly reflective, never simply asks:
"Shall I go on living?" but: "For what quality of
living, for what ideal good, shall I aim? And what
is open for me, in my situation, to achieve?" And
his judgment will ultimately reflect his view of
human nature, its relation to the total environment
as conceived, and his evaluation of the options open

77

to him at a certain stage of human development in relation to environment-Environment. So when we are considering the good for man, we are also evaluating the nature of the Realm in which persons, with their activity-potentials for value and disvalue, arrive and survive. (I am not, of course, claiming that this is a self-conscious, continuous process for all, or even any, persons; but I do suggest that most persons have more evaluations and convictions on these matters than they articulate.)

(f) Perhaps an over-simplified, personal note may illuminate, not justify, the approach that I have been suggesting for determining what the good for man is. In my early adolescence my religious conversion "made all things new." I became convinced that the Jesus-way of life as recorded in the Gospels (independently of other interpretations) marked a unique way of conceiving the meaning of man's life. As I grew older, I became increasingly convinced that nothing is ever done lastingly in this kind of world without the kind of love that becomes supremely creative in forgiveness. But what does it mean to love my neighbor, to forgive? What values are at stake in ethical choices?

The issues I have been discussing became a center of reflection. To speak of love of God or neighbor was to speak vacuously, as "in tongues,"--unless I could decide what kind of personality I should encourage by my feeling, thought, and action--given what persons, as I conceived them, could become. The fact is that I simply do not know what to choose, whether I try to love either my friend or my enemy, unless I am guided by some pattern of values, that is, an ideal already breaking up into modes of experience and behavior that are 'good,' as tested by myself and others whose authority I accept provisionally. Again, it is a will-o'-the-wisp to think that the good can be achieved simply by removing all conflict, frustration, or anxiety from human living. Those thinkers, religious men or world-sages, who suggest that the good life is impossible to achieve until we are able to move above the conflict of

78

human desires and the anxieties this entails are
under the spell of the conception of 'peace' that,
as we shall increasingly see, misconstrues the nature
of the actual dynamics of value-realization. They
exaggerate some desires and some value-disvalues,
rather than seeing the creative compenetration
possible in the variety of human values.

There is no intent, in such a brief statement,
to set aside in one fell stroke the teachings of great
mystics in every religious tradition. Nevertheless,
expecially in a study that concerns itself with the
nature of good, it is pertinent to remark that,
whatever control of sense and desire is deemed necessary for a peace above sense and desire, when mystics
return to themselves they do not empty themselves of
sensations and desires but develop a keener awareness
of balance (or of priorities), given the interrelation
of desires. It is a basic network of values that will
impress us as we gradually fill in the conception of
the good.

4.   What Does Oughting Refer to?

(a)   At this point I can hear a critic ask: But how
do you get from wants, from criticism of wants, and
so on, to the ought to choose the ideal that, according to you, seems to result from reflection?
If, indeed, ideals have no status independent of the
wanting-knowing person, is 'ought' any more than a
derivative of, or consequence of, 'knowing' what
you critically want? Here my answer will be very
direct, for space will not allow the discussion deserved and which I have undertaken elsewhere.[1]

I agree with this putting of the question because I am sensitive to the difference between wanting
and oughting and, above all, regard the latter as an
ineluctable and irreducible human experience. Wanting
is never oughting, and, I hold, cannot become oughting.
That is why, among the activity-potentials of the
person, I stipulated oughting also.

79

To elaborate all too briefly, I put it to myself: Add wanting upon wanting, can I ever arrive
at oughting-experience? Can I take seriously the
idea that <u>oughting</u> can be the product of a history
of wantings without hiding the impossible under
the word "gradually"? If <u>gradualness</u> can perform
this qualitative change from wanting to oughting
experience, then maybe sensing can "gradually"
become thinking? Surely not!

I suggest that no amount of appealing to
'evolution' can suppress the puzzling question:
Will my psychological alchemy, even over eons of
time, bring about the experience of oughting from
affective-conative wanting? My answer, reflecting
the challenge already made to those who would derive
respect from fear, sympathy from some other emotion,
is that such suggestions cannot support confrontation
with <u>ought</u> or <u>oughting</u> as experienced. <u>Want</u> an apple
is one thing; <u>prefer</u> an apple to a pear is another
thing. Each such experience has its own quality. By
comparing and contrasting and eventually evaluating
these value-claims, can we develop oughting, let
alone <u>an</u> ought from even such criticized value-claims?
Again, if you insist on a psychological alchemy that
produces oughting from these and other such ingredients,
then why stop there? Why not concoct thinking, for
example, from anger; anger from the color red? Oughting
as experienced has no <u>conative</u> impetus; our word for
capturing it is "imperative." That is, we find ourselves lured invisibly, we know not how or whence,
not simply by wanting but by the imperative best.

(b) But the words "oughting" and "imperative,"
alas, have gained not only the connotation of "strong
wanting" but also of "psychological must." Yet, I
submit that "oughting" is no more "musting" than
wanting. This imperative "oughting" has its own
quality, its own kind of urgency, but it is not "power."
The imperative (ought) makes itself felt always in a
context where choice is deemed possible. Its "cry"
is not stentorian; its power no thundering clap that
shatters the psychic atmosphere. Bishop Butler
neatly expressed its unique place in our psychic life

when he (in Sermon II of his classic <u>Five</u> <u>Sermons</u>, 1726) said: "Had it strength, as it has right; had it power, as it has manifest authority, it would absolutely govern the world."

Perhaps I can present a situation that for me is a kind of acid test of what must seem to some I have simply affirmed dogmatically--the irreducible, unique 'cry' in oughting. Suppose that I find myself wanting $\underline{x}$-value (be it apple or justice), and that I also find myself wanting $\underline{y}$-value (say pear, mercy, and so on). I also find that I cannot have both at once; there are conflicts with other values. And, although I think that $\underline{x}$ is better than $\underline{y}$-value, I still want $\underline{y}$ very much. Let me now assume that I can decide: $\underline{x}$ is better than $\underline{y}$. My whole thesis about oughting turns on what happens now. At choice-point, when I believe that $\underline{y}$-value is within my reach, but is not the better alternative, I never experience: I ought to choose $\underline{y}$! Never, never, never! I may find later that my will-agency will not actualize (by will-power) <u>the approved $\underline{x}$-value</u>! I may even decide that my judgment of $\underline{x}$ as being better than $\underline{y}$ was ill-advised, or even a subterfuge with unconscious roots. No matter, at choice-point, still approving $\underline{y}$ more than $\underline{x}$, I experience 'I ought to choose $\underline{x}$,' not, I ought to choose $\underline{y}$. And if I choose $\underline{y}$, my guilty conscience sets to work clearing itself by proving to its own satisfaction that $\underline{y}$ <u>was</u> <u>better</u> after all.

If my reader ever experiences <u>oughting</u> to do $\underline{y}$ when he seriously means: '$\underline{x}$ is better than $\underline{y}$,' we are at a parting of the ways. Our disagreement may grow when I conceptualize my view in the words: <u>Oughting</u> <u>is the imperative experience a person has at choice-</u> <u>point as he decides that any value is better than</u> <u>any other value.</u> The imperative (not a <u>must</u>, not the stronger or alluring <u>want</u>) he experiences can be expressed: <u>I ought to choose the best I know.</u> He may not actually choose the best, but at choice-point he recognizes that did his imperative have the power as it has the authority it would rule his world! It may be, however, that several other remarks will at least clarify these affirmations.

(c) The distinction between what I experience as the
<u>authority</u> of ought and what I experience as compelling
or compulsive is clear once I turn my attention to it,
although I often say: "I must," when <u>as erlebt</u> the
experience is of oughting some value. Of course,
there are many times when a <u>particular</u> value that
began in my experience as 'a must'--learned from my
parents, say--is re-interpreted as the better of the
alternatives. Then that <u>must</u> is no longer <u>that</u> <u>must</u>
but that ought. It is remarkable that once an authoritarian <u>x</u>-value gains my own approval, it gains
<u>authority</u> over me, even if in fact it turns out that
I cannot actualize it. Each of us, I submit, can on
reflection note the difference between what has authority and what is authoritarian (I ought, not I
must, if...).

(d) I come to elusive but all-important ingredients
in the total ought-situation. If we do all we can
to actualize, say, <u>x</u>-value deemed the best, we experience <u>moral</u> <u>approval</u>, and this whether there be
<u>social</u> <u>approval</u> or not. Again, we may have learned
that an <u>x</u> <u>is</u> <u>best</u> in a social context, but the moral
authority of <u>x</u> does not derive from the social pressure as such, but from our own approval of it. Thus,
we experience <u>moral</u> <u>approval</u> only when we pursue the
imperative (<u>x</u>-value is best)--whether or not there
is social approval, or whether anxieties are aroused
by social censure or by our own awareness of unwanted
consequences. The criterion of choice is not at issue
here, but only the quality, <u>moral</u> <u>approval</u>, experienced
as we try to actualize what we deem to be the best,
social approval or not.

(e) If we decide that <u>x</u> is best and then choose <u>y</u>,
we experience <u>moral</u> <u>guilt</u>, not anxiety. This experience looms large in my refusal to identify oughting
with wanting (or any other sheer, dispositional thrust
or merely imposed demand). The fact that <u>moral</u> <u>guilt</u>
can be evoked only by willed disobedience to what I
think is best, this phenomenon must remain as the criterion between <u>moral</u> <u>guilt</u> and anxiety. Moral guilt
is never anxiety.

(f) I may experience both guilt and anxiety in a
given situation, but the erlebt quality of each is
so different that I wonder how profound observers
could have gone on using 'anxiety' and 'guilt' as
synonyms and, even worse, conceived of moral guilt
as a form of, or product of, anxiety. I can only
ask: Is there in moral guilt the quality of uncertain
fear that characterizes anxiety? Anxiety is a consequence of uncertain fear of what may be the outcome
of many situations; anxiety, indeed, often attends
reflective choice of what ought to be chosen (since
consequences may not be foreseeable and controllable).
But each of us knows, I submit, the experienced difference between 'I ought to do x despite my anxiety,'
and 'I want to do x despite my anxiety,' (since I
know x is disapproved of by friends).

(g) There is much more to be said on many related
questions that arise out of the dynamic interrelations
within a person, but I have said enough perhaps to
indicate why I must reject two views of moral obligation. (I have substituted the verb "oughting" for
"moral obligation" in order to distinguish what I
ought [an obligation] from my experience of "oughting.")
Oughting is not to be defined by any particular ought,
by any particular obligation, any more than thinking
is to be defined by any particular thought.

(h-1) I have already suggested my difficulty with the
view that since oughting is experienced in connection
with some particular ought (x-value), oughting can
be assimilated to, or conflated with, the experiences
of oughting this x, that y, and so on. Thinkers who
have no difficulty with this conflation speak of what
I am calling the distinctive activity of oughting as
a unique way of knowing values. They use such terms
as 'moral consciousness,' 'moral sense,' 'moral reason,'
for their basic view: for persons to be aware of the
obligatory claim of x as such is for them to realize
that x-value cannot be any want-experience. On this
view, then, 'oughting' is an irreducible way of
'knowing' that certain values (say, mercy and justice),
given their nature, are obligatory. Oughting is
con-science.

83

Now, while many great minds through the ages have not agreed with Plato, that to know the good is to do it, they did and do think of knowing the good (and-or the right) as an irreducible kind of _moral_ cognition. As they see it, the human situation in which the unique quality of the imperative is experienced is so different from even the persistent lure of any object of desire that what I have referred to as oughting should be differently understood; it should register the imperative _in_ the moral cognition. The moral authority intrinsic to x (justice), they would have it, has its uniquely imperative claim in our _moral_ _consciousness_ because, as _moral_ _consciousness_, it is in no way reducible to desires (or a possible derivative from conative experience). Accordingly, 'ought' and 'oughting' for them characterize a non-sensory, non-conative Value (Idea-1) that is steadier than anything reducible to human dimensions. Its authority rests on the very nature of the value (good or right) as cognized; and persons who remain undeceived will know these normative values (or rights) for what they are and, in so doing, acknowledge their imperative.

Many of my readers will be aware that the history of the human struggle for goodness cannot be told apart from this view of the _moral_ _consciousness_ as involving a kinship with goodness, be it the command of God or the imperative of a Realm of Goodness (non-personally conceived). The _religious_ consciousness for so many seers has involved such moral consciousness with its discernment of imperative_s_. The awesomeness of the moral imperative--didn't Nietzsche say that man is a red-faced animal, an animal that blushes (experiences guilt)? Again, "Duty, stern daughter of the voice of God;" "Thou shalt love the Lord thy God...;" "Though I flee to the ends of the earth, Thou art there..."--such exclamations still understate that imperative experience of ought, of 'duty,' in the name of which countless persons in every age sacrifice their strongest inclinations. Conscientiousness is common to conscientious believers and to conscientious objectors; they 'can do no other.' It is no wonder that so many plead that such experience can hardly be earthborn.

84

This interpretation of the moral imperative persons experience is one that I, for one, have not found easy to resist. As already suggested, this cognitive view of the imperative is advanced also as the foundation for the objective ground of ethical values. I have, in substitution, claimed that oughting is _sui generis_, whether or not it be the voice of God. But I have also urged that what is (the) good (or right), _what_ is the best, is not _given_ to a _moral_ consciousness. The objectivity of values need not be confined to a view that defines values independently of the person and his affective-conative nature. The alternative view of objective goodness that I have in mind will be expounded in the next chapter. Here, agreeing with the cognitivist that the imperative is irreducible to wanting, I have disagreed that the imperative to the best (oughting) depends on any particular moral cognition of the best and its status.

(h-2) In this context I need hardly explain my resistance to a second view of both oughting and of objectivity of value, that might be called _the social view_. On this view, any ought and oughting, any value and the imperative, are products of social interaction and social learning. Any specific _ought_ is the introjection of social demands, or a product of identification with parents or other authority-figures. And the experience of 'oughting' is really a consolidated growth from _wanting-musting_.

I have myself argued that the person, in his affective-conative-cognitive development, depends on others. It would be silly to deny that social influences result in demands for social approval that become second nature in their power over us. Moreover, the guiding and 'pressuring' influences of others are strong factors in evaluating particular value-claims. But whether value-claims are initially 'I want _x_,' or consequences of 'we want _x_,' or both, I suggest that they are still wants and not oughts. I submit once more that it has not been shown by what psychological osmosis 'pressures' become anything but _musts_, and that _wants_ become anything but wants.

Consider: "_If_ I want this, I had better..." Do such deliberations about affective-conative alternatives produce an I ought or only an I must (or close equivalent)? The answer, I persist, is no. Rather have I suggested that a particular value-claim, 'I want x,' socially influenced or not, becomes 'I ought to choose x' only when, for whatever reason, the experient decides that this x is best.

(h-3)As I see it, then, to move from 'conscience' as vox Dei to conscience as the vox gentium or vox societatis does not alter the experience of 'oughting the best I know.' If 'conscience' be defined as a particular, acquired complex of values by which a person guides his choices, it gets its authority not from its derivation from society but from the person's conviction that it is best. Only then does 'I want x' evoke the imperative-experience (oughting).

The view I have been expanding recognizes the influence of society on individual development and on actual evaluations; but it reserves 'moral authority' to a distinctive activity-potential of the person. Again, without denying the introjection of others' commands, it accords them 'must'-value but not 'ought-value' (until the person assents to a 'must-value' as best). One might say, all too briefly, that within our breasts there is both a second nature must-conscience and an ought-consciousness; that their vying with each other respectively produces both anxiety and guilt, both social approval and moral approval.

One final consideration in passing, and putting largely phenomenological questions aside. If indeed the person's experience of oughting is no more and no less than the product of his social conditioning, how do we go about explaining the person who conscientiously resists what his society approves, who, indeed, stands against the very society that supposedly produced his 'oughting' and 'oughts'? That would remain a puzzle indeed!

(i) How, then, do I answer the question with which this section started: How do you get from the value-claims (originating in want) to the imperative of ought? For indeed, in my view, there is no ought in the premises as such of any value-deliberations and conclusions; no oughting decides the relation between value-claims and value-possibilities; any deliberation considers only what is and what will be (see next chapter). My answer: Ought is present in the conclusion because it is from the beginning in the matrix of the person engaged in evaluating his value-claims. Whatever else we say about what he ought, his oughting is in his activity-potential to ought the best he knows, whether he does so or not. It is the person himself who, having decided that x is better than alternatives, finds himself affirming, "I ought to choose x."

It is the person himself who experiences moral guilt and moral approval as he proceeds to act or not to act on his imperative to do the best he knows. And, incidentally, in finding oughting co-existing with knowing, with affective-conative ongoings, and with willing, we can understand why persons of the greatest moral sincerity and intelligence can, in the name of their own particular evaluations of value-claims and value-possibilities, criticize the evalu-ations and norms of others; it is in the name of 'conscience' that they stand against each other.

5.   Reflective Overview on the Essence of Moral Agent

We are by no means finished with our attempt to define the essence of a person. But it will be help-ful to draw together and comment further on theses and problems that are relevant to that question and immediately relevant to our task of defining the good in the next chapter.

First, the person's activity-potentials are not simply juxtaposed, for they are distinctive dimensions of his conscious experience (which may or may not be related to processes-events in his body and unconscious).

87

Second, to focus thus on constitutive or un-learned activities within the personal Gestalt does not mean that, as the person matures and learns by interaction with his environments, he becomes in every way the product of them. My thesis is that learned attitudes, sentiments, traits (and other formative structures that are more or less system-atically organized in his personality) could not occur did he not have the kind of constitution he has. The person, who did not create himself, sur-vives because of indissoluble links with 'the possibilities' beyond himself; he is no isolated, windowless monad.

Third, in a mine field of controversy, I have focused on what all scholars would agree is sufficient-ly distinctive about man--his search for truth and his search for the good. However, I have emphasized that the search for truth is a bad joke unless persons are free (within limits): first, to allow the evidence to appear in the court of reason and, second, to allow the reasoning person to be able to weave the relevant data into a system that conforms to the laws of logic and of experiential coherence. Yet, in my interpretation of the experience of will-agency, and in my relating it to will-power, I have protected both personal initiative and the influence of one's history, of culture, and of factors beyond one's power.

Fourth, the relatively 'raw material' for thinking is not only the sensory patterns in their comparatively refractory quality and order, it is also the affective-conative predispositions that initially and persis-tently, but not rigidly, orient the person to certain meaning-situations (food, suffering, novelty).

Fifth, accordingly, both the sensory givens with their qualitative hedonic tones and the unlearned af-fective-conative wants are the minimal, relatively raw materials to be, as it were, expressed and adapted by the personal Gestalt. Whatever the person confronts, these telic raw materials are contributing factors in the telic responses that go into the organizing and reorganizing of his environment(s).

Sixth, value-claims, therefore, be they truth-claims or health-claims, are the person's conscious response to complexes of wanting with their variable sensory, imaginary, ideational, and hedonic components. Any pattern of the person's adaptation and expression reflects the kinds of decisions he has made as he constantly interacts with sustaining, converging, challenging, threatening, and destructive environment-Environment.

Seventh, owing to the maturation of his own complex nature and to such interchange, there are conflicts, sequences, priorities, in short, options amomg his value-claims that need evaluation. At this point the person may, of course, be overcome by factors too strong for his will-agency, but, if my reading of experience is correct, once a person has decided that x-value is better than y-value, he experiences 'I ought to choose the x-value' (the best I know). Oughting I have introduced as an activity-potential that is not reducible either to wanting or any (hypothetical) must, nor to an introjection of social pressures, nor to a unique way of knowing what is good or right.

Eighth, I am aware that to emphasize capacities that are irreducibly personal and the roots of personal change is to attack the claims of respected scholars who hold that social interaction can produce, for example, the 'higher' conative dispositions, will-agency, the sense of obligation. Such scholars in their less critical moments sometimes make a strong appeal to evolution as if it could be an independent principle of explanation rather than a description of what occurs.

Ninth, when such evolutionary conceptions are married to psycho-social interpretations of human developments, the burden of proof seems to be placed these days on those of us who will not accept the view that I have maintained. But I insist that the 'will to survive' becomes a mischievous, theoretical will-o'-the-wisp if we forget that, for persons, especially, it must be defined by the very affective-conative factors and other activity-potentials that distinguish the personal Gestalt.

I must add that I am not unmindful of the long
ages when earlier hominids appeared to carry on their
particular forms of the will-to-live in other climes.
Whether they had the full potential that I have so
far attributed to persons I leave to competent re-
searchers. But I enter a <u>caveat</u>. The interpretations of 'the beginnings' become enlightening only
when we also ask: Beginnings of what? For until we
know that a goal is reached, we hardly know how to
select what 'beginning,' in a given instance, refers to.

Tenth, the application of this <u>caveat</u> is especially relevant to my claim that 'oughting' is
irreducible among the activity-potentials. When I
consider the many 'bests' that persons have confronted in the course of their history, and in so
many environments, I am often tempted to capitulate
and agree that 'oughting' (as well as specific
'oughts') are the products of learning--social
learning, in particular. But then I cannot resist
asking: If there were no phase of human experience
during those same ages that held persons imperatively
to the best they could know, would the human saga not
lack its dramatic and creative heroes? "Here I stand,
I can do no other"!--despite excruciating pain, the
forfeiting of what seemed to make life worthwhile,
the doubts of intimate friends, and the fear of
hurting them--is this imperative loyalty to an inner
drummer not among the transformers and builders of
the national and social environment that persons
live in today?

I have now stated basic theses regarding the
roots of the life good to live. From these roots
does a pattern of values arise that is central to
human fulfillment--whatever that means? In the
next chapter we shall see.

90

Notes

[1]   The discussion of value-theory and the good life
in this and the next chapter condenses the broader
discussion in Bertocci and Millard, PATG, and in
other writings and essays (Bertocci, PGI). As here
presented this view of obligation and of values
profits from, but in significant respects would be
disapproved by, those I have learned the most from,
particularly: Brightman, Moral Laws, 1933; R. Ulich,
Conditions of Civilized Living, 1946; R. B. Perry,
General Theory of Value, 1926 and Realms of Value,
1954; Tennant, PT, vol. 1; Nicolai Hartmann, Ethics,
3 volumes, 1932; C. I. Lewis, On Analysis of Knowledge
and Valuation, 1946; W. H. Werkmeister, Man and His
Values, 1967; Blanshard, RAG; RAB.

Chapter Five

THE LIFE GOOD TO LIVE: FOR PERSONS

Before us now is the framework of human capacities that make for both good and evil in the "fighter
for ends." I believe there is a framework of values
that so develops the person's psycho-physiological
potential that he can resist evil as he develops the
life good to live.[1] The value-and-disvalue claims
that persons experience are indeed varied, enticing,
confusing, and urgent. Yet we are not bound to fail
in the attempt to discriminate a skeletal pattern
that will support human ventures in seeking the best.
This framework of interpenetrating values can be comprehensive without homogenizing the good--a firm and
steady frame that will not become rigid and dull. But
we do need to keep before us the dynamics within the
personal Gestalter as he seeks to appraise the variety
of value-claims issuing from his interaction with
environment-Environment.

1. Survival and Health Values

(a) From the moment a person is conceived to the time
when he can begin to choose quality of survival, his
complex psycho-physiological nature has already been
sustaining itself by drawing from the environment-Environment what is needed for survival. But, from
early infancy on he becomes increasingly aware of
conflict among his affective-conative tendencies,
including conflicts with his natural and social
environment. At the same time his ability to make
more reflective appraisals can also increase. What
will he postpone, modify, reject in the light of his
conception of what is and will be available to him?
What are the conditions that underlie one gratification and not another?

Once we begin to talk about a minimum standard
of health we are already probing for some connection
among values that, presumably, will prevent not only

physical weakness and painful disease but also specific qualities of depression, despair, and mental
dullness. Indeed, when we observe a minimum of
"human" (humane) quality, we speak of living "like
an animal." We refer to a terminally ill person
as a "vegetable."

In other words, we distinguish <u>survival</u> <u>values</u>
from <u>health</u> <u>values</u> as we focus on a person's ability
to cope with everyday problems without obstinate
physical and mental distress. We deplore in our
fellows any weaknesses that seem to issue from failure
to follow cues that, given their chronological age,
we expect them to note.

(b) This search for health-quality in survival will
take account of the actual relations between value-
claims and value-possibilities, relations that are
not made up by persons' wanting alone. The excess
sugar that I enjoy is a value-claim because I want
it, but its worth in relation to other value-claims
is not made up entirely by me; nor are the value-
possibilities in the sugars I absorb and those already
in my body. I pay, willy-nilly, for excess sweets--
perhaps in diabetes. But it is not my wanting sugar-
taste that makes it excessive. What makes sugar excessive (and a value-claim a disvalue-claim) is
what happens to me because of the relation of sugar-
to-my-body. I get diabetes not solely because I
want sugar but because of a certain relation of my
sugar-intake to the sugar-tolerance of my body. That
value-disvalue possibility exists before my first
taste of sugar.

Thus, even at this very first level of value-
appraisal, it should be noticed that our values in
being person-related are not relativ<u>istic</u>, or
dependent simply on our wants. Indeed, even the
<u>prima</u> <u>facie</u> qualities of value-experience are not
created by us; our unlearned conative predispositions
find themselves being gratified by some "objects" and
not others. So, also, the <u>relations</u> among value-
claims and their realization <u>are</u> <u>not</u> the products
only of our wanting them, individually or socially.

Further exploration will indicate that our dependable values consist of relationships among value-claims that our critical evaluation brings to light. And these dependable values may well be clues to the fact that the Realm supports some patterns of values and not others.

Much needs to be done to discover even the main roads to such a conclusion. But, confirming my earlier suggestion, what the 'objectivity' of values means here is not that some values or ideals (like justice, mercy, beauty) exist independently of persons. Rather does it mean that persons, in discovering a pattern of values they require for their expression and adaptation, are experiencing and developing patterns not solely of their own making as they interact with each other and with the Realm. Nor, as we proceed, should we forget that each person's imperative to the best is absolute, once he has decided what is best, and that even if he cannot reach that best this does not render the objectivity of an anthropic pattern of values a rootless concept.

2. Quality of Survival and Truth-Values

(a) We have already seen that even the choice among sheer survival values calls for some definition of healthy survival. This, in turn, witnesses to some interdependence among the value-experiences that are rooted in our psycho-physiological needs and abilities. Yet, as persons, we cannot depend on our reflex and other innate predispositions for survival. We require truth-values to guide us in sorting and sifting that will avoid fruitless conflict within our natures and between us and environments-Environment.

But avoidance of conflict, prevention of illness are not health. In other words, given the developmental nature of persons, both their survival and quality of survival require practical and theoretical knowledge--such, for example, as will render intelligent their care of each other especially during periods of helplessness and illness. Persons become healthy insofar

95

as they discover and choose the values that, connected with each other or mutually supportive, become the bases for further value-realization. But
this knowledge is not available apart from self-
disciplined exploration of the values and value-
possibilities that go together and make for health.
For example, a person has to learn that the hedonic
tone of some "foods" cannot be relied upon to provide
what is required for health. A certain kind of cola
may not be "the drink for you."

(b) It is often said that we must survive in order
to think. Our analysis shows that persons will not
survive unless they do think. Truth-seeking has a
nuclear value because thereby we identify the best
means of relating all value-claims in the various
areas of our lives. We cannot stop, any more than
Socrates himself did, with his insight "the unexamined life is not worth living." We must go on to
ferret out the very sources and the exact conditions
of interrelations between values. To think is more
than to entertain ideas in a "grand" style; it is
to become reasonable, or as experientially coherent
as we can.

3. Character Values and the Good

(a) We have already emphasized that thinking out the
answer to human problems, and not the least when there
is a conflict of values dear to us, requires the activity of will-agency. Value-claims do not sort
themselves out, neither does thinking always initiate
or sustain itself. So the person experiences value-
claims whose further value and interrelations are not
clear. Moreover, he experiences 'I ought to choose
the best' as the priorities among his alternatives
emerge. In his "cool" moments he is always confronted
with the task of organizing his potential so that he
may know how to actualize the values he acknowledges
as best. The thesis I shall here develop is that the
person as _moral_ _agent_, under the imperative to the
best, wills into being qualities of response--that

are learned dispositions required if his organizing of value-claims is to have some inner structure. This inner skeleton of dispositions is dependent more on him than on values that are available to him in the ambient in which he lives. The values of these dispositions, dependent so much more on his willed choice than are other values, I shall refer to as the moral values and moral disvalues (virtues and vices) that make up a person's character-- his moral backbone, as we sometimes say. But some distinctions must be emphasized.

(b) "Character," in its descriptive, psychological sense, refers to what may be expected of an individual because he is "built the way he is." To say: "That is characteristic of him" (he is polite, he is sincere), is to say that he has certain dispositions (traits) that transcend any particular environment. That is, the person who has acquired the trait of politeness can be depended on in different situations to express that trait in some suitable way.

The psychologist of personality in evaluating character is not, primarily at least, concerned with whether a person's character is morally good or bad. His focus is on character as a unique, more or less organized, set of traits, traits that, good or bad, have prepared the person to respond in this or that way to situations that evoke those traits in him. Psychologically, the trait of neatness will tempt a person to "tidy up" a situation that disturbs him but not the untidy person. Thus, to know a person's traits, and to know how they are connected with each other, is to know much more about what environments he will be especially sensitive to, and what his response is likely to be.

But sooner or later we need to ask what traits, what quality and what organization of traits is better than another as we seek the life good to live. I shall propose then a family of traits, moral values (virtue-traits) since they ought to be willed, as the nucleus of a moral character. Before proceeding we should note that "character," used non-valuationally in psychology, used ethically as a norm in ethical choice, both stress selectivity and organization which yield stability. We often speak of a person's having a strong character-- meaning that his inner organization is such that he can withstand temptation, even at a sacrifice, to stray from what he thinks is best. I shall use the word "character" in the ethical sense since I am seeking especially those (cardinal) virtue-traits that are the backbone or musculature involved in the realization of values that are available to persons. Thus this backbone of (cardinal) virtues defines the person's ongoing willingness to sacrifice for his acknowledged ideals.

(c) To avoid misunderstanding: character is not an isolable "entity" in moral development. Yet, without the traits--virtue-traits and vice-traits--a person chooses to develop in his quest for varied and mutually supportive values, a crucial ingredient in the life good to live is missing. I stress: virtues and vices do not simply happen to a person. Indeed, a person may have developed traits before he comes to reflect upon their value, but by deciding "will-fully" to choose some and not others he is engaging in the moral struggle as he chooses the larger context of values and disvalues. For example, a person who does not develop honesty, courage, kindness will not be able to evaluate and choose among value-claims that do not depend initially on his choice. Substitute dishonesty, cowardice and cruelty for the former and you have characteristic dispositions that will probably dis- courage the actualization of acknowledged values within his power.

(d) Another comment is now in order. If moral char- acter is the crucible within which these virtues are willed and sustained, and if they are vital to the choice and organization of other values open to a person, these virtues do not simply stand side by side with other values (such as health, work, rec- reation, friendship, beauty, holiness) to be con- sidered in the total life good to live, the summum bonum. Thus a person, without any choice involved, may experience values in certain sunsets, in certain

98

games, companions, kinds of work, and so on indefinitely. However, he will himself need deliberately to choose to be honest, courageous, kind as he interrelates his non-willed value experience. Will he be honest with the friend who is not aware of a fault? Will he face courageously certain risks in his work? A person without a strong, moral character is readily victimized by most alluring values. Still, he may be a strong character, virtuous to more than a fault, because his sensitivity to the variety of values in human existence is all too narrow.

Accordingly, part of the moral agent's task is to integrate the virtues in character not only in relation to each other but to the other values that make his life good to live (ethical values, inclusive of the moral). I shall make much of what seems to me to be the inescapable fact that most values in the lives of persons cannot be achieved, sustained, and increased, independently of the virtues that go into the formulation and realization of the summum bonum. But character is not enough!

(e) Elsewhere I have elaborated on the scheme of virtues that form the person's moral backbone. Such cardinal virtues as honesty, courage, gratitude, humility, meekness, kindness, fairness, tolerance, forgiveness, for example, are vital to the realization of an adequate pattern of values--but little more than a hint of the line of reasoning can be suggested here. I have already suggested that certain virtues form, to persist in the figure, a moral backbone; they support and increase the realization of values. For example, the pattern of values that encourages health is possible only for the person who is willing to discipline himself by sacrificing some values--for instance, luxuries earned by extra work. Plato long ago reminded us that it takes courage to forgo pleasures as well as to face known risks. And we all know the courage it takes to be honest with ourselves about our own shortcomings, to be appreciative of the achievements of competitors, let alone to be kind and forgiving when the situation, despite our resentment, calls for kindness and forgiveness.

Once we pursue the interrelation of moral values
with each other in the pursuit of values we see that
it is not too much to consider character the moral
crucible of value-actualization and organization. In
our discussion of survival-values and health-values
we have already noted that health depends upon the
discovery of truth and its disciplined application
to the actualization of health-values. Of course,
both health-values and truth-values are interrelated
with other values, not the least of them economic
values; but sooner or later these and other values
depend upon honesty, courage, humility and fairness,
for example. I have already stressed that the discovery of truth calls for the willingness to forgo
desired conclusions when the evidence does not adequately support them; and without courage a person
will not bear the disappointments that occur in the
search for truth; nor will he withstand the disapproval
of those who fear and denigrate his claims.

Thus, to hold, as I do, that the taproot of all
other virtues is honesty is no casual claim. Without
honesty there can be no courage; without courage no
honesty; and without both other cardinal virtues
(such as gratitude and humility, let alone fairness
and forgiveness), will not be developed or sustained.
Consequently, the pattern of values loses conprehen-
siveness and vitality. The interpenetration of
virtues (better the compenetration, to borrow Philip
Phenix's word²), and of virtues and values with each
other, is inescapable. I should defend a nuclear
family of moral values--a basic pattern of compene-
tration--yet with a hospitality to relatives and
friends of such values, and a certain tolerance in
the way interrelations are realized in concrete choice-
situations.

(f) Nowhere is this interweaving more critical and
difficult than in relating knowledge to virtue.
Knowledge may be virtue, but only if we recognize
that in order to achieve it honesty, courage, fairness and tolerance are required. These values are
necessary, also, if knowledge is to be true to itself
in practice. But, as already mentioned, we must immediately add that the virtues, even if developed,

become narrow if persons' eyes are not opened to the varied contexts of living. Persons of strong character are often insensitive to values available to themselves and also rigid in their denial of such values when attested by others. The persistent pursuit of comprehensive harmony among values is not likely to engage persons who are unwilling to gird themselves for the creative effort to appreciate new dimensions of values for themselves and for others.

Indeed, the ethics of belief takes root in the imperative: reasonableness ought never to be thrown to the winds nor subjugated to the wish to believe. It is reasonableness that investigates our relationships to each other and to the environment when there is any likelihood that there are value-possibilities open to courageous spirits. But history is marked, alas, by the vain efforts even of our "representative men" to go to the limit in a given direction without kindness, gratitude, humility, meekness, tolerance, and forgiveness--with reasonable compenetration.

4. Affiliative Values

(a) Even as we speak of the interrelation of health-values, truth-values, and character-values, we become aware of another most pervasive value-experience in the human drama. Affiliative values--a broad name for value and value-possibilities in relations with human beings--are no mere luxury! To be sure, meaningful solitude is important to insight into the reaches of our own being. Yet, without the different levels of human warmth and companionship we are beset by the loneliness that affects our health and shrivels up whole areas of our emotional and intellectual potential. We often underrate the importance to our living of the small affections, the little services we render each other in the mutual acknowledgment of our reciprocal needs as well as of our intrinsic rights as persons.

Yet even the affiliative values need pillars of support. These are the (minimal) virtues that

101

uniquely develop, sustain, and increase the quality
of affiliation: gratitude, kindness, humility, meekness, tolerance, fairness, and forgiveness. Which
of us could grow in self-confidence and trust without
knowing that there are others committed both to help
us to fulfill our needs and to care for us when we
are lost? At the same time, for a person to know that
he can so care for others that he can depend on himself to go 'the second mile' of understanding is for
him to be ready to participate in those values--family
and friendships, for example--without which human
existence becomes conniving prudence. Nor must we
forget that so much of the actual value of work and
economic goods, of recreation, depends upon the
quality of affiliation these involve. When there is
no honesty, kindness, gratitude, courage, fairness,
and tolerance, not to speak of humility and meekness,
then, indeed, 'Hell is other people.'

(b) I have been suggesting that neither values nor
virtues live independently of each other, and I have
been emphasizing the centrality of the cognitive
effort and the quality of knowledge (wisdom) required
for value-evaluation. We cannot underestimate the
dependence of the quality of a person's intellectual
progress on the quality of affiliative values. From
his first floundering trials and errors as a child
to his disciplined reflections based on cautious
methods of inquiry, the course of a person's intellectual life is influenced (not necessarily determined) by the standards of intellectual appreciation
of his social affiliations. It is not a simple
matter to develop intellectual self-confidence in
a climate that discourages the responsible probing
without which a person will not discover the quality
of his own abilities. Yet, in any environment a
person must be willing to accept his own limitations
and the fact of his interdependence with others, even
as he comes to recognize his needed cognitive skills.
The growth of intellectual power, the achievement of
a well-stocked mind--this is good sport and calls for
good sportsmanship by no means reserved for athletes.

(c) In this vein, let us point out that the discovery

102

of truth requires the responsive cooperation of both the investigator and those who are affected by what may be discovered. How often do investigations falter when they begin to hit too close to home! 'Truth' and 'fact' are ultimately fertilized by the values of the economic, social, and political community that must continue to support agencies of learning. The search for wisdom, as well as the search for information, demands risks for all concerned. The tree of knowledge develops new branches not only if it can withstand the winds of prejudice and the storms of superstition, but also if it is pruned judiciously by those who care for its growth. If the truth-seeker loses sight of the larger, social terrain in which the tree grows, his very scholarship may become arrogant and be diminished by his failure to recognize that both his shortcomings and his successes depend upon the implicit trust of others. At the same time the scholar will sacrifice social approval and peace of mind for the sake of truths that disturb the habits, prejudices, and cherished values of those who have helped to make him the investigator he is.

(d)   The life good to live, we are seeing, is rooted both in the prima facie value-claims that are tied to our primary and acquired wants and in the actual relations we discover among them and among the possibilities in ourselves and our world. So far we have been forced to take note of the interrelationship between the values (value-realms!) of survival, health, economics, truth, and affiliation, and to emphasize that moral values in character are themselves compenetrating factors in the creation of value-horizons.

In this book I can no more than call attention to the varieties of aesthetic value—without which every other quality of survival suffers. Aesthetic values, in my view, add their own ranges of quality to human creativity and satisfaction. We ought always to challenge the demand so often heard that artistic works be subject to the prevailing standards of truth and goodness, especially if those demands fail to take into account the artist's own conception of novel,

103

aesthetic values. At the same time I should wish to
argue that to see each dimension of value-experience
for what it is also involves seeing its relation to
other values that may be supported or threatened.
Art must, in one sense, be 'for art's sake'; in another sense it cannot be, and never, in fact, turns
out to be, especially in the great works of art. Such
tensions or conflicts are of the very stuff of creativity, be it aesthetic or moral. But, pity the
person who knows not the dimensions of imagination
his aesthetic life needs, and the help of artists in
the growth of his aesthetic values.

5. Co-Creativity in Value-Realization: Altruism

In view of the conflict inherent in the human
situation, we must now face the problem of a fair
"distribution" of values and disvalues among human
beings as a matter of policy.

(a) We have already, of course, recognized the interdependence of persons, and that the term "affiliative
values" refers broadly to all those values that arise
from relationships involving others. As we recognized
that the quality of affiliative values influences
health and truth values, we became aware that "sharing"
values requires some guidelines. Once more, I limit
myself to a major theme.

Persons can build no stable set of values without
insight into themselves in relation to their environments. In this sense, truth is indispensable to
quality in any area of life. Honesty, the disposition
to find and convey truth, I have consequently regarded
as the taproot virtue. This does not solve the
question of the distribution of values and disvalues
within a life and between persons, but it requires
that we be honest about the sources of value and disvalue. We will not boast, for example, like some
"self-made men," or Dickens's Mr. Bounderby in Hard
Times, that we earned values that are in fact unearned

increments of effort or provided for us by others. Furthermore, honesty, the taproot virtue of life as a whole, grows into justness (fairness) as the trunk of affiliative values. And for good reason.

Plato, I think, was essentially correct in seeing that there can be no justice to others unless each person can develop his best abilities and will live with others mainly on the basis of what he can contribute to the association. A person who guides his life by desire or interest alone will not discover what he can do best; nor is he likely to be a good judge of the worth of others. It is the doctor's skill, not his interest in being a doctor for whatever purposes, upon which the patient places his basic trust.

Fairness to self and to others is dependent on honestly sharing strengths and weaknesses, and doing so in a way that will encourage the values and minimize the effects of disvalues. At the same time, neither the individual person nor the State can approach justness by sheer suppression or repression of desires, feelings, and emotions.

(b) This Platonic emphasis upon "justice" in the individual and in the State as the ideal of discovering what persons can do best and in relation to each other's best is, I suggest, the indispensable insight that distinguishes human community from human collectivism, or, from its opposite, individualism. For it builds the conception of the good of each and of the good for all on the need to pursue what persons can do without suppressing individuality or, on the other hand, indulging a person's desires as such.

Let me support this contention in terms of the conception of the theory of value I have been advancing. Each person, we have seen, cannot but evaluate as he chooses among value-claims. In so doing he trusts his reason. But other persons also are reason-capable; there is no reasonable justification for trusting one's own and distrusting the reason of others arbitrarily. To appeal to a person's reason is neither to disregard his ability nor his desires, nor to minimize his achievements and interests.

What began as a Platonic insight is strengthened by Kant's strongest ethical insight, as I see it. For to treat oneself as a person, to treat others as persons, is to treat them as capable of reasoning. It is to rely on the use of reasoning--not on the use of power as _power_--in service of a reasoned appraisal of what each person can make of himself in relation to his reasoned appraisals of others, and _vice versa_. A reasonable person cannot treat another arbitrarily like a mindless thing or only as a means to his own ends. For a reasoning person, as such, the power he reasonably achieves in his own life must be consistent with his allowing others to reasonably achieve power in theirs. The guiding principle in altruism and justice, therefore, is mutual respect for one another as reason-capable persons.

One cannot emphasize enough that reason-capable persons cannot, in principle, treat themselves or each other as if they are beings whose actions result only from the powers regnant in a situation. If persons reject reasonableness, there is no other appeal open to them but sheer power, physical or emotive. Power, as sheer power of any sort, may overcome, but it does not make right. Persons beaten, however subtly, into submission, may seem to consent to what they had opposed, but "convinced" against their reason, they still remain of the same opinion.

(c) I come, then, to some value-conclusions that will be crucial to all else in this study. Among persons power can never be the test of goodness, human or divine. To be sure, power--to act, to fulfill, to restrain, to control--is critical to the full definition of _the good_ (the _summum bonum_). Values that compose the good, I have submitted, have their origin in human wanting. Wants are evaluated in turn by their relation to each other and by their efficacy in relation to environment-Environment. Hence, there can be no question about the importance of power within the good life. The good life will be effective, will have power; but power is, as power, not the sufficient norm for goodness.

(d) Accordingly, the issue we all face is: what power is good? Justice has to do with the acquiring of one's own values in proper relation to those of others in this kind of world. Hence, the problem of choice, grounded in the nature of the human situation, is the problem of making reasonable decisions about value-claims and about dependable values--for ourselves in relation to others in environment-Environment. The question is never: Why should I keep for myself what another also has reasonable claim to?--but: Granted that we both need to criticize our values and to actualize them reasonably, what shall guide me in apportioning and sharing values and disvalues that can be shared?

(e) Justice, it becomes clear, is not a concession that a reflective, self-centered, and selfish person makes prudentially to other (presumably) equally self-centered and selfish persons. Justice stems from the recognition that until any reason-capable person has good grounds for treating other persons as means only to his own ends, he has no reason for denying to other persons the values that, so far as can be reasonably ascertained, are important to the fulfillment of their potential as persons.

If this line of reasoning is correct, we have located a normative principle to which persons are morally obligated, an ought-principle in personal affairs that is as reasonably valid as the laws that guide the growth of plants and animals, or those that guide us in understanding the relationship of things. This principle of ethical justice (not identical with political justice but the norm for it) is not imposed upon persons but derived from their criticized attempts to conserve and increase their values as wanting-thinking-oughting persons in their environment-Environment.

A brief summary and a hint of the argument to

follow: If (i) persons arrive in environments that are relevant to the Realm; if (ii) persons survive with quality only as they define values that actualize their own potential in relation to each other and to their environment; and, if (iii) to do this they must respect each other as co-creators of value, then we cannot treat the anthropic principle of justice as irrelevant to our reasoned conception of the Realm. We shall make use of this conclusion in a larger context, but now we must take a closer look at justice and co-creation.

6.   Co-Creativity and Love

(a)   The implementing of the principle of justice is the art of living; the sharing of goods and evils justly is neither an easy nor a hopeless task.   There are discoverable guidelines, and three may be mentioned here.

First, justice never means equal sharing in the mathematical sense of equality.   Every person is unique in ability and wants, and he requires an honest appraisal of his abilities and needs in relation to the abilities and needs of others.   The most difficult problem in ethical choice is the evaluating, for ourselves and for each other, of the priorities that are reasonable options at a given time and at a given stage of development, individual and social.

To be aware of this difficulty encourages a fundamental policy decision: Persons who respect each other as persons will engage as responsive-responsible participants in making value-decisions and in developing ideals that, as far as possible, will protect and increase their common values and so distribute the burdens of disvalues that evils will, at least, be quarantined. This communitarian, democratic ideal guides the development of democratic methods.   It recommends itself because persons affected by decisions thus participate in decision-making.   In so doing they charge themselves with abiding by common agreements until "the mind of the community" can be changed by deliberate, mutual criticism.

Second, one thing only will keep justice from becoming an exercise in futility. That is the exercise öf a _formalistic personalism_. However, the treating of persons as ends in themselves becomes a relatively empty formula if there is no pattern of values to guide us in the art of evaluating the optimum values open to persons in varying situations. I purposely have avoided such terms as "altruistic living" or "love"; I have not contraposed "altruism" to "egoism" because both the sentimentality and ambiguity connected with these terms so readily mislead even sincere persons. Mistakes in helping--or hurting--persons are inevitable. But we invite them when we acclaim "respect for persons" without having some conception of the quality and scope of values that are long-run goals and short-run objectives.

This concern for a norm of personal growth has dominated this inquiry into the constitution of persons as a basis for their values and their relationships. The concern for justice is not simply the concern to be related to others--how can any person avoid interdependence in any case! Justice needs guidance by the patterns of values open to persons so that responsive-responsible agents, recognizing that mathematical equality is not even possible, can do all in their power to establish the kinds of goals that will be creative compromises as they commit themselves to mutual growth in value-realization. The bearers of value are persons who, remaining sensitive to the needs of others for value-realization, never condone blindness or encourage rigid distribution.

Third, in this whole process there are the failures rooted in purposeful choice as well as those stemming from accident and ignorance. Honesty about evils stemming from human ignorance and weakness, honesty about the evils that beset persons through no clear choice of their own, calls for kindness and mercy. Moreover, justice without insightful

forgiveness is never adequate. Those who purposely
hurt others call for consideration that reinforces
our realization that there is no neat formula for
sharing the resources and weaknesses among persons.
No matter how much evil is quarantined by kindness,
those who suffer it will still bear unmerited
burdens; and we encourage weakness, not strength,
by repressing the unmerited suffering of persons.

(b) It is this all but inevitable human situation
that calls for another moral value as persons will-
fully inflict pain and disvalue upon others unjustly.
I have just said that justice without forgiveness is
never enough. I add: Justice without forgiveness
is blind to what the human situation calls for. The
human obligation is to forgive and to accept forgiveness is no indulgent "extra." Yet it has no
place for sentimentality. For persons do willfully
choose to hurt others; they do destroy value without
warrant, and in so doing they create situations in
which the innocent need protection and the evildoers
at least constraint. (In this discussion I am
omitting the virtue of <u>repentance</u> in its complicated,
dynamic relation to forgiveness and the full meaning
of both; although I should not in principle let
forgiveness depend on repentance.)

Honesty, accordingly, requires a wise appraisal
of the damage done, the realization that the culprit
cannot be allowed to go on hurting others and himself. Honesty also calls for the evaluation of legal
and moral guilt. Forgiveness in such situations does
not cast the claims of justice aside; rather does it
become sensitive to what the facts relevant to growth
in that situation require. Honesty faces the fact
that vindictive punishment is unlikely to strengthen
either culprit or victim. Facing the facts requires
that persons courageously take the kinds of risks that
help the guilty and the innocent to regain respect
for the good in each other.

Forgiveness, then, is the extension of justice;
it is the virtue developed as persons concern themselves with quarantining the purposed evils and with

liberating the possibilities of goodness in the cul-
prits who, as persons, are still, after all, ends
in themselves. If the evildoer can have confidence
that the evil he has consciously committed will not
stand as an irremovable obstacle to the realization
of new values still possible in his life, he is much
more likely to become more constructive. Forgiveness
fosters a moral atmosphere in which evil does not fester.
To be sure, the more persons are involved, the more
difficult it is to be creative in the effort to be
redemptive rather than vindictive. But the fact remains that vindictive justice, because it has to
depend so much on sheer prohibitive power, cannot
be trusted to re-create the qualities of mutual trust
and responsibility. For this re-creation of possible
values in critical, yet hopeful, mutual respect, what
is required is love--the source of co-creative value
among persons.[3]

(c) It will be noticed that I have not referred to
love--steadfast love--as a virtue. For, without being
unaware of the many uses and contexts of the word, I
would reserve it for a more embracing orientation--
a style of life that grows out of the fundamental
awareness that free persons can hurt and help each
other, that they need to help each other beyond the
demands of a calculating justice and deserved kindness.
Each of us knows how vulnerable he is to both the
gross and the subtle temptations to increase his goods
at the expense of others; we know how great the temptation then becomes to protect oneself against vindictive punishment. We exacerbate evil in the attempt
to escape from punishments that seem greater than
our capacity to bear. Legal guilt aside, and aware
of our moral guilt, we require new trust in ourselves,
even when we can make some amends.

In this situation to know that others are willing
to care for us to the peak of redemptive forgiveness--
to know this is to experience hope that we can rescue
ourselves from possible disaster and gain a constructive
place in the community. Accordingly, if justness is
concern for honest co-creativity in value-realization,
love is that purposeful, steadfast disposition to care

for persons with a view to their growth in value-realization. Love has its roots in that steadfast concern that creativity in human affairs springs from growing self-respect and trust in others that is no "mere sentiment."

Again, without for a moment forgetting affective-emotive factors in loving, I am purposefully referring more inclusively to the loving person as one who cares in particular that the evildoer be able to renew his effort in the confidence that values are still open to him as a person-in-community. Love, sentimental and unsentimental, is not love without commitment to redemptive forgiveness, to the growth of persons at the stage where they can renew faith in them-selves and reach for values open to them. Love is honesty with self that is so rugged and so sensitive that a person can say: Who am I that I should not be mindful of him, and try to help in generating new hope? Not for nothing did St. Paul link faith and love with hope.

7. Pattern, Creativity, and Uniqueness in the Life Good to Live

(a) We have in these pages moved from an outline of the kind of constitutive activities which distinguish a person to an outline of the basic kinds of choices that he ought to make, if he, given his nature, is to heed mutually sustaining and complementary trends in the actualization of his activity-potentials. There are problems that persons cannot avoid, and they require strengths (virtues) for dealing with them in any arena of living. There are consequences of choices, good and bad, that they themselves do not create.

Hence, for persons the question never is: Will there be conflict?--but: What is the quality of conflict, and what can be realized? In discovering, for example, the interrelationship of survival and health values with truth-values and affiliative values, we cannot miss the constant, dynamic influence

112

of character-values (such as courage, kindness, justness, and forgiveness). Even in this limited analysis
a network of values is discernible that is immanent
as persons adjust and express their affective-conative
predispositions in the light of conceived value-possibilities. In sum, insofar as the person, as person,
faces universal problems of choice within the scope
of his flexible but finite activities, and insofar as
he does not misconstrue the nature of environment-Environment, we may expect certain patterns of value
(including virtues) to be staples in the life good
to live.

(b) Thus to stress the ligaments among values may
seem to invite blindness to variety and neglect of
spontaneity of value-experiences. I can only try to
be constantly aware of the fact that abstract terms
will not capture lived-experience--neither in the more
observable affective-conative arteries that live,
grow, and change, in unique persons, nor in specific
stages of moral growth. Nevertheless, I must still
submit that there is no substitute for such a comprehensive framework of values and virtues as guide
and support for the person in both exploring and
enjoying varieties of value. I have been very selective, but those values stressed are not mere "extras,"
but, with others here omitted, remain the musculature
of the varied human Gestalten of value-actualization.

Some critics might refer to our effort, somewhat
disdainfully, as "another bag of values," or "another
list of virtues." But I must confess that I always
wonder whether such thinkers have pursued the dynamics
of the compenetration of value-realization. Are they
sufficiently aware of their own value-priorities to
justify them? I have hardly hinted at the interrelation of the economic and recreational values and of
aesthetic values, with health, affiliative, truth,
and moral values. Nor have I mentioned the particular
virtues a person has to possess to be creative in
different areas of his life, vocational or avocational.
But when concrete choices have to be made at different
levels, or dimensions, of self-conscious choice, how
does one make reflective choices apart from some governing, ideal pattern of values for resolving conflicts?

113

(c) Accordingly, to point to the pattern and framework of value-realization is by no means to suppose
that unique persons will orchestrate their value-
motifs differently as they go about expressing and
adapting themselves--at home, in school, work-
center, recreation areas, art centers, and in their
social, political, and religious ventures. To insist that virtues are not islands in the life good
to live, to point to a moral musculature in any
reasoned pursuit of values, is simply to realize
that persons cannot in this kind of Environment
sustain their value-pursuits as "unstructured
ecstasies," or self-indulgent and self-pitying
pastimes.

Moreover, if we are correct that persons are
indeed free within limits to participate in the
shaping of their lives, then their qualitative freedom, their qualitative creativity, will have a place
in it for their own uniqueness, even at the points
where co-creativity means deliberate sacrifice. The
human condition of change, conflict, decay, growth,
and surprise calls for quarantining evils once they
occur, for conserving values by increasing them,
for keeping patterns of value from rigor mortis.
No imaginative observation of the dynamics of value-
actualization among persons will minimize the creative
power of forgiveness deepened by a sense of humor.
Nevertheless, just as a flag cannot wave without
being attached to a flagpole, so the freedoms in
value-appreciation cannot but be enhanced by the
sustaining, co-creative control involved in the
pursuit of values in vocation and in religion. To
these sources of con-centration of values, we now turn.

8. Value-Creation and Vocation

(a) A person's vocation is too often identified with
the job by which he "earns his living." A job, indeed,
is the main source of economic stability. Moreover,
day in and day out, the person's job is the locus of
much of his social life; what that job is constantly
affects the range and quality of his value-realization.

A person's <u>vocation</u>, however, is the center of his purposeful commitment; it embraces large segments of his value-strivings. Fortunate is the person whose job fits in with his vocation. A doctor's care of his patients may be part of his vocation--the dedication of his insight and skill to improve the health of the community. Again, the many details of tending to a house and caring for the needs of her own and the children of others as members of a community may be part of a mother's sense of vocation--to be the cultural center of a home.

Vocation, then, calls for constant attention to the organization of values in one's life, to the continual orchestration of values within one's life and in relation to others. The life good to live shifts its point of choice as the priorities of "this vocation" emerge; the person may discover what he can do best as he moves from gratifying wants to more wholesome satisfactions. But, as we have seen, satisfaction may increase creative tension when values are appraised in relation to abilities and to demands made by relevant environment. Hence, conflict, tension, frustration, and anxiety are always part of the human lot.

So we return to the path of wisdom. To realize that to pursue the good, <u>never</u> a mere flight from frustration and anxiety, <u>never</u> a denial of all desires and attendant conflicts, is to face full-front the question: Which sacrifice, which suffering, which orchestration of good-and-evil is most worthwhile? For to idolize security is both to worship a false god and to encourage the clever, pseudo-creative, cunning patching together of value-experiences.

(b) To put this theme positively: The attempt to understand and appreciate the relationship of values and their quality to each other, to evaluate the quality of value-claims and the contexts that support them, suggests the kind of harmony sought for by the creator of a symphony. The musical metaphor is not accidental. For I have in mind the way in which the different themes or motifs of a symphony at once sup-

port and challenge each other as they contribute
to an immanent purpose. The task facing the
composer, realizing that some musical possibilities
must be sacrificed in a given Opus (vocation), is
the problem of orchestrating as richly as possible
the musical instrumentation available to him.   To
be sure, the human, compenetrating network of values,
this symphony of values, is always an unfinished one.
Yet, this symphonic analogy may still capture what
actually takes place in the life of persons who try
to weave together the many contexts of value they
experience.

(c) In this weaving, persons cannot escape insecurity.
The great seduction is to think that security ("peace")
is the ideal of the good life. For if we keep our
gaze on what actually occurs within the human situation,
not security but creativity bears the greatest promise.
This creativity faces the inevitable insecurity of
conflicts: it is creative insecurity. Here, I am
simply naming what we have already encountered, the
vocation of overcoming and minimizing destructive
disvalues within the pursuit of the more inclusive,
tensive harmonies; yes, unfinished symphonies.

(d) Such creative insecurity, as intrinsic to the
ideal of the good, vies with the conception of the
summum bonum as "divine" peace, or "serenity" without
tension. With point we are told that the ideal, the
divine, the perfect peace, is without insecurity;
in itself it knows no change because there is nothing
good that can be added to the quality of divine being.
By contrast, "the completeness" that persons seek is,
unfortunately, never "finished." I shall later resist
the particular line of reasoning that sets up this
notion of perfection as the meaning of perfect being,
even for God. Here I shall only plead that, without
denying the value of experiences of peace and serenity,
these cannot actually frame the human ideal of perfection. If our analysis is correct, the "perfection"
that persons do experience is that which I call
'creative insecurity." Why? Because creativity-in-
self-actualization is impossible without undergoing
the inevitable conflict and insecurity in the human
situation, indeed in the achievement of vocation.

116

I leave the discussion at this point with two
views of perfection: one, the classical, that stresses
the completeness that is rich with harmony; another,
the "perfect" that our study finds in tensive, creative insecurity--the human awareness that goodness
consists in the constant dedication to the unfinished,
but by no means unstructured, symphony of values.

9. Religious Experience, the Good, and Creative
    Insecurity

(a) To make this anthropic creative insecurity central to the life good to live, I have been told,
does not ring true to the experience of believers
in every age. In the end, even this attempt to find
the good, not _here_ alone or _there_ alone, but in a
growing symphony of values, will keep the human
venture man-centered or Nature-centered; it will be
seduced into idolatry. At best, my critics maintain,
I have advanced a view of the good that is a humane
naturalism. Why? Because I have not appreciated the
full impact of a dimension of value, the experience
of the holy, or the experience of union with the
One. I have already hinted that, in the end, what
critics attribute to me is _not my view_, but my final
reply will have to be this book as a whole. Let me
here, however, sharpen one of the points involved
in this complaint.

(b) The religious believer I have in mind will
probably argue with my emphasis in the presentation
of vocation. Yes, he will argue, vocation as creative insecurity unifies a person's energies; its
fruits grow from the challenge of a goal for his
living that keeps both abilities and interests
reaching beyond his immediate grasp. Let a serious
illness, however, keep a person from the pursuit of
vocation, and his need for security will reinstate
itself. For, having lost that sense of wholeness
that his vocation provided, he yearns for a life
and a universe that has a challenging center. He
still may go on being "useful"; he may even be
spared the feeling that he is parasitic. But his

117

roots now seem to be withering with no hope of real revival. So also, my unfinished symphony of values, with its adulation of creative insecurity, having lost that vital one-ness with the divine, will be, for all my protestation, like the evaporating "perfume of an empty vase"! [4]

What this religious experient is saying can be emphasized by another analogy. Unless these compenetrating values find their center in an inspiring sense of union with the Perfect, they will lose what two married persons lose when their love for each other stops inspiring their lives. As long as they loved each other their lives grew together--for better, for worse--as they participated in the crises and daily routines of their existence. Let their love "wear out"--they may still go on respecting each other as persons, they may accept their responsibilities to each other dutifully--as good friends! But they will be the first to tell you that "everything is different."

To summarize, I am told that perhaps this "dutiful" and "creative" relation is all that can be in a world in which there is no kinship with "the Center." Moreover, even one who captures the connotation of personal vocation as rooted in the dimensions of religious dedication will be likely to find that "my" unfinished symphony of values will be sustained in its creativity. One may still continue to make music in bits and snatches, here and there, heroically, but the inner sustaining rhythm has been broken for good.

(c) As we shall see, in the end I shall find it reasonable to challenge this "perfect peace" as the norm for the religious dimensions of life. But the question behind the analysis in this chapter is this: Do other dimensions of value depend on the religious experience for their value and validity? My answer has been, and still is: No. And I have tried to show that a network of values takes root in, and is nourished by, the wants and abilities of persons as they interact with each other and environment-Environment.

(d)   But even at this point it would still be fool-
hardy to deny that a person's religious experience
and belief can make a considerable difference to
every phase of a person's value experience--the
specific difference depending on how his belief comes,
in fact, to influence countless other values.   I have,
indeed, stressed mutual hospitality within the organization of values as the obligation to keep the variety
of value experiences in sensitive relation to each
other. For, as we saw in the first chapter: the religious experience does not come with a final set of
beliefs attached to it, and claims rooted in it cannot dictate with final authority the worth of other
values. The morality of reasonable living consists
in weaving together, without contradiction and as
comprehensively as possible, the varied data of fact
and value. This cannot be accomplished without being
sensitive to any ties, including those claimed by
religious experients, that link human experiences
with each other and with the Realm. But to be sensitive to claims is not to bow before them, especially
when they are as complex as the religious claim--or
creative insecurity, or love--is.

10. Reflective Overview

(a) Our discussion in this chapter does not, of course,
prove the goodness of the Realm of Eligibility. But
we are more aware of what the goodness of persons
opens before us. We have not recoiled when faced
with the fact that probably for every person in the
world there are thousands of stars and trillions of
molecules. We have not denied the solid quality of
reasonable probability available by way of scientific discipline. But neither have we neglected to
note that this quality of reasonable probability results from the enterprise of persons who share an
underlying trust in the order of Environment, and who,
therefore, treat neither themselves nor their reason
as alien ghosts. Reflective scholars are free agents
who preside over the meanings to be assigned to data
in the context of their affective-conative lives.

119

They, too, experience obligation to the best they know. None of us who dares to investigate himself or "his world" is an eviscerated observer; nor can he forever declare a moratorium on questions about the larger meaning of his ventures for his own further thought, action, and appreciation.

(b) What our unfinished symphony of values impresses upon us is that persons, aware of the challenges rooted in their sensory, affective, conative, and emotive experiencing, are willing, in fact, regularly to make choices that are fraught with both anxiety and guilt; they forgo some near-values for distant ones in trust and hope, but not without sacrifice. By and large, despite heaps of superficial evidence to the contrary, they go on living in the conviction that just surviving is not the thing, that what one lives and dies for defines himself and points to what's "really real." Mother and father, teacher, doctor, lawyer--yes, they want to live, but what they regard as their dignity is not simply "survival for another day."

     The person, then, presents himself to us as a creator--an architect of worlds built not from his imagination alone; indeed, he conceives himself as a co-creator, both when he is confronted with the in-scrutable dynamics of his inner life, and when the perpetual mystery of his being and becoming in his ambient all but overcome him. Yes, it may be that the MACHINE or THE ULTIMATE CONFLICT OF POWERS has "produced," or just thrown him off, in an oasis within a mindless desert. It may be, but we have reason to look further.

(c) We seem, indeed, in this first part of this book to have centered on man and the nature of his good. But we would not look further, we would not seek to relate his values to the nature of the Realm, were it not that the creativity of persons takes the forms that it does. At the birth of creativity (not mere spontaneity) are the moral values of honesty and courage involved in any search for truth--and that search forces the person to relate himself to the Realm. The vitality and success of truth-seeking

120

is married to value-finding, and both partners join
in the self-discipline of discovering what is beyond
them--and, as we have begun to see, this creative
discipline shares the evil as well as the good within
persons and in their relation to the beyond. Yet, in
such challenge, threat, support, their creativity
lives, and that very creativity at once may enhance
and endanger the other values in their lives.

(d) So we bring this part of our book to a close with
a fundamental contention that is not nullified by a
thousand qualifications. The "pearl of great price"
in human experience is the fact that a person can,
within limits, be responsible for the direction of
such creativity as he has. Kant put an unerring
finger on this fact: the good will, he said, is the
will to do all in one's power--to achieve the good,
yes, even if it should be that Nature is "stepmotherly." (I am not presenting the Kantian view in
toto.) That creative good will is a "jewel shining
by its own light," even if it is not the sole value.[5]

    Kant knew, as we know, that the good will in its
specific creativity gives shape to other values. But
no other value, no other jewel, will diminish what
moral creativity contributes to the quality of any
truth about environment-Environment. Persons, I have
argued, legislate for themselves as they develop value-
horizons within the value-possibilities of the Realm.
Such persons are among the data that any decision
about the nature of the Realm must take into account.
If the Realm is not stepmotherly, niggardly, and impervious, such persons, if indeed the life good to
live must include co-creative membership in a community of responsive-responsible persons, will be all
the more concerned to ask: Can it be, and if so, in
what sense can we believe that the Realm of Eligibility
is good?

Notes

1 The views in this chapter are more adequately supported in Bertocci and Millard, PAG, Part III. See
also Bertocci, PGI, ch. 6, and references therein;
Blanshard, RAG.

2 Philip Phenix, _Man and His Becoming_ (W. Sloane
Assoc., 1947).

3 See Rollo May, _Love and Will_ (Norton, 1969), for
an existential psychotherapist's treatment (with
foundations in Paul Tillich's writings), and
E. A. Burtt's SPU.

4 See also G. W. Allport's relevant essays, especially in Part III of the collected essays, _Personality
and Social Encounter_, 1960; his BEC, 1955, and his
Waiting On The Lord (30 Meditations on Man and God)
ed. P. A. Bertocci (Macmillan, 1978).

5 See first section of Immanuel Kant's _Principles
of the Metaphysics of Morals_, trans. T. K. Abbot
(as in Liberal Arts Press, 1949, with introduction
by Marvin Fox).

PART II

PERSONS, COSMIC PURPOSE, AND
THE CREATOR-PERSON

Chapter Six

THE ORDER OF NATURE:
IN NATURALISTIC AND THEISTIC PERSPECTIVE

1. Reflections on the Conflict Between Theism and
    Naturalism

(a) In the process of examining persons as agents
in knowing and valuing we have already been considering some issues upon which historic and contemporary theists and naturalists divide. Historical detail must give way in this chapter to the
basic problem of interpreting the order of Nature.

Classical theism (as expressed dominantly in the
Judeo-Christian-Moslem tradition), of course, places
persons in Nature, but it insists that persons, in
accommodating themselves to the order of Nature,
cultivate their overriding loyalty to Nature's God.
For the manifold majesty of Nature is the handiwork
of God "spread out" in space and time. Nature's
laws are not impositions upon God; they are expressions of His impartial justice, His omnipotence,
and His omniscience; and they are reminders that
persons live under God's far-seeing providence.

The order of Nature, therefore, is not to stand
"between" persons and the God. God, moreover, also
makes himself available to persons directly in religious experience, in special events, and in persons
that reveal His purposes. Nature and its order, yes!
Man and his natural yearnings, yes! But never as
substitutes for appropriate and religious experiences
that witness to the sovereignty of God.

(b) I have recognized the religious experience (or
the experience of the holy) in the life of persons,
but I have suggested that, in view of serious problems

123

in interpreting such experience, we establish a broader base for further appraisal of its impact and import. Many thinkers I deeply respect would say that I have closed the highway to belief in God because I have not learned to read the spiritual compasses of men. The reader will decide this in due time. What concerns us here is whether the naturalistic perspective on Nature's order is reasonable enough to persuade us to forgo the interpretation of Nature's order by appeal to a divine Ground of that order.

(c) Naturalists, too, differ amongst themselves.[1] It is not correct to assume that a naturalist is a materialist in his final interpretation of what constitutes the ultimate nature of things. Naturalists and materialists agree in denying that there is any purpose in the universe as a whole; they are adamant in denying any cosmic Lawgiver whose authoritative demands are imposed upon persons and all that occurs in the world. Some naturalists agree with the specific views of materialists as to the nature of the ultimate non-mental beings in the world, but many regard themselves as less speculative than materialists. Naturalists usually tend to confine themselves to what is known by way of scientific method, especially as this is used in the realms of physics and chemistry, and careful extensions thereof to other realms.

Especially to be noted here is that while materialists and naturalists agree that there is no cosmic purpose or Purposer, naturalists do not feel constrained to agree that within the world there are no purposive or purposeful agents. Still, naturalists in shaping their ideal of scientific method and of truth (by the method of discovery in the physical sciences which yields quantitative, public predictable generalizations priority), have been understandably hesitant about attributing telic tendencies to subhuman beings. Moreover, they are inclined not to trust the data of conscious and self-consciousness because these are not amenable to public checking, let alone to prediction and quantitative measure. Many, not all, social scientists abide by what they regard as the proper application of such naturalistic principles to the understanding of human affairs. Often, in investigating mind-body relationships, and in dealing with such experiences as willing, oughting, and with the varieties of value experience, these social scientists have been influenced by naturalistic conclusions as well as by these scientific principles of investigation.

(d) In my discussion so far I have adopted positions that would be rejected out of hand especially by naturalists who, given their conception of scientific truth, will not relax the presumably more stringent demands for publicity, for quantitative measurement, and for prediction.

It is understandable that, once minds intent upon accuracy in observation and experimentation could feel free to explore without the constraints and censorship imposed in the name of God's will, these minds would explore (what soon became) the ways of Nature, be there a God or not. However, I need not call to mind the pleas of other thinkers, religious believers and non-believers, who, in the name of Humanity, have protested that those who enthroned this naturalistic conception of Nature as ultimate and who extended the scope of physically-oriented, scientific method to the study of persons, in theory treated persons like things. Broadly speaking, then, if naturalistic thinking is in good part dominated by the desire to free the discovery of truth and value from the inscrutable will of God, the broader, humanistic plea to evaluate the scientific enterprise itself comes from persons who protest the homogenization of the universe and the substitution of "strict" scientific method and mathematical accuracy for more adequate reasonableness as the guide to truth and value in every field of human endeavor.

(e) I have not denied to scientific method, either in the narrower or broader interpretation, the right (or obligation) to probe any sphere of the world of human experience. We cannot tell before investigating what exploration will bring; we need to know what can be known by the strictest ideal. But, I have protested,

125

in the name of an accuracy which is adequacy to the
variety of actual data, the imperiousness of what has
often been a new orthodoxy in the approach to solving
human problems. I continue to reject 'scientistic'
censorship that declares certain kinds of phenomena
and hypotheses as initially 'out of bounds' since
they are not amenable to 'scientific method' or call
into doubt 'scientifically established' fact. In
particular, in the discussion so far, I have resisted
conclusions about the nature of persons that belittled
or bypassed, as hopelessly untrustworthy 'scientifically,
the inspection of human consciousness and self-consciousness.

Indeed, would a comprehensive or adequately
accurate procedure minimize data that are available
to us only in human beings, namely, persons' own
reports of what they are conscious? Of course, man's
place in Nature is to be considered in terms of
principles that guide the development of living organisms in evolutionary process; of course, these
developments, in turn, are to be considered in terms
of the laws that govern the physico-chemical order.
But limiting ourselves to considerations based upon
this "strict" approach to the understanding of man
is singularly self-deceptive; and imperialistic
scientism goes far beyond the scientific concern to
keep hypotheses related to data. For, unless we
have a fairly adequate description of their experience, one that only persons themselves can provide,
how shall we guide attempts to correlate conscious
experiences with whatever is not consciously experienced? The twitching nerve is not in pain; the
conscious person is conscious of pain "in his finger."

So, by all means, let us follow every trace,
notice every link, be sensitive to the dynamics of
every pattern that relates persons to the subhuman
orders of being and to the physical world. But let
us remember that philosophies, theologies, sciences,
arts are not "fields of study" independent of persons
who are activated by goals at once theoretical and
practical. Persons themselves cannot escape the
unique fact that they are guided by norms of truth
and value that give meaning to their existence;

yes, norms that have so often led them to sacrifice
survival itself in the name of a higher loyalty. A
goodly number have often "sacrificed" in the conviction that in so doing they were being grasped by a
deeper Dimension of being, one that lay "beyond" and
"within," yet could not be known by reference to
physical and biological dimensions alone.

(f) I can neither grant direct knowledge of the
supernatural, nor grant finality to prescriptions
presumably emanating therefrom. I cannot substitute
for such direct knowledge a naturalistic interpretation of things, persons, and values that tends to deny
or minimize telic agency in persons and teleological
explanation of phenomena. What is left for me to do?
In the remainder of this book I shall try to show
that, without accepting religious or scientific-
naturalistic imperialism, we can, with our ideal of
reasonable probability continuing to guide us, arrive
at a specific teleological view of the Realm that is
more coherent than alternatives. In this chapter I
ask whether the naturalistic interpretation of the
order of Nature, so often accepted by theists and nontheists alike, does meet the requirements of experiential coherence.

2.   On Grounding the Order of Nature

(a) Nontheists and theists alike agree that we can
depend upon events in Nature to occur with uniformity.
Some theists will reserve a place for miracles, some
naturalists will reserve a place for unpredictable
'emergents,' but both reservations become meaningless
apart from commitment to the dependable, causal sequences in Nature. Both theists and naturalists agree,
accordingly, that our present ignorance of the causes
of event b does not mean that b has no causes, or that
once we discover these causes we may not anticipate
the same effect under the same conditions. Indeed,
for all of us the presupposition of daily living is:
given the uniformity of Nature--a causes b under
certain conditions--we shall expect b when those conditions recur. For example, the scientific prepara-

127

tions for the sending of exploratory equipment to Mars
rest on the presupposition that what occurs on that
planet can be expected to respond in predictable ways
to given tests, since the conditions on Mars apply on
Earth. Accordingly, the tests for the presence of
living organisms on Mars are the same as those on
Earth--although we may not expect to find the same
species.

A second example brings out even more dramatically
what is entailed by the conviction that the causal
patterns in all of Nature are uniform. When the first
American astronauts returned to Earth from the moon
they were quarantined for a certain number of days.
Why? In order to assure the death of any unknown,
harmful bacteria that the astronauts might have
brought back to Earth with them. It would have been
at best interesting, at worst disastrous, if it turned
out that some harmful bacteria from the moon could
survive for more than the earthly limit! Our faith
in the uniformity of Nature ruled our quarantine procedures. Over and over again, then, reflection on
what we even mean by Nature rests on the presupposition
that inferences, based on cautious analogy with what
is already known, can move safely to the unknown. Why?
Because Nature, as we presume it to be, is a uniform,
universal Order.

(b) The naturalist, however, will in principle grant
no exception to this presumable "finding." Most
theists appeal to the uniformity of Nature also--it
is the trustworthiness of God!--but they in principle
hold that the God of Nature and History can suspend
these laws sometimes, if to do so is to further His
purposes. Those who believe in such suspension of
law for a special purpose still, of course, appeal
to orderly processes for the fulfillment of the miracle.
Both naturalist and theist protect the human enterprise
against what they regard as the inadequately justified
allegations made by each other about the total order
of being (Realm). But both also insist that the large-
scale order of Nature will become more evident to him
who knows how to observe what is there. Of course,
since God's will cannot be observed as such, a scientist,

128

for his purposes, may be a-theous, not necessarily atheistic, as he refers not to God's laws but to the principle of the uniformity of Nature. It is the naturalistic interpretation of the uniformity of Nature as requiring nothing nonnatural (or supernatural) that must now be evaluated.

(c) The principle of uniformity, as we have seen, articulates the fact that, given a, b, c connected to d, e, f in one part of Nature, then, unless one has grounds for assuming different conditions, the presence of a, b, c anywhere else will be connected to d, e, f. I am using the word "connected" to mean, at least, dependable sequence, that is, to suggest a bond between a, b, c, d, e, f, and not between a, b, c and x, y, z. For example, the scratching of a match on a certain kind of surface will produce a flame anywhere in Nature if the same conditions prevail. That such "connection" may be predicted is all that the scientist (not the naturalist) requires for the kind of understanding or explanation in his province. The scientist's reference to the principle of uniformity is not to something other than the connections and the regularities observed or observable.

Note: The principle of uniformity does not make connections possible; it articulates what the scientist has observed as the basis for this principle, namely, that actual existents do regularly occur or recur under certain conditions. It is the naturalistic interpretation of this order of Nature as being the pattern and structure of all there is, and as requiring no further interpretation, that raises questions that engage proponents of the cosmological argument for God (hereafter cosmologists).

(d) What, then, calls for further interpretation? Essentially the fact that there is recurrence of orderly change of the sort we all live by. The cosmologist hypothesizes that the very possibility of Nature (or uniform order) is more coherently interpreted if Nature is conceived of as the manifestation of an intrinsically unified Ground. The basic reasoning he advances, I present as follows:

(e) What we notice in the order of being-events (here-after beings or events) in Nature is that no one being and no one relationship between events is self-suf-ficient (or self-caused). The match, and the flame it produces under certain conditions, these and their effects on their surroundings are what we observe. But, there is nothing about them that __must__ exist. For example, there is nothing about __this__ __order__ (flame following scratching of match) that __must__ __be__ __what__ it is. __This__ order of beings, this __relation__ between them, is, accordingly, not a __must__ in any logically necessary sense. The same thinking applies to the larger order of beings that they, in turn, depend on, for neither beings nor their relations must be what they are.

Let us be clear about the situation that char-acterizes all the beings that compose Nature, __once__ __we realize that all beings and their relations are__ never self-sufficient beings but contingent. The cosmologist asks the clarifying questions: Can a Nature composed of contingent beings be itself any-thing but contingent? Can Nature as we know it now, Nature as order at any point in Universe-history, be anything but the kind of contingency exemplified by our match-flame relation? The cosmologist says "no." But this conclusion and its full meaning do not always dawn upon us because we keep on depending on the (order of) Nature as if nothing, no beings and no pattern of relations among them is ever contingent.

Yet let us reflect: If everything in Nature is contingent, then what we now depend on as Nature and any equivalent form of Nature need not exist. I re-peat, we often __read__ __into__ __Nature__ what is not permissible on this __naturalistic__ view. But if Nature is defined only by the innumerable contingent events in the past and present, __then there is no reasonable basis for__ __predicting__, as both naturalist and nonnaturalist confidently do, __innumerable events in the future__. The cosmologist's basic contention, accordingly, is: If, as the naturalist contends, there is no iota of anything but contingency for all the events in Nature, then we must conclude that the whole of Nature is con-tingent; Nature, in no particular way, nor as a whole, __must__ exist.

(f)   But I can hear distinguished opponents immediately
point out that an elementary, logical mistake has been
committed by the cosmologist.[2]   For **what applies to the**
parts need not apply to the whole. Nature, as a whole,
is not contingent even if all the parts are. We need
not, therefore, account for the order of Nature by appeal to anything other than Nature as is.

(g)   This rejoinder seems unanswerable, but let the
cosmologist take a closer look. If, indeed, each
"member" of the world is essentially contingent, can
anything but contingency characterize the whole? If
all members of a committee are blind, surely the committee as a whole will not enjoy sight! It is enough
to give the cosmologist a case of the shudders to think
that nothing about any part, or about any whole, must
be or continue to be! For then his trust in an orderly
world, his belief in the uniformity of Nature--in
short, the fundamental premise of our practical and
theoretical lives--is unfounded!

(h)   I shall suggest that other conclusions that the
classical cosmologist has drawn are false, but here
he stands on firm ground. He is affirming that, if
Nature is indeed an order of predictable beings and
relationships, the kind of reliance we place upon it
calls for more than utter and complete contingency.
How can this be without the hypothesis that some non-
contingent being, that is a self-sufficient being,
related (in some way) to all other beings, provides
the bond that makes prediction--or the principle of
uniformity--possible?

     To put the cosmologist's counter-interpretation
of the order of Nature positively: the network of contingent beings and their relations that we call the
uniformity of Nature has its root in a unitary Ground
(to be further defined) that itself depends on nothing
but itself for its existence (is, therefore, self-
sufficient). In terms of my earlier figure, Nature,
which is the joint-product of persons who anthropically
construct their natural environment in response to
the dependable sensory patterns, is uniformly dependable
because the Environment or Realm is a self-sufficient,
unified Ground of beings-in-relations. There is no

more reasonable way of accounting for the success of scientific method and its roots in the belief that the order of Nature is _uniform_. It is not surprising that some naturalists, responding to their own reflective need to ground the dependability of scientific method, now turn to ultimate and self-sufficient ground(s). Many at least move, if somewhat reluctantly, toward the more speculative, yet more clear-cut, alternative to any form of theistic belief, materialism.

3. The Ground as Unitary

(a) Ancient and modern materialists have in common the view that there are atomic or subatomic beings (or fields of energy or being-events) whose nature it is to be what they are--whose existence is self-sufficient. The Nature we now know is the product of motions among 'ultimates' that form the compounds and patterns that we take to be the laws of Nature. So far the materialist and the cosmologist agree; something eternal, something self-sufficient there must be. But the materialist claims that these ultimates cannot be said to be governed by, or to express, any self-sufficient and unchanging Being or Pattern.

For the materialist, then, our natural environment and all that depends on it is consequently contingent. This contingent, lawful order is (in contrast to the cosmologist's view) the product of the ways in which the ultimate, non-contingent being-events happen to combine. The laws that we do know and live by are, indeed, our descriptive generalizations of what goes with what in the world. But these laws are not the _ultimate law_ of things; they constitute no unchanging Ground, no Structure of the Realm. The materialist's ultimate, unchanging beings, with their own movements, are what they are, go whither they go, combine as they do, and whatever dependence they have consists in the combinations they happen to be in now and in any that occur.

(b) What will not escape the more attentive mind,

however, is that materialists keep referring to "the
ways" generated and, presumably, inherent in the
combinations or patterns of movements. If we do
grant self-sufficient being-events or patterns that
have no unifying ground, and if we accept the natural
environment as the present exhibition of 'combinations
of events and patterns,' we still may be puzzled at
the continuing orderly exhibition without which Nature
loses its intrinsic meaning. The materialist, in
short, denies that the laws of Nature are the necessary
result of, or are related to, any more unified, over-
arching, or immanent, or interpenetrating Order; and
yet he goes on insisting upon the predictable order
and uniformity of Nature! In the last analysis, the
laws underlying the existence of Nature as we know
it are the products of non-lawful "meetings" that took
place "once upon a time," and continued to have consequences for possible other "meetings," ending up
in the order of Nature that now prevails.

(c) The issue between cosmologist and materialist,
thus, is not about the necessity of positing some
non-contingent, self-existence in ultimate being(s),
but about the nature of that ultimacy, if we are to
give the most reasonable interpretation of the lawful order that we actually discover in our natural
order. At this point there are three considerations
that weigh heavily with the cosmologist.

i.   It is one thing to trace the order of being-
events that we observe to some fundamental happenstance meeting(s), after whose occurrence there is
always some prevailing order that determines future
relationships. On this interpretation, the physicist,
chemist, biologist, astronomer and geologist may
dutifully observe the regularities in their respective
and interrelated realms, and consequently postulate
the uniformity of sequences upon which confidence in
present, past, or future descriptions rests. Again,
scientists enjoying this confidence need not, as
scientists, concern themselves with the question of
the ultimate foundation of this confidence. But once
we reflect upon these materialistic-naturalistic
foundations for that confidence in the regularities

in our world, they leave much to be desired theoretically. For now, as scientists and as knowing-wanting-
persons, we must realize how implausible is the theory
of a dependable order of Nature, if that order is the
contingent product of meetings among self-existent
being-events that by definition involve no universal
pattern of order.

Indeed, we ask ourselves at this point why we
should reasonably accept contingency for all ultimate
"orders" when we govern our reasonable practice by
search for the covering laws by which we explain
the relation of events to each other in the present
natural world. After all, the imperative, theoretical
issue goes beyond any scientifically expedient explanation. It involves the wisdom of accepting a naturalistic-materialistic grounding of dependable order on
what, in the absence of order among ultimates, we,
in any other analogous situation, would hardly expect
to be dependable. Is the cosmologist's theoretical
alternative not more reasonable because it does
ground the proximate orders of our environment in an
intrinsically unitary Ground?

ii. Let us, at this philosophical level, take another
look, with the cosmologist, at the ultimate ingredients
of things that constitute the Realm on the materialistic hypothesis. We should notice that, despite individual differences, the self-existent beings, being-
events, or fields of energy, are of the same kind,
namely non-mental; that all the 'elements' of the
world move; that they all have a common environment,
space and time (or involve a space-time structure).
This closer look reveals that what is being inferred
are universal similarities, similarities that pervade
these ultimate beings. Without these similarities
there, presumably, would be no initial meetings, let
alone any continuing, dependable meetings that we know
as the lawful order of Nature.

The cosmologist cannot but be impressed by such
universal similarities that are themselves not contingent
and yet postulated in order to enlighten us about the
presumably purposeless order of Nature. Consequently,
the cosmologist reflects that even for the materialist

134

it is theoretically rather awkward to understand the
order of the world without attributing common and
constitutive similarities and relationships to the
ultimates that are non-contingent and not constituted
by their relationships.

In other words, some pervasive unifying principle
is actually required by both materialist and cosmologist
if the order of Nature is to be nothing but a constant
surprise. Again, it may seem reasonable, at the descriptive level, to say that the order of Nature as
we know it now is grounded in contingencies. But to
hold that the ultimate constitutive factors of these
contingencies are themselves in their nature and relationships contingent is anomalous. For, on any
view, some structure(s) is self-existent, some structure
is non-contingent; and, as self-existent, it is un-
changed by the contingencies of combinations (or relations). Otherwise, we have no good reason to refer to
a _universe_ in any serious sense, either as Nature, or
as Ground, or as Realm. What, pray, "theoretical
emergency" drives us to change our daily rules of
rooting one order in another order, and end up with
the claim that in the final nature of things order
stems from non-order?

iii. If we must affirm some universal structure(s)
without which other 'dependent' orders cannot be
understood, then we all face the question: What is
the most reasonable way of conceiving the relation
of ultimate structure(s) whose own unity is the
continuous ground of the order of Nature as we know
it?

The cosmologist's essential answer: The Ultimate,
that both our theory and practice require, cannot Itself be composed of other structures. It is a Ground.
However, as unified and unifying Ground, it is _not_
to be conceived of as another unity alongside the
contingent orders. That is, apart from some _initiating_
and sustaining relation of the ultimate Structure to
the contingent, the continuing orders that we know
become opaque to our intelligence. Unless there be
a common, self-existent Ground, itself related to

135.

the connections that ground our daily experience and our scientific projections, the success of our practice and our guiding theory is arbitrary. Why accept the arbitrary at this point if there is any reasonably more illuminating answer? From now on the question must be: How is that Ground to be conceived in its relation to all we depend upon in our experience?

(d) At this point, then, the cosmologist properly presses his demand for a _sustaining_ Ground. In an approach to that problem, the cosmologist, aware that his own answers are neither easy nor coercive, asks us, however, to bear in mind the alternative to acceptance of a sustaining Ground. He wonders once more: Is it plausible to reduce "all there is" to ultimate being-events that come and go with no inherent or dependable connection with each other? He replies: If all the most remote elements of any "world" are in their relations "unfastened," as it were, from each other or from orders dependent on them, we must face the consequences of this thoroughgoing pluralism. For, once more, nothing ultimate _must_ go with anything, or can be reasonably depended on to go with anything. Thus, neither the ultimate contingent happenings, nor the dependent-things-in-relation resulting therefrom, that in time compose what we observe in the natural world, need recur at all.

The cosmologist, then, contemplating this granular 'pluriverse' in which nothing has to be _or_ recur, cannot avoid another case of the shudders. For now the ultimate 'pluralism' of self-existent elements is, in fact, a "neutral" word for chaos; in actuality no one has an intellectual right to expect anything to recur dependably. Faced with what, in the last analysis, is a junk-heap world, indeed, a junk-heap that may not even continue to be a junk-heap, the cosmologist knows what is intolerable if theory and practice are to harmonize. His basic alternative is a Unitary Being-related-to-all-other beings-and-relations as the Ground (Realm of Eligibility) for an orderly Nature (environment). Such an alternative has the inestimable advantage: it establishes a reasonable basis for the trust in the uniformity of Nature. The cosmologist's task is now to propose what the essence of that unifying Ground is.

4. The Ground as Creator

(a) One persistent view of the actual relation of the Ground to all other beings--one that has and does recommend itself to many religious minds and to some acute philosophers East and West--is that the Ground is expressed in all finite beings, including Nature, although the Ground is not exhausted by all of these modes of being. The Ultimate, the Realm, the Ground is an Absolute One, and all orders of existence have their being in and through it. No matter to what degree we finite beings appear to have independence and autonomy, once we transcend "imagination" and come to understand the rational structure immanent in all beings, or once we feel the indescribable Unity of all, we cannot avoid the conviction that It is an unchanging One. Thus, in essence, while this One is instantiated in finite beings in myriad ways, it is never to be simply identified with them. On this view the only cogent way to avoid the chaos of ultimate plurality is to achieve an adequate conception of the one Ground and its ways of being.[3]

(b) I shall not deal with the difficult questions having to do with the ways in which the One _is_ the changing Many and yet in itself _is_ an undifferentiated, unchanging One. The view is so welcome, especially when we are overcome by the problems of sheer pluralism! It may not be turned aside by pointing to the mysteriousness of a One that expresses itself in its gradations. Any view of the relation of the One to the Many faces difficulties. But assuming, as I myself have been unable to do, that any Monistic Absolutist can succeed in explaining why, on his view, individuality in the non-human world is not annulled, I shall have to make my last line of defense against any ultimate Monism that of the classical theist. He finds Monism unable to render the freedom of persons intelligible if persons are indeed instantiations of the Absolute.

(c) In chapters eight and nine I shall propose a view
of the person that will call for further articulation
of the relation of the Ground to persons in particular.
Here it must suffice, given the conception of the
person's will-agency, willpower, and of oughting, as
I proposed above, to say that the creativity of the
person is unintelligible apart from his own history.
In any case, before adopting Monism as the best
solution to the problems of ultimate pluralism, we
do well to examine the classical theistic view that
would save the person as the finite crucible of
autonomy in value-becoming. For classical theists,
such individuality is so precious that they resist
even the doctrine of emanation of individuals from
a Ground. What classical theists require is a view
of the Ground that is indeed not exhausted by its
immanence in the Many but that is still so related
to them that self-experienced individuality and
freedom, when and where it occurs, is not annulled.
However, the Ground must not be one more being
alongside other beings who do not depend on it. This
would gainsay the cosmologist's whole argument that
all contingent beings-and-relations require the unity
and continuity of their existence to be related to
their Ground.

(d) The alternative that classical theists have
turned to is admittedly mysterious. They propose
that the Ground is Creator of all that depends on
It for its being and continuance. But the notion
of Creator has been the source of much dispute, and
not the least because of what is intended by the
meaning creatio ex nihilo. When translated literally
(and removed from the context of the philosophical
issues confronted), "creation out of nothing" understandably is unintelligible. It is not surprising
that great Greek and Eastern philosophers simply turned
their backs on even the hint of "something coming
from nothing." But the creationist-theist is well
aware that he is pointing to a relationship which,
like other ultimate relations, is mysterious in
terms of how it occurs. The sanction for this admittedly mysterious way of "relating" the One and
the Many lies in the evidence for individuality and

freedom, such as that we have presented, data so
pressing as to resist all temptation to their annulment in the One.

In order to avoid the difficulty of creation
"out of nothing," some have urged that the only alternative for the theist is to follow the Plato of
the Timaeus. The created world would then be the
product of an eternal Demi-urge who "persuades" some
co-eternal "unformed" being to take on the finite
shapes and forms that come as close as possible to
the co-eternal Forms or Ideas that guide his "creating." So, why not say simply that a cosmic Architect
and Lover of the Good, in creating, has always created
not "out of nothing" but out of some relatively amor-
phous "stuff" that is not part of Himself and yet
yields to His will (up to a point)? The resulting
world-order has the advantage of fitting in, presumably, with our human experience of "creation"--
something made out of something else.

(e) This view, however, has the same underlying difficulty that we face when we think that co-eternal
ultimates (two, a dozen, or an infinite number), can
come together to produce as orderly a world as we
have. Even in the case of two co-eternal Beings, do
we have the slightest ground for supposing that they,
who by definition do not depend upon each other in
any way, would enter into the kinds of relations that
produce the world-orders known to us? Inescapably,
neither millions, nor two, non-related, co-eternal
ultimates can be reasonably supposed to ground world-
order, even if a co-eternal "Architect" be among them.
For by definition the ultimates have nothing that
grounds orderly, recurrent connections.

It is in this larger theoretical context that the
theistic doctrine of creatio ex nihilo takes on positive meaning. Creatio ex nihilo, however mysterious,
is the alternative to unacceptable, ultimate dualism,
pluralism, monism, or emanationism. Indeed, the cosmologist can join the voices insisting that from
nothing, nothing comes. For he proposes that the
doctrine of creatio means that the self-sufficient,

eternal God (who is <u>not</u> nothing) creates the world--
and <u>not</u> from or out of nothing, nor out of something
else, nor even out of himself. The self-sufficient
Ground brings into being <u>what</u> <u>was</u> <u>not</u> <u>in</u> <u>being</u> <u>before</u>.
To create is to bring into being out of no preexisting
stuff. The doctrine is indeed difficult, but no more
so than that of the other alternatives; but, I, for
one, am driven to it by the individuality and freedom
we observe in the created. Indeed, in my view <u>creatio</u>,
<u>ex</u> <u>or</u> <u>ab</u> <u>nihilo</u>, is no more explicable than the free-
dom and individuality we are seeking to ground without
losing it (or other relations we need not discuss here).

(f) The classical theistic cosmologist, then, postu-
lates a self-sufficient, unchanging Creator who is
the Source of all dependent beings, but not because
He can take nothing and make something <u>out</u> <u>of</u> or <u>from</u>
<u>it</u>. To be a Creator is to be the kind of Being who
brings into being what would not be existent at all
otherwise; to create persons is "to posit" beings
with delegated autonomy consistent with the scope of
their potential. But any created being as created
is limited and contingent. The Creator-Ground alone
is self-sufficient; all dependent beings, whether
by creation or not, depend on His uncreated nature.

5. The Ground as Contemporaneous Creator and
   Omnitemporal

(a) Thus far the classical theistic cosmologist seems
to be on firm ground. A Creator-Ground enables us
to account reasonably for the contingent order of Nature
without annulling the relative autonomy of any crea-
tures--and especially persons--who depend for so much
of their existence on the dependability of Nature. It
is also plausible for the classical theist to hold
that the Creator-Ground is a cosmic Mind, arguing from
analogy with the fact that minds are unities, given
to establishing and "creating" orders.

(b) The next step is a leap that gives pause. To
move from a Creator-Ground to a Creator-Mind, or

Creator-Person, that is omnipotent, omniscient, and all-good, is to leap (as Kant in particular pointed out) beyond the evidence actually presented. Each of the qualifications or attributes of the Creator-Ground needs definition that accords with the evidence it is intended to illuminate. For instance, classical cosmologists hold that in having reached a self-sufficient Creator-Ground who is an unchanging (eternal, self-sufficient), omnipotent, omniscient and all-good Mind or Person, they are defining what a perfect Being, or Perfection, is.

But is such a conception of perfection indeed self-evident? And are the definitions and justifications of the attributes themselves self-evident? Much of our remaining task will be to indicate what may be reasonably held to be the nature of the Creator-Ground and of perfection. I draw this chapter to a close by calling attention to a basic, often misconceived, tenet of the classical cosmologist that I think requires a different interpretation. The question of whether the Creator can be reasonably held to be a Person I reserve for later clarification, although the two concepts have overlapped in our discussion.

(c) I have been using the term "Creator-Ground" rather than the more familiar "First Cause." I have done so to emphasize that "Cause" is not used in the Humean sense, namely for a member of a customary sequence of events that has no necessary, let alone productive, relations with any other. And "First" means not first in time, but the self-sufficient Agency without which, at any point in history, any other agencies and orders become unintelligible. The word "First," in short, means first in order of importance to the being and becoming of others. First Cause refers, in creationist theism, to the Creator as the contemporaneous productive Agency transcending, but related to, the orders that depend upon its Agency.

The whole intent of the cosmological argument is lost on us if we do not realize that without this ongoing, contemporaneous Creator-Ground there would be no cosmos. Again, without this contemporaneous

Agent, the unity-continuity that underlies our thinking
about the uniformity of Nature and an orderly world
becomes opaque.

(d) But the classical theistic cosmologist takes a
step that can and should be questioned, as is my
intent even as I try to draw up an alternative. The
classical cosmologist, in part influenced by his conception of perfection as unchanging, and in part convinced that orderly change must presuppose a permanent
being who would hold, as it were, the beginnings and
the ends of events together, interprets this Creator-
Ground as unchanging in every respect. The Creator-
Ground is nontemporal; It is the Alpha that is Omega,
despite the fact that much change occurs between Alpha,
in any scheme we experience, and what Omega would be.

(e) I have sometimes referred to the Creator-Ground
as It because what requires argument, even granted
that It is a Mind or Person, is clarification of what
these terms are to embrace. I shall defend a particular view of person that may guide our thinking about
the way in which a permanent Ground can be a Creator-
Ground that transcends and yet is immanent in its
creations. But be the Creator-Ground a person or not,
I must here confess that I am to be numbered among
those who cannot understand how the Creator-Ground,
immanent in the changes of the world that call for
a cosmic Agency as their contemporaneous Ground, is
Himself exempt from some change even as a transcendent
Being. Hence, even at this early stage of the argument, I suggest that the contemporaneous Creator-
Ground, who is the source of order in change, cannot
be exempt from change. The Creator-Ground is
changing, and we must work out a plausible conception
of a unified Ground that is at the same time a contemporaneous Creator. For the order of the world as
we know it is indeed an order of change among being-
events related to each other. The Ground, without
which that order of change cannot be, must be self-
existent and eternal but not unchanging in every
respect; it is neither nontemporal nor temporal, but
omnitemporal.[4]

142

The charge that unless the Ultimate is an unchanging One the universe will crumble into chaos
we shall keep constantly in mind as we try to develop
an acceptable view of the Ground. We shall build on
the essential argument of this chapter:namely, a
unifying Ground is a self-existent unity that can be
more reasonably understood as a Creator-Unity. But
our next step is to ask this question: Is the concept of orderly world that we have been dealing with
an abstract way of designating a teleological order
which we can more clearly conceive as a Creator-
Purposer?

6. Reflective Overview

The cosmological argument for God has been presented in this chapter as a more reasonable, but
not demonstrative, interpretation of the order of
Nature or Environment. In essence what has been
suggested is:

i. That the naturalistic-materialistic interpretation of Nature is an interpretation that leaves much
to be desired theoretically, once we expose the
assumptions involved in a reasonable view of the uniformity of Nature that both scientists and nonsci-
entists live by.

ii. The Ground of the uniformity of Nature must be
so related to it that the reliability of the changing
order in which we trust is forthcoming. The Ground,
the First Cause, for reasons set forth, is both
transcendent and immanent; what is grounded in It
does not exhaust its nature, but It, in turn, is not
another being "alongside" all other beings. The
term "Creator" is attached to Ground in order to
focus on this immanence and transcendence in a way
that articulates the individualities in existence,
and especially the kind we know in ourselves as
agent-persons.

iii. Once we disabuse ourselves of the notion of perfection as meaning unchanging in every respect (and

143

assumed correlates), once we persist in justifying any attributes of God only by evidence especially relevant to it, we can move to the view denied the classical cosmologist: the cosmic Ground is indeed One--a contemporaneous Creator-Ground, some aspects of whose nature are affected by the kind of temporal world we know. Hence, if we have succeeded in exposing the weakness of a materialistic-naturalistic interpretation of the cosmic order, we have also realized that what we say about any Ground will depend upon the particular quality of order explained by the Creator-Ground. And here we turn to the qualities of order referred to in natural, organic, and human history: the cosmo-teleological-ethical realms of order.

Notes

1   See E.S. Brightman, Nature and Values, 1933, and POR, as well as PAR; and for representative, systematic presentation of varied materialistic and naturalistic presentations, see the works of George Santayana, John Dewey, and Roy Wood Sellars.

2   A strong critique of the cosmological argument is Milton K. Munitz, The Mystery of Existence, 1965; strong defense in E.L. Mascall, Existence and Analogy, 1949, and He Who Is, 1966, and James F. Ross, PT, 1969.

3   For distinguished differing expositions of the monistic view, see C.A. Campbell, Selfhood and Godhood, 1957; and John N. Findlay, The Discipline of the Cave, 1966; The Transcendence of the Cave, 1967.

4   In Bertocci, PGI, there is a defense of temporalistic creationism, and related theses that mark disagreement with Tennant, PT, vol. 2, a powerful defense of traditional theism on teleological grounds; but the thesis I present is strongly influenced by E.S. Brightman, IPOR, and the works of A.N. Whitehead, Charles Hartshorne, and Ivor Leclerc. See also my "The Idea of Creation in Religion" in Dictionary of the History of Ideas, ed. Philip P. Wiener, 1970.

Chapter Seven

IS THERE PURPOSE IN NATURAL AND HUMAN HISTORY?

1. The Underlying Theme of Cosmo-Teleological Reasoning for God

(a) Reasoning that approaches the existence of God from the dependable order of Nature, reasoning that focuses on the manifold forms of design in Nature has often been kept from proceeding to legitimate conclusions by a seemingly irremovable roadblock. It continues to be set up by those who examine thinking about God with a preconceived idea of what God (and perfection) must be. Such thinkers condemn the cosmological and the teleological arguments, separately or together, because they presumably do not culminate in a God worthy of worship. They concede that the arguments at their best, and, especially, when supplemented by the moral argument for God, could appear as impressive indications of a Perfect Being. But the paths themselves cannot possibly attain the summit of Perfection which is imperfectly comprehended, necessarily, by finite persons in a finite world.

Thus, as pointed out in the last chapter, once the order of Nature was seen to require a First Cause, that Cause was assumed to meet the requirements of Perfection. The task then became, first, to show how a self-sufficient, immutable, omnipotent, omniscient, impassive, all-good God (that is, "perfect") could be related to the finite changing forms of natural and human history. Second, by the magnificent display of particular and widespread designs within and between things, plants, animals, and man, eminent thinkers were overcome by God's wisdom, goodness, and power. Yet the catastrophes in Nature and the evils in human history provided evidence of an opposite kind. How effect a reconciliation, especially to a Perfect Being, one that they simply assumed to exemplify the only possible form of Perfection worthy of worship?

In fact, then, cosmological and teleological
reasoning tended to resolve itself into a search for
evidence of a _certain kind_ of God rather than a
search for ways of understanding the data actually
presented in the realms of physical, organic, and
human history as a whole.

(b) Hence, in respected and influential quarters,
the venture in these pages may be deemed, perhaps,
a very interesting one, but destined to fail the
demands of both intellect and heart for Perfection.
At best, I might reach the "God of the philosopher.."!
But I counter by asking for the source of the _impri-
matur_ on what is called "the God of the religious
consciousness" as differentiated from "the God of
the philosopher." And I propose that we try to see
whether this distinction may not be question-begging
and even self-serving.

My contention, to begin with, is that the classical view of Perfection can be challenged in the name
of the human experiencing of perfection. Moreover,
by proposing the idea of a contemporaneous, omnitemporal Creator-Ground, I have begun to avoid the
theoretical "patching" to which the classical theist
resorts in order to sustain his fixed notion of
Perfection in the face of the changing, multifarious
orders of existence and, in particular, of evils that
stand in stark opposition to that notion of Perfection. My intention, in pursuing the evidence available in cosmological, teleological, moral, and religious data, is to see what kind of Realm we live in,
by what kind of Creator-Ground our purposes are
"guided," and to leave open the question of whether
the quality of Person-Ground I shall suggest is worthy
of worship. Let me caution the reader that until we
have examined the notion of person and confronted the
problem of good-and-evil the meaning of Creator-Person
or Creator-Ground must remain ambiguous (except as
we have already made it clear). But, minimal to
that notion of Creator and Person, is the assumptive
analogy that, at the very least, the Creator is
aware of his own being and what He is doing.

146

(c) The teleological argument I shall be actually
continuing to expound is no appendage to, or comple-
ment of, any other.[1] Why? Because it is neither
dependent on, nor confined to, the particular instances of design or segments of purposive order in
Nature and in human experience--such as caught the
imagination of exponents of the "narrower" teleological argument. While such designs as a whole
must continue to impress, so much in the array of
interrelated parts of living organisms and so much
in their supposed prefitted adaptation to specific
environments can, indeed, be understood without
reference either to finite purposive action or to
the controlling creation of a cosmic Designer that
the impressiveness loses its cogency even as reasonable argument for a cosmic Creator. The "wider"
teleological argument that I shall be expounding
will point to the network of orderly relationships
without which we cannot reasonably understand persons
and their values as they actually appear and grow
in relation to the physical and biological environments that bespeak their interrelation with the
Realm. The argument, I grant, is not logically
coercive, but its reasonable probability consists
in its cumulative, theoretical impressiveness as
a better alternative to other interpretations of
man, Nature, and God.

The great philosophical theologian, F. R. Tennant,
paved the way for this orientation. In his neglected
but far-reaching and searching development of a more
wholesome empiricism, particularly as presented in
his masterly two volumes of Philosophical Theology,
1928, 1930, Tennant realized that the narrower
teleological argument could be given a wider scope
if we take into fuller account the areas of value-
experience, and if we profit from a more comprehensive and critical analysis of the epistemic assumptions that underlie all efforts of man as knower-
valuer and agent. Accordingly, his "wider teleological argument," by a scrupulous critique of the
kinds of evidence available in the varied yet interconnected dimension of human experience, supports the
judgment, "and God saw that it was good."

147

Tennant's work, as he himself says, cannot be read as one runs, but he who studies both volumes of Philosophical Theology may well concur with the verdict of the unconvinced critic, C. D. Broad, who nevertheless stated: "If a system of speculative philosophy cannot be established by Dr. Tennant's method, I agree that it is still less likely to be established by any other...; it leads to a form of theism which is intellectually and morally respectable and in practice inoffensive...."[2] I have suggested elsewhere that Tennant can be defended against Broad and other critics. On the other hand, I differ with Tennant on certain aspects of his theory of man and God.

(d) However, before developing the next phase of this wider teleological argument, I would avoid misunderstanding by making several partly repetitive comments. I do not concede that the narrower teleological argument was mistaken in its unwillingness to think that coordinated and harmonious wholes can be dismissed as accidental juxtapositions or as combinations that only suggest design. To be sure, the fundamental weakness of the narrower teleology, as illustrated in the Genesis account of creation, consists in the affirmation that the actual fit of living beings to their environment required a Creator. Biological evolutionists are able to explain these formations by hypothesizing that the present species are the product of an agelong sorting process carried out, not by a planning Creator but by a non-purposive "natural selection." A neutral natural and living environment, according to this hypothesis, "favors" those species which can adapt themselves and which, therefore, can survive and breed in territories advantageous to them.

Nevertheless, while such appeals to "the survival of the fit" or to "natural selection" are plausible substitutes for the Creator at the segmental scientific or philosophical levels of descriptive explanation, the discussion that these substitutes have evoked among interpreters witnesses to the simplistic crudities of "evolutionists" similar to those of biblical "creationists." At this stage

in cultural history we cannot hide the fact that
Nature, as conceived by most evolutionists, does
not "select" or "favor" anything. Once living beings
arrived the structures of Nature "allow" those organisms to survive which have more ability than their
competitors to modify their ways of adaptation. To
explain the survival of a species as due to the "survival of the fit" is like explaining it by the "will
of God"--both explanations simply dub the surviving
as "the fit," or as "God's choice," respectively.

Nor is the simplistic theory of "natural selection" saved when the process of "mutation" is added
to natural selection. Evolutionists explain changes
at some points in biological evolution that cannot
be anticipated or cannot be understood in terms of
the usual process of selective adaptation. These
(discontinuous) mutations, as is well known, do not
necessarily improve the likelihood of survival. But,
again, one point should not have to be stressed at
this stage in the history of reflection. This theory
of evolution, supposedly discrediting any theistic
creationism, only discredited a teleological theism
that depended on specific divine acts pre-forming or
pre-ordering certain organic harmonies.

To be sure, the whole evolutionary movement
supported the strides already made in the physical
sciences by opening the door to human observation,
experiment, and hypothesis; it discouraged "anticipations of Nature," or any fixed convictions about
natural events based on the conviction that they were
ordained as such by a Will that is inscrutable. Insofar as theism, in the name of "conserving" and
"saving" facts and values, actually discourages human
observation and reflection, it loses and deserves to
lose--indeed, should be strenuously opposed by--the
community of persons who are courageous enough, imaginative enough, and self-disciplined enough to explore
every nook and cranny of existence and value. But a
more adequate conception of empiricism by no means
closes the door to considerations emphasizing not so
much special design in particular products but the
evolutionary process as a whole and, not the least,
the place of persons in relation to the more comprehensive historical process.

2. The Reason in Teleological Explanation

(a) Fundamental evidence favoring the wider teleological theism that I shall expound is already before
us in the suggestion that the unity and uniformity
of Nature, so congenial to human theory and practice,
are not blind, accidental sequences either in the
human or the nonhuman areas. One point I need to
emphasize more fully is that human endowment could
not organize and relate itself to being-events, in
both the inorganic and the organic spheres, if there
were not support in these spheres relevant to it.
It is the evidence of such support that calls for a
cosmic Ground that is not simply a principle of Order,
or the reified Uniformity of Things.

What remains the stubborn fact is that the cosmos
we know as persons is not any cosmos, and the ideals
that undergird our development in knowing, valuing,
and acting, are not any ideals. 'Cosmos,' as such,
does not attain to accurate or full meaning as this
Cosmos apart from the persons actually observing and
affecting and being-affected-by their observations
and reflections. The collocations observed by persons
that enable them to speak of a common physico-chemical
environment for living beings and persons, these collocations themselves are at once not isolable from
persons nor the artifice of persons.

Collocations there are, we also infer, that make
possible what persons understand as their environment,
the very environment in which they and their ideals
are involved, in shaping and being shaped. It is the
ultimate support for this dynamic interaction and
interchange, it is this kind of order, in the last
analysis a valuational teleology, that calls for a
Creator-Ground whose unity and continuity are informed
by some patterns of goals but not by other patterns.
To think concretely about these pyramidal, differentiated orders of being, and to jump to the conclusion
that "creative" means Creator is natural but needs
further support. A more cautious inspection sees
persons, in their being, becoming, and fulfillment,
in relation to these pyramidal physico-chemical-biological orders but not restricted to them.

(b)   I have made several statements that call for
further comment.   I shall not retract the contention
that our minds do not, in fact, fully understand any
instance of order apart from relation to an end, goal,
or ideal.   The notion of order, in abstraction from
purpose, is just that--an abstraction.   We may, of
course, simply focus on the mechanisms which together
make a bicycle work, but the way in which we observe
what takes place actually reflects our purpose in
observing the end for which the bicycle was made.
And both the end and the means that help us to understand the bicycle are related to the goals guiding
persons in other areas of their lives.

Again, the person observing how a saw cuts through
certain kinds of lumber may disregard questions concerning natural resources (the indiscriminate cutting
of these trees) and other factors that do not relate
to his immediate purpose of noting how effective the
saw is and what it does to this particular kind of
lumber.   But since not only the sawing but other particular calculations involving trees are also related
to the safety of persons--such considerations will,
sooner or later, influence the degree of value we come
to place on this kind of sawing and on this species
of trees in the light of their consequences for a
larger pattern of values not hitherto considered. I
am simply saying what Plato long ago taught in the
Phaedo, namely, that any change and its order remains
incompletely understood until we know its end or what
it is good for.   The end or value, although not observable as such, is yet immanent in the orders of
change and explains them.   Like Plato, the teleologist
maintains that we understand phenomena the better the
more we understand the goal.   To explain teleologi-
cally is also to place some value on the order-of-
changes taking place.

(c)   There is, in short, nothing arbitrary about my
contention that the cosmological argument is itself
a part of a wider, cumulative, teleological argument.
The God of Genesis I did not, in a "later observation,"
after having created the heavens and the earth and the
orders of living beings, simply realize that "it was
good."   Again, there is no objection to the scientific

purpose that limits the biological evolutionist to "explaining" evolution by natural selection, the survival of the fit, and mutations. But "understanding" and "explanation" in the wider teleological argument requires that we seek a motif that will enable us to relate the orders of the physical, biological, and human spheres into a larger pattern that recognizes both the "inexorable" linkage of these orders and any aim that gives further coherent meaning and valuational unity to them.

When the scientist himself moves beyond the observation of regularities (beyond explanation by classification of occurrences or their assimilation to prior observations), to the hypothesizing of some principle (such as natural selection), he is taking a significant step. He is himself on the way to explanation in terms of the more coherent hypotheses-- in this instance, one involving the goal(s) for the orders-in-change-and-development. Such thinking, in terms of goals, is not itself subject to scientific tests. For scientific tests can only be confined to the happenings within the environment as defined by scientific aims. The teleologist is moving beyond correlations and laws to "subsurface connections," as Henry Margenau puts it in The Nature of Reality, 1950. Again, the teleologist, in reaching for an hypothesis that defines the purpose of the whole, expresses the full aim of human explanation, and this by extending desirable yet segmental purposes, halted at other levels of human effort, to the most inclusive goal or pattern of ideals.

(d) Accordingly, in terms of my explicit argument so far, it is the cosmologist who, in fact, takes the first steps in our wider teleological argument. For he maintains that we can avoid unintelligibility in positing a sheer many-ness of ultimate, disconnected being-events by hypothesizing a contemporaneous, goal-oriented Creator-Ground to explain the unity-continuity of the orders of being. More coherence is achieved when the temporalistic theist substitutes for the classical Creator-Ground the telic, omnitemporal Creator-Ground. For the temporalistic theist

allows the transcendent Creator to maintain his
act-ive unity without rendering unintelligible his
unifying-ordering immanence in the changes in natural
and human history. Still more coherence is achieved
when the teleologist explains orderly sequences and
connections as more integral phases of a total pattern
that neither neglects nor ignores the values of persons who both know and act in the environment (that
is still open to segmental "scientific explanation"
without reference to goals).

(e) Of course, the teleologist's work is not done
until he has been able to show that his hypothesis
as to the goal is as inclusive as he claims. I shall
presently begin to extend my suggestion that persons
as knowing-agent-valuers, no mere addenda to the
cosmological concern, contribute to theoretical
issues that our search for greater experiential coherence confronts.

One more objection must be faced. A question
is sometimes raised, often as if it could stop all
further inquiries: How can we possibly know that
the world-order as known to us is not an oasis in
a desert of chaos? How do we know that the Creator
of this world-order has not already failed many
times as a cosmos-maker, or, in terms of our metaphor, that the Realm of Eligibility has not already
allowed and sustained many patterns of order, and
some more significant than this one? The answer,
of course, is that we do not know for sure. But the
question is framed in a context that would force us
to miss the explanation open to us. It suggests that
if only we could have watched a Creator create worlds,
as one would throw dice, we could establish some
statistical probability upon which to base our interpretation of this world and the significance of its
orders.

Three brief comments may at least indicate why
such a line of objection will not bring this inquiry
to a halt. First, we are not seeking _statistical_
probability, but the _reasonable_ probability (some
prefer to say "likelihood") that will guide our

thought and action concerning what is vouchsafed us,
the kind of probability that guides us daily when we
have few or no statistical probabilities as bases for
making significant choices. Second, the ground for
trusting statistical probabilities is not itself
based on the kind of statistical probability now being
demanded of the teleologist; indeed, it itself presupposes a reasonable trust in this and other ways
of knowing dependable relations between ourselves and
the world. Third, in any case, neither the objector
nor the teleologist is witness to the worlds being
thrown like dice. Both are confined to developing
noncoercive hypotheses that, short of direct, unmedi-
ated knowing, of logical proof, and statistical
ratios, may increase the reasonable adequacy of our
hypotheses regarding the environment that is the
product of our knowing-acting interaction within the
Realm. In what follows in this chapter we bring together what has remained too long asunder.

3. The Collocation of Things and Persons as
    Agent-Knowers

(a) Given the theme in the first "cosmological" link
of the wider teleological argument, the second link
articulates expressly the thesis running through much
of what we have been saying. Despite human failures
in knowing, the fact remains that our cognitive
grasp is trustworthy enough to warrant our efforts
to widen its scope. Bringing forward our figure of
piano keyboard in relation to the soundboard (Realm),
we can say that our keyboard--in this instance, sensory,
memorial, imaginative experiences and our reasoned
weaving of them together with our affective-conative
thrusts--does 'correspond' to the Realm as far as we
have gone. Often goaded on by conditions forced upon
us, our cognitive probing, as persons intent on coherence, may indeed be pertinent to only a segment of
the eligibilities of the Realm. But it certainly is
not alien to them!

     I have already cautioned against thinking that

'correspondence' means a mirroring of Eligibilities. No more is intended than the relevance of the patterns of our known world (environment) to the Realm. More suggestive is what we have in mind when we say that many of our cognitive keys "open" the locks of the Realm. Perhaps our best way of understanding 'correspondence' is suggested by what we reasonably mean when we say that we know <u>what</u> is in another's mind. Thus, if my students express what they attribute to me in words different from mine and expressing their own interest, they may still <u>convey</u> much of the pattern of meaning I had in mind, enriched (or not) with their own contribution. I may judge that one student grasps my meaning better than another. But there is never a point-to-point correspondence between what is going on in their minds and mine. If, somehow, their minds could be present to me directly, it would still be mine that would selectively interpret what I took to be present. Similarly, to know the Realm by way of piano keys that our ancestors and we have developed is never to know the Realm point-for-point; <u>but</u> neither is it to distrust <u>in principle</u> that what we do weave together as coherently as possible at a certain stage in history is our best guide, in thought and action, as we live in relation to the Realm in terms of our environments. And Nature (as physical environment), in our most warranted constructions, is our reliable keyboard, segmental as it is, for much that we can take the Realm to be.

(b) Creativity, therefore, in this <u>cognitive</u> context, does not produce human, imaginative wish-fulfillment or day-dreaming. For, in the historical development of our clue(s), both our own natures and their development are at work with the Realm in ways and degrees that remain a problem for constant investigation. <u>What</u> we claim the Realm to be finds support in the Realm--without which, in the last analysis, knowing-agents could neither be, become, nor know. Our sciences still are in this sense our magnificent creations; they are expressions of creative, disciplined human awareness that relate our interests to what in environment-Environment will gratify and satisfy us as persons.

It is this total, human, cognitive enterprise,

heritage and hope that the teleologist will not attribute to cosmic happenstance. He believes our compasses may be trusted; but compasses point without mirroring, even as persons, with their help, continue to direct their interactions with the Realm.

(c) A possible retort at this point: "What you call cognitive evidence for cosmic teleology can be explained by the very fact that man has his roots and his branches 'sifted out' by a non-purposeful Realm." Without denying the influence of evolutionary dynamics already referred to, we need not accept the (often crypto-teleological) assumptions in much talk about the mind-less order of things, if we keep before us the kind and quality of knower-actor and of knowing. Say what one will, the so-called purposeless Realm being referred to had to its credit the fact that it allowed such persons to arrive with their activity-potentials; and then to survive on condition that they could discipline themselves in accordance with certain trends in being-events and not others. Persons did what not even the "highest" animals could do. Such animals are so largely confined to their built-in, relatively rigid, affective-conative tendencies that they lack the capacity for symbolic creations that free a mind from the immediacies of sensory and conative experience. They, therefore, cannot "evolve" the compasses which persons "find" and "construct."

To argue that persons can do all this merely because of evolution and environmental pressure is to claim that something can grow where, so far as we know, nothing was sowed. To reply that the arrival of the unique powers of persons is an emergent, or that they are mutations is to label, not solve, the problem. For what we are trying to understand is the very arrival of the kind of living being who survives as he makes demands that require a quality of relevance of "thought to thing" that knows no parallel in, is no shadow of, anything in the sub-personal world. Even if biological evolution in the subhuman species could be described-explained without reference to interlocking ends, we still would

156

have to account for persons with their telic ventures and symbolic creations.

(d) It is in these circumstances that the teleological theist hypothesizes that the Creator _creates_ the new kind of agent-knower in relation to patterns of order already existent in the subhuman and nonhuman realms; yes, _creates_ the new kind of agent-knower who has problems to solve, values to experience, appreciate, criticize, and organize at a level not heretofore existent.

Having said this, and with a view to the problem of evil later, I hasten to point out here that the personal cognitive creativity we have been taking into account is subject to further appraisal. Nowhere on earth is there a being who can become the fraud, the cognitive cheat, the betraying liar, that a person can become. To such evil purpose can he connive with the use of his unique powers that we may be glad he was endowed with no more! On the other hand, if persons are to overcome evils that stem from the sheer complexity of the natural world and the labyrinthine course of human growth, they require more power than they have. So, granted that some limitation of cognitive power is necessary, can any of us propose that the cognitive endowment of persons is the best possible in relation to the demands made upon persons at some given point in human history?

All in all, granting that persons even with their present cognitive power do purposely hurt themselves, do enslave and injure other persons, do rationalize their needless cruelty to subhuman creatures, and are so shortsighted in their use of natural resources, there still is no erasing a _fact_! With more cognitive power man _could_ avoid or further mitigate disasters in every area of his life, and he _could_ enlarge the horizons of knowledge and value eligible to him. Hence, what I am considering questionable cognitive values need more interpretation because of the possible consequences for good and evil that new increments of ability for free persons make possible.

(e) Accordingly, our tentative verdict at this point in the cumulative, teleological argument is this. For all the support that the Realm has given to the person as the kind of cognitive creature he is, there are catastrophic, natural and man-made events so much beyond his power to cope with that we cannot minimize the fact that his present cognitive endowment involves a mixture of good and evil that hardly suggests "victory" for persons-in-the-Realm.

In more theistic terms, at this stage of our argument can we hold that the Creator, whose purposes embrace human cognition, has endowed persons so well that, even if they so willed, they would escape the kind of suffering that remains a constant threat to the values they have realized with so much effort? I, for one, even at this stage of the argument, have to bear in mind that a Being who could have created but did <u>not</u> create a more benign increment of cognitive creativity, can not be said to have the "infinite" qualities that would make this vale of tears more worthwhile.

This judgment must remain tentative. For the underlying premise of our argument, always to be kept in mind, is that reasoning presupposes the will-agency so important to the moral backbone of every human venture in value-realization. The fact remains that reason as we know it is not neutral to the ongoing matrix of human life; and we are aware (a) of its links with the vitality of living and psychic forces within persons, and (b) of its links with the physico-chemical-biological forces that require us to look beyond them. Experiential coherence may not take us to as much of truth and value as we could use, but it will resist the conclusion that undermines its trust in itself, namely, that the Realm is neutral to our anthropic reaching and grasping.

4. Moral Creativity and Its Roots

(a) The theme for which I have been laying the

foundations is that the good in human experience be-
speaks such structures, patterns, trends, as make for
that quality of good in the Realm. Reason, we have
seen, imaginatively organizes the sensory-perceptual
patterns related to the person's varied affective-
conative demands. And reason does this not only
in accordance with the logical demands intrinsic
to its own nature but also in accordance with the
moral imperative: I ought to choose the best I know.
I ought to choose the best I know!--this is the moral
absolute imposed not from without, but exerting its
authority at those junctures in a person's experience
that seem to provide an option within his power. The
moral venture of the person--I ought, I will, therefore, I am!--is no addendum to some substratum impervious to, or indifferent to, its creativity. It
is this kind of creativity that arrives to choose,
within limits, the quality of survival open to
persons.

(b) And we have found that the moral-ethical pattern
of personal actualization is related to the person's
own givens; that his possible and actual development
is also related to the givens of others and their
possible and actual development. Individually and
together in their environment-Environment, persons
find themselves in more or less forced and optional
ways deciding what will be best in their individual
and social responses to the environment-Environment.

Again, to refer to specific moral-ethical patterns of the person is not a simple addition to the
affective-conative, sensory-perceptual, and logico-
reasonable dynamics of personal existence. For to
reason about values is selectively to weave together
into compossible, comprehensive patterns the relatively unformed and indeterminate stuff of life, at
given stages of development, in terms of some conceived promise. Neither the activity, willing, nor
specific choices occur within a vacuum; and evaluation does not create ex nihilo. As we have seen,
the moral-ethical life, originating in private,
critical, and uncritical selection, becomes increasingly and consciously interpersonal; it incor-
porates itself in customs, institutions, and laws;

it consists in creative fusions of what is and may
be, and this in ways that depend on the efforts of
persons.

(c)   What now needs special emphasis is that the
person as a reason-capable agent, experiencing and
exploring the norms of reason and the imperative to
the best, brings into being (as he matures, learns,
and purposely creates), an ethical environment for
which he is responsible in a measure that has no
parallel at other distinguishable levels of the
"worlds" he lives in.   The moral-ethical keyboard
witnesses to his moral creativity.   For the unfinished symphony of values is the normative appraisal of what is reasonably open to persons as they
basically are, and can become, in view of their common natures and of the kinds of problems they face
within the parameters of environment-Environment.

(d)   The consequence of this line of reasoning is
that, while persons participate in the organization
of the values involved in the growth of their personalities, these values and disvalues are joint-products
of their own capabilities of being-becoming in interaction with the environment-Environment.   Accordingly,
their judgments of the human good are judgments about
what Environment invites and encourages, about what
(moral-ethical) environment is better expressing what
Environment and persons can be.   For the patterns of
value and disvalue are related to persons, to persons
whose problems of choice basically arise from what
man has made of man in environment-Environment. The
good, anthropically conceived and participated in,
does not define man alone any more than "physical
laws" do.   But the good does depend more on his
creative self-discipline.

Another way of putting this theme is to say that,
since the pattern of value-realization envisioned in
the unfinished symphony makes for the development of
personalities capable of tensive growth, and since
it forestalls unnecessary conflict and disvalues, we
can reasonably believe that this unfinished symphony
is consonant with value-making in the Realm.   More

160

concretely, if the ideals of Justice and Love-unto-Forgiveness generate certain value-orientations and not others, these ideals are characterizations of persons-in-relation-to-Environment; they are not ideals to which the Realm is impervious or neutral. There is no logical proof here, I reiterate. But why should some such symphony, discovered, as it is, as persons among persons interact with each other and with Environment, why should some such symphony not probe even further what the Realm of Eligibility seems not only to allow but to prefer?

Once more our tale will not be told until we evaluate the factors within and beyond man's control that make for evil. But we may remind ourselves that the persons who appear in the Realm that makes possible their survival are the same persons whose basic nature and whose value-realization are involved in appraisals of Its trends in relation to human knowing and acting. To assume that persons and their values are addenda to either a neutral or indifferent Realm is logically possible, but stubborn and hardly plausible, if we would weave together the considerations we have had before us.

Moreover, any judgment that sets dysteleology and evils against _any_ cosmic design, and this because of a preferred or preconceived idea of what is _the_ worthy design, must in intellectual fairness not leave the court of reason. For dysteleology must not be extirpated from the considerations upon which our wider teleological argument is built. Persons are of the quality they are because, given the scope of their sensory experiencing, given the scope of their primary affective-conative tendencies, and given the amenability of these capacities to the working of reason, they, as persons, do selectively respond to some and not to other factors in the Realm. In so doing persons develop foundational conceptions that help to structure the environments without which judgments of disvalue and dysteleology are impossible. Such moral-ethical valuations upon which persons base their knowledge and guide their actions are themselves expressive of their dependent and yet creative relation to that Realm.

161

Accordingly, if our analysis is correct, appraisals of evil require a more fundamental, ethical framework. Persons appear in a realm that makes the quality of their survival a task for creative self-discipline. As they undertake this task, persons sound the depths of their own being in relation to the Realm as they conceive it in the light of the environments already made possible and still open to further criticism. If, then, they find that "not everything goes," that some patterns of value (keyboards) sustain and encourage creativity in depth and breadth; if, more specifically, it is true that reasoned creativity in the form of forgiving love is indispensable to the more lasting resolutions of human problems, we may, indeed, reasonably infer that such creativity, especially when it informs the spirit and laws of human communities, witnesses to a dominant trend in the cosmic Purpose in relation to persons.

At this point in our reasoning, I conclude there are sufficient grounds for deciding that the human search for the best is no cry in a wilderness—nor is it an echo of Things as They Are. We have already found reason to suppose that this human search is a creative witness to a larger task, sometimes in the midst of sound and fury, to be sure. Yet it is also sustained and inspired by the blessedness of creative insecurity.

5. Reflective Overview

The issues that still lie ahead presuppose the pattern that has thus far been woven in the attempt to discover the nature and purpose of the Realm. The six strands in our weaving thus far may now be succinctly put:

First, whatever the biological continuities between persons and animals, at least the unique personal activities of reasoning, of wanting, of willing, of oughting, introduce us to a new level of cosmic development—a kind of being who can participate in

162

shaping what his own development will be. The fulfillment of a person's constitutive activity-potentials
require his own choice, sensitive to goals he conceives
to be best in the light of the constraints and opportunities afforded by the family, by the customs and
laws of his social environment, and by the nonhuman
order of things.

Second, persons do not grope about, pushed simply
by strongest needs within the parameters of sensory
experiences that they can do little about. In the
activity of thinking they experience the logical norm
of consistency, and they gradually forge, as they take
into account the dynamics in the varied sensory and
non-sensory areas of their living, the norms that will
conform to their own demand for experiential coherence.
This cognitive imperative is partner to the moral
imperative to choose the best available theoretical
and practical alternative. However, persons all too
often find themselves oughting the best, yet deciding
not to will it; they often will the best they know
and find that they do not have the willpower to realize
it.

Third, it is this kind of being who can come to
the realization that an (unfinished) symphony of values
will enable him to appreciate most fully his own potential in this kind of Environment. Since these ideals
have their roots and their fulfillments in the interaction of persons with each other in this Realm not
of their own making, we may regard persons-and-their-
values to be the most comprehensive clue to the drift
of the unifying Creator-Ground as it is so far vouchsafed us.

Fourth, since I cannot myself grant that the nature
of the Realm is directly grasped by any one dimension
of personal being--sensory, rational, ethical, aesthetic,
or religious--it is to the mutually supportive network
of values that I look for the most comprehensive insight into what the Realm can be in relation to persons.
All the more, then, must the moral-ethical network
remain sensitive to the thrusts of every aspect of
personal experience. In interpreting our experience

163

as a whole we can leave no stone unturned, but the stones are never without contexts that require reasoned interpretations. Persons actualize value-and-disvalue possibilities in every dimension of their experiencing, within the scope of lawful interaction with the Realm. In so doing they creatively add their contributions for better or worse; they create _their_ environments, eligible to them in the Realm and expressive of both-- in degrees hard to ascertain, to be sure. But we cannot but venture that man's constitution and the nature of his mutually sustaining and creative cardinal values are at once expressive of motifs in his "created" and possible environments. Yet, no symphony of values is complete or orchestrated once and for all. No pattern is closed to further criticism when persons confront the new data that challenge present organizations and orchestrations of values.

Fifth, the Realm of Eligibility cannot be understood simply as the unified Ground of dependable sequences with no teleological drift. For, given the considerations adduced, we cannot reasonably infer that the cosmic, contemporaneous Creator-Ground of 'order' is neutral or indifferent to the quality of persons and their ideals. Basically, to conclude that the Realm is rational in other areas of human experience, but neutral to human ventures in value, is to suppose that _reasoned interpretation_ can be reasonably satisfied with the hypothesis of a cosmic indifference to values. To do so is to undermine persons' own authority, rooted as it is in value, in every area.

Sixth, and finally, this interpretation accords with our earlier thesis that the most reasonable interpretation of regularities looks to the end that, immanent in them, renders them the regularities that they are anthropically. All the more, then, must we remind ourselves that we are considering which of the anthropic hypotheses at hand is more coherent with the available evidence. In any case, we have no reason to assume that the hypotheses of non-teleology are already established and that the burden of proof rests on the teleologist.

Indeed, we now press the deeper meaning of an earlier contention: if any hypothesis is to be trusted as 'corresponding' to the Realm beyond the claimants, then we require ground for trusting the honest and disciplined efforts of claimants in discovering the truth about themselves in the universe. If the most disciplined knowers, let alone Everyman, have no telic kinship with the Realm, why should they claim a stronger basis for trust in their views? For they discredit knowing at the same moment that they demand that we credit _their_ own knowing in _their_ own, presumably cogent, anthropic conclusion.

Again, we have no logical proof of our hypothesis that persons and their creative achievement of values are the goal that best illuminates all that has gone on before. But the data on which we have been building our hypothesis about the Ground of world-order-and-human-values so warrant our theory and practice. The Creator-Ground reasonably undergirds the courage to believe that our dependable values are trustworthy soundings of both our own natures and of the creative changes in the evolutionary order.

Realm of Eligibility, Environment, Ground, Creator--each emphasizes a way of conceiving the unity and continuity in the interrelated order of our universe. What now lies ahead is further justification of our use of the concept "Person" for the Creator-Ground and a rounding out of the reasons for attributing goodness to Him. As we attempt this, the argument we have just reviewed will be related to new problems.

Notes

1   The argument of this chapter is strongly influenced
by F. R. Tennant's PT, a systematic philosophical
theology second to none, and, to my mind, the best
systematic answer to Humean and Kantian critiques of
the argument.   I have expounded it in my EAG, and
argued for it in my Introduction to Philosophy of
Religion, 1940.   But in the present instance I expound it in my own way and tie it in more closely
with cosmological and ethical data, as a basis for
conclusions about the nature of God.   Delton Scudder's
Tennant's Philosophical Theology (Yale), 1940, is the
best systematic critique.   The criticism and evaluations of natural theology or empirical arguments
(even like Tennant's) found in John Hick's works is
in mind as I develop the argument as a whole.
Frederick Ferré's excellent essay, "Design Argument,"
and John Hick's essay, "F. R. Tennant," in Encyclopedia
of Philosophy are very helpful.

2   C. D. Broad, Mind, 39, 1930, 483, 484.   See my
discussion of Broad's objections in EAG, chapter 6.

Chapter Eight

THE ESSENCE OF THE PERSON AND THE COSMIC SITUATION

1. The Aim in This Chapter

In each chapter of this book, I have, perforce, encroached upon conclusions that await further support. In particular, the context and the language readily connoted that the cosmic Ground and Creator is a Person. But what it means to be a person, finite or infinite, has always been subject to debate. In our own day controversy about the finite person is even more extensive. For, if at one time the understanding of the person was the special domain of metaphysics, ethics, theology, and jurisprudence, today proposals rooted in the work in physics, chemistry, and biology, as well as in psychology and the social sciences, have been forwarded as providing better foundations for properly understanding the person.[1]

My earlier discussion and conclusions, related to these lively controversies, are germane to the view of the essence of the person to be proposed here.[2] I hardly need warn that other scholars, who agree that in the finite person we find the best clue in microcosm to the nature of the Cosmic Ground, disagree with the temporalistic view of the finite person I shall advance.

In general, I have much sympathy with those who hesitate to attribute to God the notion of person. I hasten to add that if 'person' had the same connotation and denotation for me as it has for them, I should join their ranks. But, when I restate for myself what the essence of the finite person is, and when I consider the problems we face theoretically and practically in trying to conceive the essential structure of the cosmos, I keep coming back to the person as our best clue. At the outset, then, let us disabuse ourselves of the notion that the motivation for considering God a person is to draw on those human connotations that are not only familiar but

167

also fit our emotional and ethical wishes as weak
and sinful human beings. I shall be concerned with
those characteristics of personal being that seem
necessary to an adequate conception of the person,
be there a Ground or not. And we shall need to be
cautious when I move from this analogate to the
nature of the Ground.

2. The Person Not Identical with Body

'Person' does not refer to male or female human
characteristics. Physiological differences are
important to what I shall call the <u>total person</u>, but
no person can be identified completely with "his"
body. "Male" and "female" do not appear in the definition of the essential person as that quality of
conscious being (self, mind, psyche, soul, spirit)
who is capable of self-consciousness or self-awareness, of reasoning, and of acknowledging ideals. If
there are animals that can be so characterized, it
would not disturb my essential thesis; nor will it
disturb my essential thesis if many beings with human
bodies are incapable of experiencing the "normal"
quality of those activity-potentials that I earlier
distinguished as defining the unified matrix of the
person, namely: sensing, remembering, reasoning,
imagining, feeling, emoting, wanting, willing,
oughting, and aesthetic and religious experiencing.

The relationship of these activities to physiological and to unconscious factors is best determined
by analysis of the particular operation of these
activities in specific situations. I shall not argue
the mind-body or consciousness-unconsciousness relation
here. However, my refusal to identify conscious activities with either bodily or unconscious processes
takes root in the realization that whatever we can
know about bodily and unconscious correlations or
derivations cannot but be guided by reasoned explica-
tion of conscious activity-potentials as experienced.
As experienced (<u>erlebt</u>) they exhibit characteristics
and dynamics of their own that may indeed be corre-

lated with events beyond themselves, but these correlations are confirmed by what we consciously experience. For example, how otherwise would we find
the bodily correlates of conscious logical consistency
in the pushes within electrical brain-fields; how
conceive the dynamics of the emotions in those of
glandular chemistry, or of the inferred unconscious,
if we give up the guidance of our conscious experience?

Accordingly, the essence of the person is here
defined in conscious terms, not in order to settle
larger questions regarding bodily conditions for their
arrival, scope, and continuity, but for reasons such
as those just indicated. My reader may wish to try
to define the essence himself in physiological terms
alone and to see if he can avoid reference to what he
consciously experiences himself to be in these activities. So I proceed here to focus on a view of the
essential unity and continuity of the person by reference to what we actually experience ourselves as
being in consciousness--and without suggesting that
to distinguish essence is enough to characterize and
understand any total person (that would include analysis
of conscious-selfconscious unity in relation to bodily
and unconscious processes).

3. The Person as Self-Identifying Unity-in-Continuity

(a) Conscious experiencing occurs in succession.
But, as Borden Parker Bowne phrased an historic insight, in order for there to be a succession of experiences there must be an experience of succession. For
example, if I am to utter the successive words in a
sentence, if I am to know them as successive, then I
must be the same speaker and knower in some sense at
the end of my sentence as at the beginning. Yet,
since each word and each sound as experienced is different, I cannot be identical in any mathematical
sense at the end of the sentence as I was at the beginning.

Moreover, I know the words as my words; as

169

William James said, consciousness is "owned." Hence, whatever else I say in specific description or interpretation of personal activities, the unity and continuity of the person experiencing himself as "the same" is undeniable. Even the person proposing that he is not the same at the end of the sentence as he was at the beginning can know this only if he is in some sense the same owner of his utterances from beginning to end.

(b) The reader will already be reminded of the basic theme in our cosmological considerations. Nature, defined as the unity and continuity of spatial and temporal order in change, called, we said, for a unifying, contemporaneous Ground. In our individual experiencing of our own unity and continuity, we cannot deny, without affirming a contemporaneous "I," a person who is the same, yet different, and contemporaneous with his changing experiences.

As I have already hinted, the identity of person is open to more than one interpretation, and earlier, in affirming the Ground, I resisted the conception that the One could be unchanging and yet be immanent in Its changing world. (Were we to turn for light on the nature of personal identity to an "identical" brain, we should not escape parallel problems.) It is all the more imperative to seek the most experientially coherent account of what is involved in personal identity.

(c) Great thinkers have found the unity and continuity in our experience of change theoretically impenetrable unless they postulated, or inferred, an unchanging soul or mind (a pure ego) identical with itself at every "stage" in any succession--Alpha is Omega. What recommends this view is the realization that unless unity is an ultimate (in any system of thought) no way of "fixing" being or thought exists. A collection is a collection, at some point, of unities. Unity (identity) is no combination of other unities. Unity does not happen to the experient as the result of additions or subtractions from any "stream" of experiences. Such _ontic_ unity, as

170

opposed to _functional_ unity only, cannot be built up as "experiences" are somehow identified with a distinctive purpose. Why? Because we would then still need to understand why _this_ purpose can become unitary and unifying if there is no directive unity common to the experiences that "become" that purpose.

The essential thrust of this view I cannot but accept. So, I join in pressing that only an intrinsic, irreducible unity explains the very possibility of undergoing or knowing succession. A sequence, _a_ succession, is otherwise no more than happenings. However, I cannot any longer believe that the 'substantive' conception of unity-identity, of unity-continuity, can meet a most telling objection. Can this unity, immanent (continuant) in _its_ changes, be unaffected by them? My answer is "no": an un-changing, unity-continuity simply cannot be the unity in, or of, its changing experiences and remain _identical in the logical sense_, (A _is_ _A_). But, once I give up this view, can I suggest one that has its merits without its woeful weakness?

(d) The personalistic temporalism[2] that I shall briefly present modifies the substantive view of the mind that tended to dominate the thought of Borden Parker Bowne (1847-1910), the father of personalistic idealism in the United States, and of Frederick R. Tennant (1866-1957) in England. It is influenced especially by Edgar S. Brightman, Bowne's most creative follower, and by Charles Hartshorne, Alfred North Whitehead's most constructive disciple, and by the contemporary discussion among their followers.

I have set aside the nontemporal (substantive) view of personal identity in favor of what might be called a process-view. But I also find unacceptable Hartshorne's view of personal identity as process. Personal identity for Hartshorne consists of "persistent" linear "trends of becoming" that occur in a complexly ordered society of psychic unities that make up our bodies.[3] The identify of any person is thus the product of a unique series of psychic, unified moments that cumulatively form a route that is that person. Each moment of self-experience is "pregnant with its past" as it moves from its present unified experience to its future.

This process-view has the strong merit of keeping unity-continuity selectively related to change in itself and its environment. But, can this cumulatively growing unity, once we look at it carefully--a unity that issues from the series of psychic events--actually explain the self-identifying unity each of us is? Aren't we back at <u>there can be no succession of psychic events without an experiencing psyche</u>? Hartshorne does tell us that at every moment there is a given telic unity that is succeeded by another which it helps to shape, and this does mean that in his view the unchanging soul gives way to a dominant route of selective moments. But again, is this enough? For can this continuity of linear trend become what I know as <u>my</u> continuity? I cannot see that it does, or that <u>my</u> differences with Hartshorne are mainly semantic. Why?

For Hartshorne each unitary moment grasps its immediate past as its datum, and it continues to do so selectively as personal identity comes into being. But I do not see how a present unity can "grasp" a past that is "no longer" as it moves into a future that is "not yet." There seems, miraculously, to be a route, a trend of becoming, that is successive neither via intrinsic self-identity nor by supposedly continuous becoming. What we need is an identity that is real without being unchanging, and also that enables us to conceive of unity-continuity that becomes a continuity (a persistent, dominant route) without impossibly grasping what is gone forever, a past.

(e) Here Brightman's insight (making use of H. Bergson's <u>durée</u>) is my point of departure. Each of us cannot deny his experience as a datum-person, namely, that durational, complex unity of activity-potentials with its dominant telic thrust in any <u>now</u>. Of the datum-person, the psychic <u>now</u> with its complex unity, there can be no doubt; to <u>deny</u> it is to affirm it. But I cannot be logically certain of my future ("not yet").

This complex moment, this _now_, however, is no
abstract, mathematical point-instance. It endures
_as_ this moment with its dominant _tend_ency, and it
expresses its telic demand in any moment of interaction with whatever is its ambient. (This telic
tendency is articulated in our theory of the person's
affective-conative nature.) Consequently, any datum-
person is no logical identity even in a _now_, for any
now (datum-person)is selecting (within limits) what
can be assimilated in his effective ambience. This
means that in every _now_, _for a person to be is to_
become; the _person is being-becoming in his own_
unique, active-passive way, and not in any other.

(f) I can hear the question: How can you get out of
this isolated, encapsulated _now_? The question is
obdurate. Am I, indeed, confined to a solipsism of
the present moment, to use Santayana's term? How,
in particular, is continuity possible with my past
if I am always in a _now_ and every past is _no_ _longer_?
Am I not also confined, as I suggest process-views
of the person are, to "drops" of experience, or
"slices" of being, to "nows" unconnected with each
other?

Were this the case, I should return to the continuity of memory that seems to be protected by the
rejected view of the unchanging, substantive person.
But, 'memory' is a word for the problem we are facing,
namely, how is the unity-continuity in remembering
to be conceived? The unchanging, substantive soul
presumably provides continuity (memory); it "owns"
its changing memories. But, can 'memory' be a unity
of its changing memories and still be unchanging?
My answer is "no." At the same time, how can I reject
the route-conception of personal identity and still
account for what I experience, myself identify_ing_
unity-in-continuity? Not unless I can avoid resorting
to a present grasping (impossibly) a past that by
definition exists no longer.

(g) The solution I suggest for the problem begins
by appealing to a neglected experience of the datum-
person that is also undeniable. It is the experience

173

of recognizing, that is, the experiencing of again,
that attends many experiences.[4] That I experience
again does not itself guarantee that any particular
claim about what I recognize is true. Here, as
elsewhere, what is held to be true must be coherent
with relevant evidence. But the qualitative experience of again, that is an undeniable ingredient
of so many experiences in any now, is the experience
"in" the now that evokes my belief that my now is
continuous with my past. Included in the again-ex-
perience is me-again--self-recognition. Accordingly,
given the experience of recognition of me-again in
the datum-person, and granted that what I am-was is
still open to criticism, I have the experiential base
for my assurance that my now is continuous with my
past. I express this general fact by saying that I
retain (remember) my past which I can recognize and
recall. But, neither recognition nor recall entails
my reaching back, as for Hartshorne, into what is no
longer.

(h) A new model of unity-continuity is being envisaged.
A now experience, with recognizing and reasoning as
aspects of the complex wanting-knowing now, is essential to myself as a being-becoming, datum-person.
In this now there is no past still present as originally
experienced, just as the anticipation in my now of a
future experience is not that experience. No past
can "move into the present." Why? Because there are
only telic presents (datum-persons) with their pasts
(selectively) ingredient in their presents. Accordingly,
there is no person (soul) who is the same, logically
or mathematically, from moment to moment, or, despite
this "passage" of time, "within" any now, or "between"
moments. There is only a self-identifying person--
a datum-being-becoming person, in selective interaction
with his ambient.

(i) This self-identifying person itself is no inference,
involved as it is as agent-knower in all inferences.
The "situation-experienced-and-experiencing" is the
inescapable datum-person, that is, what each experiencing person "knows" himself to be in any now. Within that now "saddle-back," or "time-span," the experi-
encing-knowing of oneself is unlike the knowing of

174

anything else. I am claiming that the activity-
potentials distinguished above exist "as," "within,"
that complex, telic matrix, conscious-selfconscious
now. There is no I or me independent of this erlebt
matrix of activities and their potentials; there is
the experiencing, active unity.

But what needs more attention is the experiential
base "in" the datum-person for his identifying himself with past "nows." I have claimed as crucial an
experience within that datum-person and adapted
H. H. Price's exposition to my thesis here. I call
attention once more to the primitive, irreducible
again in any now-matrix, to an again that is intrinsic
to, and as given as other undeniable experiences
within any datum-person. That red-again, anger-again,
face-again, and so on, and withal, me-again,--such
"brute" again-experiences, I repeat, are subject to
interpretation, and the interpretation may turn out
to be incoherent. But these irreducible, "naked"
experiences in my now are the experiential base for
my assurance and belief in my past that is, as such,
no longer.

It is very tempting to say, with H. D. Lewis,
that the "strict memory" that is involved in our
"assurance of our continual identity" would be impossible "unless the impression of the past event
contains within it a recognition of its involving
the same distinctive awareness of myself as a unique
being which I have in my experience at this moment."[5]
But in placing his stress (as I see it) on the identity
of self-past (again) and self-now, Lewis, I submit,
is resorting to an assuring inference more than to
what each of us experiences in any now. The experiencing of me-again is witness to the mystery of
my self-identifying nature, not to my self-identical
nature. The being-becoming experient (datum-person)
is, given his experience of again-ness (of himself-
again and other again-experiences), builds upon this
radical experience, as he interacts with the impinging
ambient, and develops coherently probable convictions
that are continually subject to further interpretation.

To put my thesis more positively: In my complex now-matrix, I do not experience me-again as an "atomic" again along with other agains--as if it were a feeling or a perception (as Hume proposed); nor do I experience me-again as the same as I am now. In the last analysis, each of us will want to verify such contentions for himself, of course, but I cannot but suppose that for any of us to seek himself-in-any-now in the same way that he seeks to know other beings is to invite failure.

I am not pleading for 'privileged access'; I even prefer not to prejudice the inescapable situation-experienced by saying that we know it by introspection. The datum-person must, as reasoner, interpret his present experiences in his complex now, but these interpretative and added accounts must not be substituted for the erlebt conscious undergoing in any now and "from now to next now," or "from moment to moment." I, in any now, am not identical with another moment; I am not the same I (datum-person) "in" a stream of continuing conscious experiences; but I am self-iden-tifying in any now as I experience agains. "The stream" is metaphorical, pointing to the continuity that, as known, rests on my experiences of again-ness and inferences related thereto.

What is to be resisted is the ontic view that any now passes something of itself to the next now that is not-yet; or that the datum-person can reach back ontically to a no-longer past and claim identity. In sum: self-identifying, now-unity-in-continuity is the actual durée of any datum-person; he experiences "in" his now his being-becoming, but his being-becoming is not ontically identical with his "recognized-me." That any being-becoming, datum-person is correct in what he takes himself, as recognized, to be, and in what he recalls about himself and anything else, is another matter to be approached with caution. The theory of memorial knowledge is difficult indeed, but were there no complex, self-identifying person, there would be no basis for talking about memorial knowing. But let us add a further word about the ontic situa-tion of this stipulated self-identifying person.

(j)   This datum-person, I have submitted, cannot
be an accumulative product of converging streams,
since each person would then be a collection without
any selective collector sustaining and directing the
actual course of his experience as he undergoes and
knows it. Nor is the datum-person an 'emergent' from
a purposive stream that makes _this_ rather than _that_
purposive stream what it is. If we are here to
avoid an homunculus-like soul, unaffected by the
very stream of changing experiences it supposedly
unifies, we should, I hold, rest with _the complex_
unity of the being-becoming (datum-person) experi-
encing. This datum-person, ever capable of referring
to a no-longer past and not-yet future, never moves
from one now _to_ another even as it remains a datum-
person.[6]   This primitive, initial, telic unity is
selective in responding to its ambient and yet maintains itself as self-identifying unity-continuity
_as_ it grows. A diagram that may be suggestive is:

Spiral of personal growth

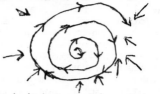

(a) the initial, telic, datum-person,
     selectively interacting with his
     ambient (stylized, statically).

(b) representing (a) accepting <u>some</u>
     thrusts of ambient and not others,
     and enlarging its selective unity.

(c) representing (a) and (b), maintaining
     its unity as it selectively ingests and
     changes. Yet (a), (b) and (c) are not
     successive; they are one initial, telic
     unity maintaining itself selectively in
     its ambient. Note that in each stage
     some of the ambient (arrows) are not
     affecting the uneven spiral of change.

This "spiral of growth" is intended to illustrate the initial unity-continuity of the datum-person and the telic (uneven) selectivity involved in its very being as a wanting-knowing agent responding to refractory factors in its ambients. The diagram is also to suggest (i) that a datum-person (a) from its initial coming into being, (ii) is affected by the environments that co-exist with it, although it selects what it "prefers," and (iii) that (b), (c), and so on, are its own successive moments as affected by its assimilative-rejective responses to its ambients.

Thus, any datum-person maintains himself by accepting "nourishment" from his environment, but only the nourishment his own nature can accept. Accordingly, the continuity of the person's unity is not a series of which he is the product, molded (without self-agency, or without being affected), in the nurturing, challenging, converging, threatening environment. Whence the resultant ontic conception: the datum-person does not pass into a future out of the past and present; he does not pass at all! Rather is he the constant now that is never an identical, but always a self-identifying, datum as he interacts with the ambient-- that is, as he "enlarges" the scope in his activity-potentials. His future, with which he is "pregnant" at any moment, is his present as he transforms himself (within limits), in accordance with what is eligible in the impinging environment-Environment. But at every moment--and this is not suggested by the diagram-- there is a passing away or ceasing to be, as well as a coming to be. Thus, to be a person is to be-become in accordance with what one's own nature makes possible in the environment-Environment.

(k) Finally, this "model" of the durational, being-becoming person lays stress upon the active unity that, as self-identifying, knows himself always to be the same-in-difference as he responds within his own limits to factors not of his own making. He may destroy himself, or be destroyed from without, but as long as he lives he does so by virtue of his capacity to change and to identify himself as changing. The person's crescence is his con-version, within limits, as he develops new, uneven rings of growth, as it were. <u>A person will never be ontically less than a person</u>, but the <u>quality</u> of his growth as <u>this</u> continuing person will be influenced by what he has done and what he is doing in the various relationships of his life. This forces me to distinguish between <u>ontic person</u> and qualitative, acquired <u>personality</u>; that is, to suggest the concept of <u>person-cum-personality</u>.

4.   The Person-<u>cum</u>-Personality

The intent of the discussion so far is to define the ontic personal unity-continuity "in" its activity-potentials as an irreducible experient that is neither divisible into parts nor the product of converging events. But in distinguishing between the person and his personality am I actually reverting to a view of the person as an <u>homunculus</u> (or unchanging, active entity) that, though interacting with his environments, develops personality(ies) and yet remains unaffected as a self-identifying agent?

(a) One distinguished psychologist, G. W. Allport,[7] has feared so, and it will help to clarify the distinction between <u>person</u> and <u>personality</u> if we look into the matter. Personality, says this psychologist of personality, is the unique, more or less organized psycho-physiological-behavioral system of habits, sentiments, attitudes, traits, and style of life that every individual acquires as he adjusts to, and expresses himself in, his environments. Allport fears that on my view of an agent-person, selectively interacting with his environment and developing personality(ies), the unchanging homunculus is invited back. Why not take the unique, acquired, "centered" pattern of the personality as the nuclear concept and avoid a tempting but idle homunculus?

(b) My rejoinder is that the agent-person cannot be supplanted by the organized personality in which he invests his activity-potentials as he interacts with his ambient. The <u>irreducible</u> unity-continuity of the person's activity-potentials cannot be identical with the _learned_ unity-continuity that characterizes his personality-organization(s). Of course, the learned pattern of personality is essential to the ontic person, but there is no idle homunculus involved once we bear clearly in mind that personality requires the learning person. While we may talk about "the personality doing" this and that, the fact is that the personality has no independent power of its own. For the personality neither wants, thinks, nor wills. It is learned. It is the product of the agent-person in interaction with his environment(s). Again, the person, as he organizes his responses and expressions in particular ways, is never a unity of activity-potentials impervious to the way in which they are being expressed in the personality--his personality that is the joint-product of his interaction with environments-Environment.

In sum: there would indeed be no personalit(ies) without the person, but the person is never identical with any particular stage of development of personality. The maturing person cannot but be influenced by the environments in which he is nurtured, challenged, threatened. However, it is he who identifies himself as involved in these changes and yet not exhausted by them. He may never claim: "My developed, learned, expressive 'structures' are all I am, and I can become no other." On the other hand, he must admit: "Neither can I discard this organization of personality (or segment of it) 'at will,' as I might discard my coat. For this is my way of living 'in-with' myself in relation to what is non-I. My personality, always in the forming at some point, is also what I 'carry with me' into new situations, and I do not find it easy to change myself-as-these-developed-formations. Yet to be 'myself' at all, I must be he who does not find it easy to change the person-in-personality. I distinguish myself as the agent-continuant, shaping and being shaped by what I become; and yet I, as agent-continuant, am not necessarily confined to, or forever committed to, this organization of myself (as this orchestration of my values)."

181

(c)   Perhaps more flesh and blood can be put on this abstract rendering of the person as (i) being-becoming and (ii) being-becoming in some expression-adaptation or other, by referring to the person-_cum_-personalities, Saul and Paul. We may say that the agent-person, born in a given cultural context, becomes the personality, Saul. Saul is what that agent-person became, yet Saul did not meet enough of the demands required by the person-_cum_-Saul. Still the personality-Saul was not readily discarded in the conversion to Paul. In his future personality (Paul), much that had been gratifying and satisfying to the person-_cum_-personality, Saul, is selectively retained. Hence, person-_cum_-Saul, especially after undergoing certain experiences, begins to shape the Paul-personality. Accordingly, the being-becoming person who became Saul is the person still alive in the "new" personality, Paul.

If this analysis is correct, any being-becoming person with his activity-potentials cannot be understood as encapsulated against changes in his expressions, or as an unchanging 'substantive self' or 'idle' homunculus. A person transcends and is immanent in his personalities; his personalities are built in relation to an Environment that is mediated by the culture impinging upon him, and to which he responds selectively. His personality(ies) are his ways of dealing with his own nature and potential within the "received" situation. And by "dealing," I mean both reactive, adaptive, and creative--the mix to be determined in adequate study of a particular person-_cum_-personality.

(d)   Before turning to the possible relevance of this model of the person, as self-identifying being-becoming, to the Creator-Ground, let us see whether this notion of being-becoming-_cum_-personality fits the main plan of the person living in his unfinished symphony of values, including moral values or virtues.

The ontically unified being-becoming confronts his nonrational sensory experiences and his primary affective-conative tendencies as, relatively speaking, raw materials to be organized in such a way that need-

182

less conflict and suffering will be avoided. For,
within the same matrix with these raw materials,
there are also, relatively speaking, form-giving
activity-potentials that I may here bring together
as logic-reasoning-willing-oughting.

No division ontically is acceptable between
sensory=affective-conative materials and the form-
giving activities. The person, mature beyond infancy, increasingly moves from what we might call his
pre-analytic, uncriticized value-claims and forma-
ations to the more critical organization involving,
respectively, both, so to speak, the former nonrational givens and the latter rational givens.
These nonrational and rational givens are better
conceived of as poles involved in the person's interaction with environments-Environment. The person
thus, sometimes gradually, or smoothly, sometimes
more precipitously, selects and forms certain patterns
of values-and-disvalues from the raw materials he cannot but deal with, especially at "crossroads" in his
history of interaction. That is to say, the person
is forever engaged in critically and uncritically
forming the personality that seems the one that will
resolve his problem. The (unfinished) symphony of
values is our candidate for the formation of personality that would be most creative (in the sense
defined above and later).

(e) What requires further notice here is that unified,
being-becoming persons are forever engaged in this
process of organizing their personalities in the light
of the ideals that express what their personalities
have not yet actualized. As persons-cum-personalities,
expressive of some more or less systematic value-
organization, they orient themselves by the total
horizon of ideals in inescapably value-laden environments. In this sense, we may say that between the
Environment and persons lie the value-laden environments expressive of, and also shaping, the persons
who are trying to discover what environment-with-
personalities is most acceptable to the Environment.
Again, to say that the person lives in a value-world
is also to say that the personality(ies) he both

183

shapes and is shaped by are his more intimate ways of shaping and being shaped by the environments he and others have formed within the eligibilities of the Realm. The realms of persons are the realms of persons-_cum_-personalities--the responses of persons, more or less creative, to what is open to them from within and from beyond themselves.

(f) Before closing this section I call special attention to a distinction in the finite person that will serve us later also in thinking about the Person-God. Abstracting from any particular matrix of sensory-affective-conative tendencies within the person, we can say that the person as being-becoming has a _nonrational given_ that is not passive or in chaotic disarray, but is relatively persistent in relatively unpredictable ways. Persons at one and the same time experience their _nonrational given_ (that imposes no specific quality of its own), and they engage their _rational given_--logical, reasonable, oughting, and willing activities--in sorting out and sifting their priorities. In short, persons build their more orderly realm of values and ideals by engaging _both_ their rational and nonrational givens. The _nonrational given_ is no more evil as such, or good as such, than is the _rational given_. The good and the evil in persons-_cum_-personalities are evaluations of the qualitative experiences, that is, the value-claims and disvalue-claims which require further evaluations as persons mature and change, and as environments change.

5. Intimations about the Cosmic Person as Creator

In the next chapter we shall consider further the relation of God to Nature and Persons. What remains in this one is to emphasize that in the conception of person as a unity of being-becoming immanent in the organizing of personality, we contemplate a unity that is also never exhausted in any one stage of development. Do we have at hand a reasonable analogate for the transcendent-immanent Creator-Ground?

(a)   Without even attempting to suggest concretely
what is the parallel for person-<u>cum</u>-personality(ies)
in the Creator-Ground, we can minimally hypothesize
that the contemporaneous Ground, omnipresent in the
stages of cosmic development, is a cosmic Person.
As <u>person</u>, He is the cosmic-Unity-Continuity of being-
becoming; as Agent-Person, He is not identical necessarily with the products or manifestations of His
sustaining agency; as Conscious-Agent, He knows what
He <u>is</u> willing and what His purposes are; as Omni-
Conscious, He knows all that can be known about Himself in relation to His creation. (It will be noted
that I have not said "omnipotent.") Setting aside
here the question of what the Creator-Person's purposes
may be, let me suggest that within His being-becoming
there is both the equivalent of the formal, rational
given (without which there would be no evaluative organization), and also the equivalent of the nonrational
Given (without which there would be no "content" in
any realm of order and value, disorder and disvalue).

(b)   Thus, both the Creator's "will" and His "reason"
are engaged in the further organization of the nonrational Given in accordance with His purpose. For
the Creator-Person, insofar as the word "create" is
taken seriously, and insofar as there is any development in Himself or in the creation that depends upon
His activities, the distinction between the rational
Given and nonrational Given is helpful in characterizing His own concrete nature at any point. It also
applies to any particular stage in our world-order,
or in any creation in which He has so far invested
His agency.

Hence, insofar as there is any truth in the cosmological contention that there is a contemporaneous
Ground omnipresent with its creations, we may, with
reason, suppose the Creator to be like the essence
of the person here presented.

(c)   More, of course, needs to be said about the
Person, but this is hardly the time to be so overcome
by the "cosmic immensities" and "the grandeur of God"
that we refuse to use the best analogue we have, <u>as</u>

185

long as we indicate what "parallels" are indicated in the finite and cosmic Creator-Person. Our intellectual responsibility is to do the best we can when we move from the known to the unknown, once we have rejected an "unknowable." If "person" can "corner the mystery," to borrow Whitehead's term, then let it, if it does so better than any other hypothesis!

I am not assuming that God's psychological states in knowing, willing, and experiencing value, are like the human in detail. But if to say that God is super-personal is in any way to deny in His being there is no equivalence to knowing, willing, and experiencing value, as known in human terms, I confess that I know not what it means to think about God. For then I find myself and others referring to "Something" that knows and does--and how can that be? All that is af-firmed so far is that, if the cosmological consider-ations advanced are taken seriously, in the unity-continuity of the being-becoming person with his rational and nonrational givens we have the best ontic Unity-Continuity of Being-Becoming.

(d) Granted an analogy between person-cum-person-ality and Person-cum-creation, can we, drawing now on the conception of the norm of goodness in person-ality, suggest that the goodness of the cosmic Person consists in His qualitative experience of achieving His goals? By analogy this entails the fulfillment of activity-potentials as this purpose-ful activity is invested in the creation and sus-taining of His purposes. In the finite person there is also the qualitative satisfaction (and dissatis-faction) with one's success in helping others to ful-fill themselves. The goodness of the Creator-Person, we may analogize, consists in the qualitative activ-ities engendered by His very being as the cosmic Person and by the success He has in fulfilling His purposes in man and in the different orders of cre-ation.

(e) In developing the teleological argument, we saw that the environment, natural and valuational, that persons have and can build, is the joint-product of persons in relation to Environment. The patterns of value, we said, are grounded in those trends in persons' own beings that, in response to trends in the Environment, are most creative in their organization and orchestration. We may, then, say that, to the extent that the Creator makes possible the order of Nature in and through which persons find so much of their own fulfillment, and to the extent that He stands ready to do all He can (with due respect for the freedom of persons) to help them further, He experiences _moral goodness_--again of an order only a cosmic Person can enjoy.

(f) Without hoping even to "fill in" what it means psychologically for the Creator-Person to "experience moral goodness" within his own being, we can, nevertheless, go one step further. The fact that His Being-Becoming is not only the source of our own being-becoming but also of the creative activity that constantly acts to make possible the quality of personal goodness--it is this fact that enables us to say that _the essence_ of personal _realization_ at once is shaped by and shapes to some extent the quality of the Creator's goodness. What all this means will be clearer after we have faced the problem of good-and-evil. Before turning to factors and phases in the natural realm and in human experience that have led minds--as generous as they are acute--to deny that goodness can be said in any reasonable way to characterize the Creator, we must consider at closer range what is involved in God's relation to the world and persons.

6. Reflective Overview

The reasoning in our cosmo-teleological-ethical argument leaves us with the hypothesis that the same Environment in which persons arrive and survive with their unique Gestalt of activity-potentials is the Environment in which persons can best organize their value-experiences in terms of creative love. We also find reason for holding that the contemporaneous

Ground of the orders of being *creates* (at least) persons *ex nihilo*.

Our method and criterion of truth require that the Ground be defined by the available data. We have suggested that the classical theist has leaned too heavily on a preconceived notion of Perfection in his treatment of the Creator-Person's relation to the changing world (and, as we shall see later, to persons in their experience of good-and-evil). What seems required first, of the personalistic theist in any case, is a tenable theory of the finite person who then may or may not become the most likely clue to his understanding of what is meant by Creator-Person.

In this chapter I have explored the ontic nature of the person and relied on the ineluctible experiencing of self-conscious persons to guide interpretation. A person cannot understand his own experiences as successive, I have argued, unless he is a self-identifying unity of being-becoming, not a self-identical experient. If this self-identifying datum-person is mysterious, so be it, in the primitive sense of mystery. At all events, this interpretation of a being-becoming person provides the analogate for guiding our understanding of the contemporaneous Creator-Ground of the changing order we call Nature.

Having expounded the distinction between the ontic person and the personality that results from the person's expressive-adaptive responses to environment-Environment, I concluded that to be a person is to be a complex unity-in-continuity of being-becoming, an agent-unity who cannot but invest his activity-potentials in the organizations that in some degree witness to his own potential in interaction with environment-Environment. In finite persons this creative process calls for a distinction between the rational and nonrational givens within the unified matrix of personal becoming. The finite person cannot be ontically less than a person, but the quality of his experience will depend upon the kind of personality(ies) he develops.

188

Why not keep this kind of essential personal being-becoming in mind as we try to identify the process in which the Creator-Person at once transcends and remains immanent in the particular organization of His inner being and in His creation? May it be that He organizes His <u>nonrational</u> <u>Given</u> in His Being-Becoming in accordance with His <u>rational</u> Given? We shall see.

The upshot of our reasoning thus far is that the Realm of Eligibility is the Creator-Person who, among His creative expressions, includes concern for such <u>quality</u> of persons-in-community as we have been proposing. God, accordingly, undergoes the equivalent to goodness at His level of experiencing self-fulfillment—a self-fulfillment that includes His concern for providing, sustaining, and implementing the conditions for the goodness persons realize as they fulfill their potential. Whether we can continue to attribute <u>goodness</u> <u>within</u> <u>God's</u> <u>experience</u> <u>and</u> <u>goodness</u> <u>in</u> <u>His</u> <u>relation</u> <u>to</u> <u>the</u> <u>realization</u> <u>of</u> <u>the</u> <u>good</u> <u>of</u> <u>persons</u> will depend on our further interpretation of what it means to be Creator-Person of the realms of order as we know them and on our evaluation of good-and-evil in cosmic and human history.

Notes

1   This chapter owes much to the writings of Brightman POR, PAR; Blanshard NOT, RAB; H.D. Lewis TEM, SAI; and John Macmurray (especially _The Agent Self_, 1957).   The works of G.W. Allport (especially PGP and BEC) provided suggestive ground for the development of my view of person-cum-personality.   I owe much to the stimulus provided by Susanne K. Langer; my essay "Susanne K. Langer's Theory of Feeling and Mind," _The Review of Metaphysics_, 23 (March 1970).   The substantive conception of the self that I have hesitantly opposed has many great philosophers behind one form of it or another; see Tennant PT, vol. 1.

2   See Brightman PAR, chapters 1-4.   See also my essays: "The Essence of a Person," _Monist_ (Jan. 1978); "Foundations of a Personalistic Psychology" in _Scientific Psychology_, eds. Benjamin B. Wolman and Ernest Nagel, 1964; "Descartes and Marcel on the Person and His Body: A Critique," _Proceedings of the Aristotelian Society_, 68 (1968).

3   My "Hartshorne on Personal Identity: A Personalistic Critique," _Process Studies_ 2 (Fall 1972), elaborates on my concern about "process" views of personal identity.

4   I am indebted to H.H. Price's analysis in _Thinking and Experience_, 1953.

5   H.D. Lewis TEM, p. 240, italics added.   See also my "Person, Personality, and Environment," _Review of Metaphysics_, 33 (June 1979); and "Does Elusive Becoming in Fact Characterize H.D. Lewis' View of the Mind," _Religious Studies_, 15 (1979).

6   See my "A Temporalistic View of Personal Mind" in _Theories of Mind_, ed. Jordan P. Scher, 1962 (repr. in PGI, chapter 2).

7   G. W. Allport PGP, chapter 6; also my "The Psychological Self, The Ego and Personality," _Psychological Review_, 52 (1945); and "Dynamic Interpersonalism and Personalistic Psychology" in _Dynamic Interpersonalism for Ministry_, ed. Orlo Strunk, 1973.

Chapter Nine

THE CREATOR-PERSON, PERSONS, AND NATURE

Our argument thus far has indicated that the physical, the biological, and the human orders of being are unified by a Creator-Person whose purposes include the co-creative activities of persons. The aim in this chapter is to follow through on what is involved in the relation of God to the orders that depend on Him for their ultimate structure.[1] I shall assume that the contemporaneous Creator is affected by the products of His creation and explore further some theses already presented along with several that require consideration now.

1. The Creator of Persons

(a) To the extent that persons are free agents, I have already argued, they cannot be identical with any other order of being, material, living or divine. At whatever point it may have been in the history of our cosmos, and under whatever conditions that were necessary for their arrival and survival, the coming into being of self-conscious, self-identifying persons calls for creatio ex nihilo. Such creation is not the "creativity" implied in those views of emergent evolution, according to which beings appear in the course of evolution whose novelty was unpredictable, presumably. The person's willed agency is more than the 'spontaneity' and 'adaptability' that characterizes all living beings, on most naturalistic views. I associate myself with that line of thinkers who have used 'creation out of, or from, nothing' to emphasize that what comes into being essentially as persons is not understandable as a form or mode of being(s) already existent. Theists grant that such creation is part of the primitive mystery that does not yield to the question: How? But they claim that 'creation' (more than 'emanation,' 'participation,' or 'instantiation') will force upon us the realization that persons, given their created nature, are free to choose within limits. Once that is understood, they grope for metaphors that seem best to suit their meaning.

191

Thus they protect the meaning of _creatio ex nihilo_ by making clear that it means not that the Creator made persons _out_ _of_ _nothing_ but that persons were _essentially_ made not _from_ something already existing, and never part of any larger whole. Thus F. R. Tennant uses the figures "planted out," "posited," to emphasize the delegated freedom of persons. In speaking of the ontic unity of the person and his self-identifying nature, I join in stressing the person's interaction with the world and his development of personality in that process. I have also emphasized the limitation of the individual person's freedom in the distinction between will-agency and will-power. In sum: to assert that persons are self-identifying beings, by no means identical with each other or any other being, is not to cut them away from others but to emphasize their distinctive activity-in-association and their moral responsibility.

(b) This is the context[2] in which I have suggested that many theists have conceded too much in holding that in God's created orders there is no example of _creatio ex nihilo_; since persons, for example, create perforce from something else. I grant that this is usually the case. However, I suggest also that in the free activity of persons there are many instances of the bringing into being of changes that are best understood not as recombination of what preexisted but as outright novelty in relation to what already existed. Reminding us, in passing, of claims to creativity in this sense by important aestheticians, I turn again to moral experience. At choice-point, I submit, the person creates in himself, in the other, what would not come into being apart from that conscious act. Once the person has created, we may be able to look backward and see what went into that creation, but the action of creation itself is the becoming without which what does come into existence makes no sense. The _how_ of creation, in the finite or the cosmic Person, _is_ in the nature of the case not open to us prior to the fact. Creation, in this theistic context, is the activity of an uncreated, self-existent Person; it is not action without relation to God's being and purpose, but in the

context of the rational and nonrational Givens constitutive of His nature.

2. The Omnitemporal Creator and the Realms of Nature

(a) The Creator-Person, I have argued, is omnitemporal and self-identifying; He is not the unchanging Alpha and Omega of classical theism. This
shift from the nontemporal to the omnitemporal is
required if we are to understand the classical thesis
itself, according to which the transcendent Creator
is also immanent in the changing order that would
not be a universe apart from His immanence. Just as
the person is engaged in and through his personality,
and yet without having his resources exhausted in
any one stage of development, so we may re-conceive
of the transcendent Person as the self-identifying
Person who is never identical with, or exhausted in,
any or all His manifestations, modes, or creations.
The contemporaneous Creator is the continuant-unity
sustaining every order of being, and in a way consistent with the quality of that order of being. However, no more than the finite person, the cosmic
Person may not be conceived of as a being who
reaches back into the no-longer (past) or into the
not-yet (future); His being-becoming _is_ His constant
self-identifying, time-binding action that is not
at the mercy of the specific orders in which He is
immanent.

(b) Such a description will, for many, pose a limit
to God's perfection. Without debating that question
now, I must point out that to introduce change and
time into God's nature is, so far as this argument
goes, not to conclude that God will ever be _less_ than
a self-identifying Person (in His own ontic nature).
But, insofar as His activities are engaged in world
history, and especially as He co-creates with free
persons, the quality of His being-becoming as He
experiences Himself in these interactions will be
affected. Again, He will never be _other_ than the
cosmic thinking-willing being: but what He thinks

and enacts will be affected by the ways of His
experiencing Himself in His developing relations
to all that He specifically undertakes.

(c) Nor is the theistic Creator-Person "simply"
another being alongside others in the universe.
For such others, without His contemporaneous being-
becoming, would be nonexistent. And I have been
suggesting that even though His constitutive resources are never exhausted by His relationships to
His products, He cannot but be affected by the way
in which He expresses that nature and purpose. In
a word, the total quality of His transcendent being-
becoming is by no means impervious to the commitments
and consequences of His immanent activity. It is
important, then, that we pay some attention to the
ways in which the Creator's relation to the order of
Nature is conceived.

(d) In the perspective of classical theism, God
creates a natural order that is nonmental--an order,
to put it very broadly, of nonmental being-events
that ultimately depends on Him for its constitution
and causal connections. What is open to debate is
whether that order is best conceived of as nonmental
(or 'material') or as mental. This debate does not
affect the theistic agreement that Nature, nonmental
or mental, in no way depends for its essential existence on the minds of observers. For Nature's
laws are so regular that they cannot ultimately be
the product of the activities of finite minds. The
debate centers on whether the regularity of Nature
and its independence of finite minds requires that
the natural world is 'surely not the stuff that minds
are made of.' Most classical theists hold to the
latter view, but theistic idealists claim that the
steadiness of the natural order is more intelligible
as the "working" of a cosmic Mind, or as the dependable interactions of mental beings who, not
identical with God, are ultimately governed by God.

     For the purposes of this book, a decision in
favor of a nonmental or a mental order of Nature is
not critical. The cosmo-teleological-ethical argument

is based on the interrelated orders, and not on whether Nature is or is not mental. In this argument, what is critical is the organization of being-events that does not depend upon, and at the same time supports, human knowing, valuing, and acting.

In this connection, however, let me define two forms of Idealism that deserve a better hearing than they have received of late, in part because Idealism has been identified (solely, but wrongly) with Ab-solute Idealism. This is the view that all of Nature, including living beings and persons, is not only dependent on God but constitutes different centers of God's own being. Theism in all its forms has rejected this conception essentially because it has no autonomy for the individuality and freedom of persons and ultimately distorts their experience of good and evil.

(e) Theistic idealists through the ages have contended that because Nature is so constant, because its organization is so intelligible mathematically, because its operations are so intimately related to the growth of self-disciplined minds, it is not the product of mind-less and nonmental beings but the relentless activity of an orderly, cosmic Mind. Nature, indeed independent in its fundamental energies from the minds of persons, is the dependable medium common to all persons. The universal "impersonality" is omnipersonal rather than nonpersonal. The subpersonal realms of order are so intimately related to the appearance and growth of persons that to consider Nature a nonmental order, interposed between the cosmic Person and finite persons, causes more problems than it solves.

This is not the place to defend even the basic tenet of a theistic, idealistic philosophy of Nature.[4] But there is one claim against this idealism of which we should disabuse ourselves. It is the claim, misguided but tenacious, that science requires a nonmental realm as the basis for its investigations. It is clear that science, as well as common sense and philosophy, requires a common, dependable order. Why that order

cannot be mental, and especially the activity of a
cosmic Mind at work, is hard to see. Much more
intelligible to me, when I reflect on the vast,
intricate, and interrelated organizations in the
inorganic and organic realms, is the view that this
common realm is the multidimensional energizing of
the cosmic Person, the expression to us, 'objectively,'
'impersonally,' of the Person's own activity. Nature
is no dream world of romantic fantasy. Persons, aware
of their interacting with each other in and through
common media, may well conceive that, underlying and
making possible their dependable interpretations,
there is something standard, the trans-individual
activity in which the cosmic Person's own inner life
makes itself manifest to persons (who are held to
its basic, orderly activities, with some leeway for
their own creative responses).

Again, the order of the inorganic world in
particular makes possible such extensive predictions,
based on the fragments open to human observation and
reflection, that, once we get beyond picture-thinking,
there is no intrinsic difficulty in conceptualizing
such harmony as the constant and steadfast activity
of the cosmic Mind. Nature could well be the Composer engaged in a vast symphonic undertaking whose
score may be in part discerned as disciplined conductors and orchestras respond to it, each according
to his own creative sensitivities and concerns, but
each constrained by the patterns in the score. But
the Creator-Composer is not necessarily confined to
a particular 'impersonal' score; and, if we are
correct, Nature, could we know it more intimately,
is the purposeful orchestration of His own activities.

For the theistic idealist, then, Nature, unlike
an ingenious cosmic watch wound up once and for all
by the Watchmaker, ticking away regardless of what
happens in history, is responsive within limits to
what created beings can do. For, Nature, as the
steady and purposeful activity of the cosmic Person,
supports rather than undermines the total, personal,
scientific effort that is generated and confirmed by
its order; it is the regularities of Nature, not its

supposed nonmental character, that human theory can grasp and use as a fundamental, predictable base for the further reflections and evaluations of persons.

(f) There are contemporary thinkers, pan-psychistic theists, who develop another historic way of thinking about the natural order. On this view, what we call inorganic, or physical, Nature is not itself the activity of Mind; it is the interactive, selective network of purposive (not purposeful) mental unities, of grades lower than the forms we know in the simplest living cells. Dependent on, but not reducible to, those 'physical' orders, are the levels of the interrelated 'organic' world, including human beings. Thus, for the pan-psychistic theist, the world--'physical,' 'organic,' 'personal'--is the vast interrelated organization of mental unities, each actualizing its own purposive thrust in interaction with the different grades of purposive unities that make up its environment. Most exponents of pan-psychistic idealism today agree with other theists in holding to a cosmic Purposer as the ultimate, sustaining,and contemporaneous source of organization.

My own reluctance to follow this otherwise welcome extension of purposive agency into the 'physical' order is rooted in the very fact that the inorganic realm is so orderly and so intelligible. This degree of regularity is more difficult to understand as the product of such "blind" spontaneous centers of purposive activity than as the product (in the theistic idealist's view) of the different 'levels' of activity of the sustaining Person.

Therefore, I am more inclined to hypothesize that the standard 'physico-chemical order' is God's energizing, but that God is Creator of the many grades of mental unity, from the organizations in the human cortex "down" to the physico-chemical realm. These orders of living beings "enjoy" telic unity and relative spontaneity within their "societies." Moreover, I am now inclined to grant that these differentiated societies may indeed account for the telic orders in plants and animals and in the human body

197

(but not mind) more intelligibly than on the usual theistic, idealistic view. In this partially pan-psychistic view of Nature and of life, the closest neighbor of my personal activity-potentials is my psychic brain-body with its orders (and such cor-relations with my personal activity-potential as we discover). Again, what I have called the datum-person interacts with the societies of psychic "cells" that make up its body. It is this body and its com-ponent purposive order that, to put it briefly, serve as the datum-person's base of interaction with the more pervasive 'physical environment' that, in turn, is ultimately the varied organization of the Person's purposeful energizing.

(g) As I have said, the basic argument for God does not depend on any one of these theistic visions of 'the created world.' My special interest in referring here to those three views of God's relation to the inorganic and organic world is twofold. It is to give more context to what it can mean to consider God the purposeful Creator of 'the physical world,' 'the organic world,' and of persons. But it is also to re-awaken, if need be, the realization that to consider God a Creator-Person is not to set Him alongside 'the created orders.' For, without His constant engagement at different levels in the realms, none of these orders, not even our own, could be sustained.

Our discussion, moreover, reinforces the con-tention that--the religious consciousness aside--what we know of God reflects His creative and dis-tinctive ways as we understand them to evolve in the kinds of order discernible in the physical, organic, and human realms. What cannot escape us is a Creator who actively is present, in different ways, as He moves to the creation of beings who can accept more respon-sibility for their own choices in their environment.

There were epochs, we know, without the spon-taneous purposiveness of living beings, but also other epochs during which purposive creatures came into be-ing in myriad gradations in relation to the steady activities in the 'physical' realm. And then there

198

were the millenia during which <u>homo sapiens</u>, a creature capable of self-conscious desire, will, reason,
and obligation came into increasing awareness of dependence upon, and relative independence of, the
orders that sustain him. 'Persons,' in our terms,
may present the saga of a sometimes failing, mainly
victorious, invincible Purposer. In any case, when
we think of the Creator's power, it cannot be in
abstraction from the course that it seems to have
taken in cosmic history. When we think of God's goodness it cannot be outside the context of action--
struggles, victories, and failures. What then of
God's omniscience?

3.   The Omniscience of the Creator and the Freedom
     of Persons

(a) An omnitemporal Creator, who has created and is
creating, who is the self-identifying Ground contemporaneous with the created orders, as He works out
His purposes in and through them in distinct, although related, ways--that Creator, I have held, is
aware of both His goals and of His achievements. I
have done little more than hint that it is reasonable to affirm that the Creator, at any moment in
history, knows what is possible and what is compossible
with His chosen goals. Yet it is of no little importance to distinguish between the Creator's own awareness of <u>all</u> possibilities and ideals and of His aware-
ness of <u>all</u> <u>that</u> <u>is</u> <u>being</u> <u>actualized</u> in world history,
insofar as what is going on depends only and entirely
upon His own activity. Omniscience, then, means that
God as Creator knows all that can be known at any
point in His own history and in creation, possible
and actual.

This definition of omniscience leaves open the
question whether God fore-knows what beings with any
degree of free choice will do. An obdurate case can
be urged against most classical theists who have in-
sisted, in order to protect God's omnipotence especially, that God, having delegated free will to persons,

does know, "before" persons exercise their choice, what that choice will be. Such theists, it seems to me, do not fully realize what the "planting out" of co-agents entails. If God already knows what the actions of free persons will be as they think about the alternatives facing them, then what difference does it make whether they think alternatives or not, since what they will do is foreordained? I submit that to fore-know a choice means that, in spite of what the "chooser" thinks, there is no actual choice, that is, one dependent on his free act. To be sure, God does know what is possible at choice-points, and He knows what is likely to take place insofar as He knows the factors in the person's personality and in the total situation that influence the realization of a given choice. But if God knows more than this, namely, the person's choice in detail of a and not b, then these are not actual alternatives for the person.

Such limitation of God's omniscience is consonant with my insistence that without human freedom even the pursuit of truth, let alone the responsibility for moral good and evil, is meaningless. To argue that God fore-knows in detail what will eventuate in a person's life at choice-point is to annul the very meaning of will-agency and responsibility. Indeed, God may know that a given choice will or will not succeed, and He may set up situations that result from that act which are hidden from the person's own insight. But if God knows what actions that person will choose in detail in every instance, it can only be because the person in fact has no will-agency.

(b) It should be plain, as I see it, that, insofar as God chose to create free agents, He chose at the same time to limit His fore-knowledge and also His power to infringe on their freedom. Classical theists have not been slow to point out that this self-limitation is still to be understood as an expression of God's omnipotent will. In this I concur, much as I will not refrain from pleading, therefore, that we define God's attributes in this context and not by an abstract conception of perfection.

However, these theists, insisting on this self-limitation of God's power, have not drawn what seems to me to be a further self-limitation resulting from God's good purpose in creating co-agents. For, I shall now suggest, this same goodness is the ground for affirming God's self-limitation: He does not know the actual quality that persons experience insofar as they are free. This point may be clearer if we review a related consideration.

(c) I have contended that we cannot define God's attributes independently of their interrelation in the carrying out of His purposes. Thus, we soon realized that, in conception, omnipotence is not sheer "all-power"; omnipotence is the power to do all that is worthwhile (all that is good). Accordingly, God's power, intent on the good purpose of delegating responsible autonomy, is limited in foreknowledge of what free agents will choose. This, in itself, is not to deny that God has the power, wisdom, and goodness to take countermeasures--consistent with respect for their freedom--to bring what persons do into line with His own creative aims.

(d) When we consider the problems of good-and-evil, I shall question whether God's omnipotence, in the self-limiting sense just defined, will serve to resolve adequately problems posed by certain types of evil. But here is the place to draw attention to a consequence of God's delegation of free will that involves the quality of God's knowledge of some phases at least of the experience of free persons.

Granted, the Creator knows more about the nature of persons than they themselves know. He is aware of all the ranges of their experience, actual and possible. But are there qualities of some human experience that God knows about, as they occur, but does not know fully? I am referring to those qualities in human experience that stem from necessary human uncertainty.

An analogy within our human experience suggests the situation. A compassionate father realizes that

his child is suffering from fright in a certain
situation--let us say that the child is painfully
ill and is frightened at the very idea of being
"sick." The father knows that the fear in this
situation is unfounded; the pain will go, and the
body will heal. He reassures the child and tries
to alleviate the distress in every way possible.
But what the father cannot know is the particular
quality of the child's suffering that stems from
the uncertainty--the unique anxiety experienced by
the child because he does not know, cannot know,
that he will get well. Or, to take another example,
the father may be kind and forgiving in a relationship with his child, but he cannot experience the
guilt as such that the child undergoes because he
has freely disobeyed his own conscience.

I am suggesting that, the general question of
freedom in relation to foreknowledge aside, there
is a more particular consequence for the Creator's
knowledge of persons as free and as limited in knowing.
Persons, created, ignorant of their own future in
detail, undergoing the consequences of their own
freedom--can their Creator know the quality, as such,
of their experiences growing out of their uncertainty?
To be sure, the 'omniscience' of the Creator-Person
requires that He know all that can be, and has been.
But why does it follow, and what meaning assigned,
to hold that even the Creator-God knows the quality
of human good and evil as experienced insofar as they
are rooted in human uncertainty? I suggest that to
say that God "suffers" or "enjoys" what persons
undergo in such situations is untenable. To be sure,
this does not mean that God cannot take measures to
cope with such situations, and especially when the
experient is prepared. And we should, in any case,
add that the quality of human fellowship with God
does not presuppose that God requires no effort on
the part of persons to prepare themselves for co-
creation. (See chapter fourteen.)

(e) To summarize, in creating persons whose very
nature calls for change that means insecurity, and
for freedom that means uncertain creativity, moral

approval, and moral guilt (and similar experiences), the Creator limited His "complete" knowledge of their inner experience. The insecurity that is part of the human situation cannot be "shared" as such by the Creator. In a world of persons, it is imperative that relations among persons (not only the relations of blame and praise but also of gratitude and ingratitude, for example) be developed in fuller awareness of what it means to be persons interacting with each other and interacting as created-creators with the Creator-Person. More adequate appreciation of the consequences of being created and being free, I am convinced, can only make us more fully aware of the humility and courage required of us in our status as persons created by Person. There is an ultimate privacy, an ultimate solitude, but not ultimate Indifference.

4. Reflections on Analogical Reference to God

(a) Everything I have said thus far in defining the Creator-Person and His attributes involves the approach to, and criterion of, truth that was set out in principle earlier. That criterion demands further articulation at this point.

(i) In proposing and defending any interpretation of our sensory and non-sensory experiences, we are confined to choosing, among alternatives or hypotheses, the one most probable in light of the evidence relevant to the problem before us. Living and thinking as we do within the mystery of the Realm, our formulations of "the" truth and "the" good will be less than demonstrative "proof," however convincing psychologically our experiences may be. If skepticism means that we never know the Ultimate(s), skeptic I am—but not if knowledge means conclusions we can support by reference to the drift in our experience, and by our presumptive knowledge as a whole.

(ii) Since in our human situation we never know as much as we would like to know, to move toward the

unknown can mean only to base ourselves on what we
know best. From the more manageable fragments of
the world within our ken, we build bridges that span
the chasm from part to whole. In the absence of
reasonable evidence to the contrary, we assume that
the ground on the other shore will be of a nature to
support our conceptual, and eventually our actual,
bridges. In developing these bridges we use the best
analogies at our disposal; concrete human reasoning
about the unknown cannot help being analogical. What
I have resisted and continue to reject is the view
that the nature of the whole is already vouchsafed
us; or that it is so far beyond our power of conception that analogical reasoning must fail.

(b) All this is relevant to the validity of my defining God's attributes by using analogical reasoning,
grounded as mine is in the activities and accomplishments of persons. Briefly, I have reasoned to a
unified Ground for the order of Nature; I have noted
that this order supports an "ascending" evolution of
purposive organisms; I have argued that the purposeful thinking and evaluative experiences of persons
are grounded in the physical and biological orders
that persons themselves understand only by coherently organizing their thinking-evaluative experience.
I have concluded that there is no better analogy than
the person for the Ground of the cumulative, inorganic,
organic, and personal orders of interrelation. But
I could not have found my "key" in the person were
the finite person not a self-identifying telic unity
of distinguishable activity-potentials that are the
contemporaneous ground of the orders that express
his own purposeful activities. However, the moment
I use this self-conscious unity of activity-potentials
for the cosmic Ground, the moment I limit myself to
the analogical core of 'reason,' 'will,' 'purpose,'
'good,' I am aware that these words (and others) cannot capture the psychological quality of the activities
that make up the cosmic Person's nature. Shall I
cease, then, using analogies? By continuing to use
them, am I in fact deceiving myself and pretending
to know what I do not know?

(c) I begin my answer by asking whether we, in our
thinking about God, are entitled <u>reasonably</u> to discontinue the line of reasoning we use on other
matters. In these, making allowance for differences-
we-know-not-what, we assume continuity based on our
partial knowledge, because the pursuit of any other
path is not consistent with our more fertile past
reasonableness in practice. So, granting that we
live by analogically designed probabilities, and allowing room for error and for growth, we proceed
consciously with our reason grown courageous. And
we try to specify, in this area especially, what
problem(s) each of the traditional attributes of
God creates for thought. I have given specific
reasons for holding that the Ground-Person is the
Creator-Person, and by no means "an additional being"--
an appendage to the inorganic, organic, and personal
orders--since it is ultimately His activity which enables us to talk about dependable interrelationships.
In any case, are not opponents of analogical reasoning
also using analogies?

     Our human alternative, I press the point, is to
aim toward analogies that are rooted in our best knowledge and are continuous with the drift of our experiences as a whole. I recall a remark A. N. Whitehead
made in a class in 1932 to the effect that a philosopher needs a kind of "metaphysical imagination" that
can see something in common between what constituted
beings as different as a crowbar and God. For
Whitehead the common, the bridge, became <u>feeling</u>,
'drops of feeling,' unified by a selective goal.
Plainly, this kind of existent needs to be imaginatively extended--all the way from what 'feeling'
might be in a crowbar, a living cell, to complex
plants and animals, to persons, and to God.

(d) Similarly, when we attribute sensitivity of some
grade to an amoeba's nature, we know that we cannot
get "inside" the amoeba to note the quality of its
experience. However, its "selective" behavior as it
accepts and rejects the morsels it ingests encourages
us to go on to say that it is purposive but not purposeful, for we have in mind the contrast within our

own experiences of transient, purposive striving and of our persistent, purposeful goal-seeking. Thus, even though we have no immediate, non-inferential knowledge of sensitivity in the amoeba, we find it more illuminating to say that the amoeba's momentary (probably memory-less) awareness is more (or less!) like certain aspects of our own experience.

We are aware that in saying "more or less" we cannot specify the actual quality, but we press our analogy to capture the direction in which the behavior takes us. When I say that an amoeba has feeling-consciousness, I mean that something like unpleasantness--as opposed to nothing like it--is present to it and "guiding" its responses. When I say that my dog can remember "more" than an amoeba and also experience "more" pleasantness, I am not suggesting that I have knowledge of the actual quality of the dog's awareness. I am indicating only that his excitement is better understood by comparison with that of a young child rather than with an amoeba's. But even the excitement of a child is an experience that I tie, by appropriate analogical links, to mine.

(e) "More or less," then, cannot but accompany our inferences from the "known" to the "unknown" when we proceed by analogies--analogies within the perimeters we at least tentatively designate. Accordingly, if we can reasonably move from the self-conscious person to the infantile and then to the subhuman on the basis of behavior, is there any reason, in principle, for rejecting this procedure in relation to the superhuman? And this especially since we have found equivalent perimeters in terms of unified, interrelated, goal-oriented organization of action? If we were to refer to the world as God's body, we move outside the perimeters of body as we know it; so I, for one, would regard such reference as "picturesque" at best. Likewise, when the Greek philosopher, Zeno, long ago reminded us not to assign blue eyes and red hair to God, he was properly pleading against illegitimate analogy. Yet it was his teacher, Parmenides, who held that God is Thought, and he defended his analogy by characterizing what he considered essential in human thought.

Accordingly, when I speak of God's thinking, willing, or purposing, I am not assuming that God's "state of mind" is a copy of the human, or correlated with processes that we can point to in the human person as a whole. But the direction of the difference between finite and cosmic Person cannot be outside the bounds of purposeful self-consciousness, and especially since, in each instance, the theoretical need is for the kind of being that is goal-oriented, contemporaneous, self-identifying. Moreover, the cosmic Person need not think discursively, or symbolically, but in His awareness there must be the equivalent of consistency in human consciousness if we are to understand our success when we think (at least) consistently.

So also, when speaking of God's will and His willing, I am not assuming the psychological context of human willing, but affirming that the activity of the self-identifying Person extends, but is not contradictory to, goal-directed will. Fully aware that a cosmic Mind is beyond our comprehension in psychological detail, I am, nevertheless, attributing the equivalent kind of activity to the Creator in order to understand the evidence adduced for the Creator to begin with.

I submit, in short, that 'talk about God' must refer to something in God within the boundaries of reasonable resolution of problems. This cannot be done if, in our fear lest we cut God to human stature, we forfeit any relevance at all to the evidence and to the human base of the analogy. Specifically, were I asked: Is God aware of the sunset? the reply would be: Certainly, but not by the way of sensory perception as persons are aware of it. But His conscious awareness of colors of the sunset cannot be such as to leave out completely the quality of color, whatever the difference of scale or intensity.

(f) To develop my earlier metaphor: if the Realm of Eligibility is the Creator-Person I have inferred, there is in His awareness the basis for what we as pianists do hear as we strike the keyboard, although

His consciousness is not limited to what we hear because we strike the keys as we do. In the Sound-board of Eligibility, in God's consciousness--not non-consciousness--and in accordance with the specific nature of that consciousness, there are the essential meanings without which there could not be the essential rational, teleological, and valuational organization integral to personal experience and growth. If all knowledge is anthropic (not anthropomorphic), if it is at all relevant to the Realm, then the measure of man and the measure of the Realm cannot be in contra-diction.

5. Reflective Overview

(a) This indication of our approach must suffice here, where our concern is to distinguish attributes of God without which our experience (including the religious experience that we shall consider in chapter fourteen), knowledge, and action would be opaque. And this is the place to reemphasize that response to the Realm in mathematical terms, in the many models used by scientists, in the images and symbols used in the varied dimensions of experience, are to be judged not by their one-to-one correspondence, but by their capacity to suggest the directions in which our responses should take us in thought and action. "Heard melodies are sweet; unheard melodies are sweeter"--this makes no literal sense, indeed no sense at all, unless we realize that what our senses grasp is not the adequate meaning either of our own existence or of the Realm. These reflections are critical for understanding the remaining attempts to understand God in His relation to persons-in-the-world.

Notes

1 This chapter extends discussion already in progress, but readers will, in addition, profit from John E. Smith's <u>Royce's Social Infinite: The Community of Interpretation</u>, 1969; and his essay in Howie and Buford, CSCI, "Creativity in Royce's Idealism." Very useful, also in the same volume, are the essays: "The Surveyor As Hero: Reflections on Ernest Hocking's Philosophy of Nature," by Leroy S. Rouner; and Richard Hocking's "The Personal Dialectic of the Impersonal." Also in Howie and Buford, CSCI, Andrew Reck's "Idealism in American Philosophy since 1900" is an excellent, succinct presentation, including theistic, personalistic idealists, such as Borden P. Bowne, Ralph T. Flewelling, Albert C. Knudson, Edgar Sheffield Brightman, and W. H. Werkmeister. I rely here mainly on Brightman's PAR; Werkmeister, BSK, and the work of Charles Hartshorne already referred to in the last chapter.

2 See my "Toward a Metaphysics of Creation," <u>The Review of Metaphysics</u>, 17 (June 1964); also chapters 12, 13, 14 in my PGI.

3 On this whole issue of grounds for describing God, see: David B. Burrell, <u>Analogy and Philosophical Language</u>, 1978; Ross, PT; H.P. Owen, <u>Concepts of Deity</u>, 1971; Gordon Kaufman, <u>God The Problem</u>, 1972; Mitchell, <u>The Justification of Belief</u>, 1973; Ian G. Barbour's <u>Myths, Models and Paradigms, a Comparative Study in Science and Religion</u>, 1974; John Macquarrie, <u>Thinking About God</u>, 1975; and Jerry H. Gill's presentation of Ian Ramsey's writings in <u>Ian Ramsey: To Speak Responsibly of God</u>, 1976.

4 See my expository summary, "Borden Parker Bowne and His Personalistic Theistic Idealism," <u>Ultimate Reality and Meaning</u> 2 (3, 1979), and "Why <u>Personalistic</u> Idealism?", <u>Idealistic Studies</u>, 10 (September 1980).

Chapter Ten

NATURE, MAN, AND GOD: A PERSON'S UNIVERSE

1. On Approaching the Mystery of Being

To be, to be-become as persons, is to live in
the midst of Mystery. There is nothing pious--be
it natural piety or religious piety--in "reverently"
declaring that the infinity of that Mystery is such
that there is no human bridge to it. Hence, we have
cautioned ourselves: from mystery nothing follows but
mystery. At the same time, we have granted that the
history of the human quest for truth shows that our
fingers will not grip to our satisfaction the Mystery
that surrounds our being-becoming.

So, in this chapter we continue to face, more
explicitly, the question: What in essence can we say
with reasonable probability about the Mystery from
the human-natural side? We expect that, as self-
conscious agents interacting with Mystery, we can
only continue to do what we always do in creative
knowing-acting; with cautious daring we let out
further the lines that promise even tentatively to
link our criticized values more firmly to our growing
knowledge and varied, developing needs. Thus, I have
argued that while no one link in our teleological
chain is by itself unbreakable, our reason cannot afford to overlook what the varied links cumulatively
suggest.

In short, we continue to live in faith that seeks
understanding and in understanding that seeks faith.
There is no test of truth for philosophy, religion,
or ethics, or science that does not sooner or later
face Mystery, acutely aware that its credential for
further travel is no more--but no less!--than an
experiential coherence. But that such experiential
coherence builds its case for probable belief on
theories--as in the theory of biological evolution,
for example--is nothing new. Without assuming in
advance what the outcome of our search for still more

comprehensive linking will be, we move to a new perspective on considerations already advanced and on
others that may require change of perspective.[1]

2.   The Uniqueness of the Ultimate as Person?

(a)   When we examined the dependable order of physical
Nature we stressed the fact that human reflection,
expressing human needs, is engaged in interpretative
organization of events without which persons cannot
at least survive, and, at best, survive well.   To
submit that physical Nature independent of our being
and knowing is a product of happenstance, and not a
collocation of being-events, runs counter to what
guides both theory and practice.   The orders that we
know, ranging from microscopic to macroscopic organizations of being-events, are such that we move with
basic confidence that there is order in the Ground
of things.   We are not arbitrary in resisting appeals
to suspend the laws we know; we find ourselves pro-
testing that what we do not yet know is in all likelihood linked to the larger, dependable system of
order upon which we already base our plans for the
future.   Our comprehensive reasoning about our
criticized beliefs concerning the far-flung, dependable sequences, past and present, have led us to
hypothesize that, in speaking about cosmos, we are
also speaking about 'contemporaneous Ground.'   But
our vision may be the clearer if the chain in which
the links appear is seen for what it draws together
so far.

(b)   Thus, our conception of the contemporaneous
Ground begins to be enriched when we see the "physical" order as the common network undergirding
other developments.   For when, at long last, living
organisms appeared on a globular speck within one
(at least) of myriad galaxies, when the orders of
organisms appeared with their myriad structures on
earth, in the skies, and in the waters, we realized
that these orders brought with them hitherto non-ex-
istent, inbuilt, telic demands to maintain themselves
and their kind, albeit unknowingly.

212

The arrival of such amazing self-perpetuating beings, whose inner arrangements enabled them to fit in with the physical order and to take advantage of other organisms, suggests to many that they were specially designed by a Mind that prepared the physical world for their appearance in accordance with larger aims of His own. But such specifically created, interlocking harmonies are properly opposed by investigators who seek to avoid appeal to an Architect-Carpenter Mind, especially when such appeal forestalls actual observation of the steps and means by which changes, reproduction, and adaptations are made.

However, this rejection of teleology seems to take on the proportions of paranoia at times; for instance, when it is assumed that in order to meet the demands of "science" telic explanation in every area of being must be rejected. Here I pass on with one comment. The very debate about whether the organic is a form of the inorganic would not take place if being-events in the (inorganic) physico-chemical order gave any (or even suggestive) inklings of being goal-oriented organisms that could heal, reproduce, and adapt themselves in about every nook and cranny of this globular speck.

In any case, once organisms appear, and once the physico-chemical world is seen to be a necessary condition for their arrival and survival, the questions must remain open: Can the kinds of being-becoming in the organic world be conceived not only to be conditioned and supported by physico-chemical events but also as different forms of (at present partly known) physico-chemical combinations? Or, are organisms actual creations that add a new dimension of orderly being-becoming to the order of the physico-chemical world, and thus encourage the conception of a distinctive, creative cosmic system?

At this point in our reasoning it must suffice for me to stand for the philosophical thesis that goal-oriented, creative organization does not preclude the understanding of those orderly processes that lend themselves to non-purposive analysis up to a certain point. Whenever purposive organisms

213

do appear in the world, cautious procedure requires
that their own structure and function guide us in
fully interpreting what takes place within them and
in their relations to environment-Environment. Outright 'reduction' of the organic to the inorganic is
far from self-evident, or a necessary interpretation
of the data.

Indeed, even at this stage of our reasoning only
dogmatism can forbid the philosophical stance that
the arrival of the fit and the survival of the fit
on this globular speck suggests that the physico-
chemical order be itself reinterpreted in the light
of the appearance and survival of telic beings.
(We have already called attention to the pan-psychistic thesis that the 'ultimates' or 'elements,'
even in the 'physico-chemical' world, are telic, that
'physical ultimates' are not beings that scurry about
within fields of forces "governed" only by "principles"
of push, but rather are aimful, beings-becoming unities.)

Whatever more ultimate probing reveals, I build
here on the differences between the organic and the
inorganic realms that remain impressive and suggestive.
Thus, the fact that the inorganic realm does not depend upon the organic and yet is open to its being
(even as it, within limits, conditions its becoming)
suggests a Ground that is responsible for ultimate
collocations--a Ground that is a Creator-Ground mindful that orders interlock as new forms of becoming
occur. I begin to think of the Creator-Ground as
purposeful Intelligence, both in order to minimize
unnecessary "mystery" and also to fortify our pursuit
of further correlations and connections.

(c) This theistic hypothesis comes into its own as
I try to give an account of the arrival and survival
of the self-conscious, interpreting-acting person.
The contemporaneous Ground renders our interpretation of the uniformity of Nature more illuminating
than a naturalistic-materialistic-humanistic interpretation. But when the intelligent, contemporaneous
Person is seen as creative in the subhuman orders

214

that support creation of agent-beings, who, in turn, can purposefully create patterns of order and value of their own, the vision of the whole loses nothing; indeed, it integrates persons into the wonder of creation. At this point I am able to reset into the pattern of the cosmo-teleological argument those environments of order and value that, depending as they do on the moral creativity of persons, shed qualitative light on the telic trend of the Cosmos.

(d) Such knowledge as persons have is a joint-product of their interaction, ultimately, with the Ground (Realm). I have claimed that what goes on in our knowing-wanting minds and what goes on beyond us stand in no one-to-one correspondence (whatever that would mean!). For some thinkers, such a contention wrecks the bark of knowledge at the outset. But we must not forget that those who claim that the knower does actually grasp the object of knowing itself (in any realm) are soon emphasizing that the keyhole of apprehension to which persons are confined is always so limited! If so, what have we actually gained by claiming direct and presumably unerring awareness of the object itself? Is it not more reasonable to admit that our knowledge-venture is restricted to the keyhole fragments, and proceed--faith and understanding engaged to each other still--to put our fragments together with a critical but optimistic bias?

In any case, there simply is no protection from errors of limitation by appeal to presumably direct experience. Whether or not we begin, as I do, with the undeniable datum-person, interacting with a Realm not of his own making, we never know finally how well the maps of our knowledge fit the ultimate terrain. And yet we may set skepticism aside because our guiding maps allow us, with reasonable probability, to continue with more comprehensive, planned action. No, we are not shut up in self-contradictory skepticism, or in "unbelievable" solipsism, by stressing that knowing is our activity and is improved by our morally responsible effort. We cannot escape the fact that we carry on our truth-value ventures, moving

from destination to destination, with maps that express our needs under the tutelage of dependable orders within us and beyond us.

I underscore this claim since it is too often
said--usually with an array of humility!--that man's
logic and reason cannot cope with affective-conative
conscious and unconscious givens, let alone with the
complexity of the sensory givens. Fortunately, the
fact remains: we, as persons with rational and nonrational givens, are toolmakers, scientists, artists,
theoreticians; we have constructed maps from pathways
and trails that set new tasks for our conative natures,
and we have found deep, intrinsic satisfactions in
the process of discovery. To be sure, we cannot forget far-reaching disappointments that result from
the cataclysms that have overtaken us; nor can we
speak as if at any one time in history persons were
not capable of inflicting unspeakable torture on each
other.

(e) But we have come once more to a watershed judgment about the intrinsic, as well as the instrumental,
worth of conscious-self-conscious beings on the universal scene. I, for one, never cease to marvel at
the significance of the sheer existence of such agent-
persons on the cosmic stage--however few they may be,
in contrast to physical elements and organisms, and
however horrible they are as they fall short of what
they can be. So I proceed to ask: Shall persons be
simply juxtaposed to a Realm that does not in any
way know itself or what goes on? Shall finite persons
be aware in their own dimensions while the Realm knows
in none? Are the orders of existence around us like
discs on a phonograph that were never recorded? Is
the Realm itself such that it turns and turns but
never knows, let alone caring about the next turn,
the next disc?

It could be! But if we are going to try at all
to follow the intellectual lines that our fullest
reason carries on elsewhere, why not affirm that
persons, yes, such as we are--with our capacities
for growth and healing and hurting that have no

similar meaning and scope among plants and animals--
why not affirm that persons are new creations, new
investments, new growing points expressive of a
Creator-Person whose knowing and caring are reflected
in different ways in the different dimensions of order?

If I seem to deplore too much the tendency to underestimate the new quality that persons bring to the
"great chain of being" because of their capacity for
self-conscious outreach, I make no apology. For I
would help to restore a sense of balance to reasoning
that "grants" the novelty of human beings and then
goes on blissfully with the assumption that such capacities are "after all" like others we already see
simulated in the subpersonal. Do persons--"after all"
indeed!--die as persons when they cease to heal in
body alone, or do they die when they lose their person-al consciousness? Which of us, who invites the
unconsciousness of sleep, does so only because he is
confident that he will return to his own person-al
consciousness? Again, which of us who tends to stress
the nearness of the person-al to the animal at its
best, would look forward to having our children or
grandchildren have the powers of animals and not of
persons?

Once we, if I may so put it, restore a sense of
the stride taken forward in cosmic history by the
appearance of persons, then world-history may itself,
by a sober, yet imaginative, comprehensive reason,
be seen as having a meaning that includes this development. Both the physico-chemical and the subhuman
organic orders take on more whole-some telic meaning
when the kind of creativity persons contribute to
world-history is no addendum.

(f) A cosmic drama--a tragedy in a deeper, more creative sense of the word--seems to have been taking
shape in world history with the Creator-Dramatist
Himself as an Actor--as we shall increasingly see.
Not to follow this line of reasoning is contrary, I
submit, to the kind of conclusion we would draw if
what we had supposed to be an electrically-linked
Computer became aware of its calculations and possi-

bilities and continued many of its operations--but
now with a view to developing subordinate self-conscious agents who themselves could participate in a
still more comprehensive order of development. So
my unwavering affirmation that a cosmic drama is
taking place is unwavering, not because it boasts of
logical proof but because there is no sufficient
reason for halting our value-judgments at the border-
line between the Realm and man-and-Nature-as-known.
Nothing less than a Creator-Person will adequately
unify the orders that already find more unity in the
very existence of conscious persons creating their
environments within Environment. The Nature we know
becomes more experientially coherent once we see that
its network also expresses the interaction of persons
with Person, involving different dimensions of their
being.

3. Why Think of the Ultimate as Person?

(a) These words are no sooner written than I hear
someone wonder how I can have escaped Spinoza's reminder that the Ultimate (Substance) can resemble
a person no more than the celestial constellation,
the Dog, can resemble a barking dog. Indeed, how
can I forget similar admonitions, for instance, of
Parmenides, Plato, Plotinus, Boehme, Eckhart, Hegel,
and of Paul Tillich, Edwin Burtt, and John Findlay
in our own time? It is more than obstinacy that
keeps me pressing the question that is at the heart
of the matter. Granted that the Ultimate is like
no earthbound person, please tell me: Does your
Ultimate know what "He" is about? And, dear Spinoza,
you who desperately avoid dichotomies and pluralities,
who will confine God to no human straitjacket, why
did you, nevertheless, insist that of all of God's
attributes there are two we must insist upon, extension and _thought_? (And would thought not have to be
much more essential--and certainly unlike--all others
in scope, since it alone would know itself and all
other attributes?) No, with full awareness that
analogical thinking in this area must be particularly
circumspect, I must confess that any religio-philo-
sophical-theological tradition whose Ultimate is in

218

no sense aware of self and of others, of what "He"
is doing and of His effects on His creatures--this
Ultimate has all the qualities I found so opaque in
Matter as Ultimate. A Universe bereft of consciousness, that Ultimate is as dead as anything can be.

This comment is not intended to be harsh, although
it may reveal inadequate sensitivity to what the critics--
historic and contemporary--of personalistic theism have
in mind. The twentieth century has seen few keener
philosophers and hospitable religious minds than E.A.
Burtt. A recent exchange with this generous and
patient friend, who understands, as few really do,
the drift of personalistic theism in the context of
world movements in philosophy and religion, writes:

> God is Infinite Wholeness. Many
> earnest persons in all parts of
> the world conceive God as a Person
> with whom an incomparably rewarding
> personal relation is possible. Mys-
> tics tell us of an ineffable radiance
> by whose warming and renewing power
> everything within our present horizon
> is creatively transformed. To them
> personhood is unacceptably cramping
> when applied to God...
>
> However God is conceived, to realize
> union with Him or to be reborn in His
> Presence is to become fully alive--
> fully ready to meet with calm faith
> and boundless energy whatever may
> befall of fulfillment or frustration,
> of joy or sorrow, from friend or enemy.
> He has always been understood by
> spiritually minded thinkers in terms
> that harmonize with this experience.

Reaching for an analogy faithful to a "Divine
Wholeness" that will harmonize today also with "a
cosmological perspective very different from that of
his forebears," Burtt draws on the scientific concept of "field." For "field" refers to an aggregate

of parts, and also has its character as a whole.
Burtt consequently thinks that "field" can meet the
spiritual seeker's growth in a Whole that "influences
what happens in the parts while the parts influence
each other in the whole." (Passages cited with permission from a manuscript in progress.)

In correspondence, I pressed the basic comment
made above, adding that the kind of complex, unified
matrix of activities that are essential to "personhood" would define the Divine Whole more experientially
than "field." A gentle reply (Letter, November 19,
1977) brings out what must underscore for any reflective spiritual seeker, not the least a personalistic
theist, the need for sensitivity to the shading of
concepts, including connotations, in any persistent
attempt to discriminate what is conveyed by terms in
this area. Professor Burtt says:

> To all that you say about 'field,' God, man,
> person, I reply 'yes.' I know full well that
> they can be interpreted in a theistic frame-
> work; many keen minds and earnest souls in-
> terpret them thus. In fact I would almost [!]
> affirm--to use Hindu terms--that one cannot
> deeply experience the truth of "nirguna"
> Brahman [the Absolute One] until he has
> vividly experienced "saguna" Brahman [the
> person-al One]. God, as I conceive God,
> is more than a person, not less. But to say
> this to a theist can't help but sound pretty
> arrogant=-it must have overtones of 'I have
> experienced all that you find true and good,
> and have gone to something greater!'

This interchange--let all sides be continually
sensitive to death by arrogance!--involves other

220

issues, but it highlights the importance of realizing
the witness to an experience that cannot be expected
to be captured by earthbound, person-restrictive
concepts. However, it is not simply that the personalistic theist seeks to protect the exemplar of individuality and agency in the finite person, and
thus rejects any interpretation of union and Whole
in which self-surrender suggests annulment of agency.
It is not that he does not grasp--I would say--in
his own experience what Dag Hammarskjöld describes
so eloquently:

> "But how, then, am I to love God?"
> "You must love Him as if He were a
> non-God, a non-Spirit, a non-Person,
> a non-Substance: love Him simply as the
> One, the pure and absolute Unity in
> which is no trace of Duality. And
> into this One, we must let ourselves
> fall continually from being into non-
> being. God helps us to do this."[2]

No, it is my hope that all that has been said about
the person as an agent who cannot survive apart from
dependence on the Creator-Ground is consonant with
this dynamics of love. In a later chapter, after we
have considered the problem of good and evil, I shall
return to the meaning of the love of God. Here I
can only accept the responsibility for making clearer
the theoretical motive for choosing the exemplar of
the person in order to render at least the a-reli-
gious dimensions of experience ultimately more intelligible.

(b) As essential to human or divine personhood I
have stressed the unified self-awareness that we
experience in the best known dimensions of experience.
And I have already demurred at the intrinsic opaqueness of "more than personal," once we realize that
the cosmic Person has that quality of self-consciousness intrinsic to a cosmic Agent. This chapter began
with the methodological caution that no concept
would adequately grasp Mystery insofar as it manifests
itself in the environments in which persons even
minimally participate. The concept of the intrinsically

unified, self-conscious person, aware of himself in
his activities and aims, does enable us to reach,
with some glimmer of intelligibility, from the microscopic to the macroscopic orders, provided we remain
aware of the distinctions to which we should be
alert as we cautiously extend our exemplar. At every
point we can add 'more' or 'less' to our attributions,
but the 'more' or 'less,' in order to be meaningful,
must be tied to something within our grasp.

The concept person will not do if it cannot be
more helpful than any other, if it does not help us
reflectively to cut below surface similarities and
differences of conceptions to functional equivalence
among beings we compare. Using our own experience
to guide us, we assign awareness to higher and lower
animals not on the basis alone of this similarity
and that difference in their appearance and behavior,
and not because any of us as persons can "enter into"
the psychic state of the animals (and perhaps plants).
When we extend to dogs, for example, affective-conative states and sensory-perceptual awareness, our
comparisons and contrasts are guided by psycho-
physiological correlations and equivalence   of
function--difficult as it is to stipulate what the
actual experiential quality probably is.   We attribute
to them awareness of scents and sounds beyond our
own experience, if in their behavior there is reasonable ground for quality of sensory sensitivity beyond
anything we can experience.

To generalize, if, on reasonable grounds, we do
not hesitate to extend what we know in ourselves to
subhuman organisms, referring even to their awareness
when the qualities of their experience are beyond us,
why should the conception of consciousness-selfcon-
sciousness of a higher kind than we can ever stipulate in psychic detail be unacceptable to us?   The
same problem remains: to justify, within the exemplars
of reasonable evidence, the extensions affirmed for
beings subpersonal and superpersonal.

In thinking about the cosmic Person our preconceived theories of the relation of consciousness to

human bodies has all but dogmatically opened or closed the pathways to conceiving what it may well be like to be a cosmic Mind. Keeping in mind my earlier discussion of the nature of personal being-becoming, of the uniquely human affective-conative dimensions, I repeat that, however correlated or not correlated they are to the body-brain, we still know them by way of the quality of our conscious experience, not by what we know about our bodies. I, therefore, would not seriously refer to a cosmic Body (even on the idealistic view of Nature) in conceiving of a cosmic Person. For, insisting that we as persons in much of our experience, including value-growth, do indeed depend on our bodily functioning and connections with the environment, I am also aware of the essential and far-flung differences, in our activity-potentials and in our value-actualization, for which the bodily dimensions are not sufficient bases and suggestive of no equivalences. But, in order to establish this point-- apart from pleading that we refrain from dogmatism-- much more than I have advanced would be in order.

(c) While, then, I shall proceed with caution to establish a kind of controlling, hopefully common, human base for our main characterization of the Creator-Ground, it would still be culturally and philosophically catastrophic if, in the end, we cut ourselves away from the "soundings" of religious and nonreligious, yet metaphysical, poets and artists (not the least, our musicians). For they so often evoke the depths and ranges of cosmically-human anguish and joy in what I have referred to above as "the drama" of being-becoming. I probably am wrong in suspecting that at the heart of their most piercing symbols and figures of speech there lies a sensitive, acute, exciting analogy. I would have nothing in these pages suggest that the ranges of artistic expression do not evoke insights into 'facts' and 'values' not otherwise open to us--that, for example, music and songs are not as expressive of What is in relation to us as is the never-to-be-surrendered grammar of concepts. Sooner or later our myths and metaphors need to be coded or decoded; sooner or later the symphonic ex-

periences of the Beethovens need to be set down in
scores--with their own _essential_ directions to conductors and musicians--if we are to grapple with them
and learn.

I return, then, having set out my own cautions,
to elaborating my grounds for affirming that the
cosmic Ground, the Creator-One, is no nonconscious
Being-Becoming; "He" is an intrinsic Unity of Consciousness (whose psychic quality is indeed outside
the parameters of finite personal experience) to
which Reason, Will, and Love-unto-Forgiveness may be
attributed without fear of contradiction. As in
other instances of analogical inference, I point
first to the central trend--in this case to self-
conscious unified, and unifying, purposeful activity.
I am not ascribing to the cosmic Unity-in-Continuity,
to the cosmic Being-Becoming, any quality that has
one-to-one correspondence with actual psychic experience of finite persons. But, without relevance
or concurrence of His attributes and ours in these
respects, we are indeed speaking "hot air" if we
try to assign meaning to the Ground that is contemporaneous with the created teleological orders of
existence as we know them.

(d) My concern at this point, moreover, cannot be
the impossible one of moving to a perfect Person
simply by erasing presumed human frailties. There
is no sword of Damocles ready to slay him who attempts to "span the yawning abyss" between finite
and infinite. Nevertheless, I find it a futile
gesture in needless appeasement to add "infinite" to
attributes of man when we apply them to God, especially
when we add no further clue as to what "infinite"
means with regard to any ascription. But I do suggest that self-conscious, purposeful Activity is the
trend-clue that accords with the complex and differentiated, interconnected orders which culminate in
persons and the values that constitute the history
of being-becoming.

In sum: my underlying procedure and criterion
of interpretation takes me to a contemporaneous

Creator-Ground, aware of Himself and His expressions
and creations. To suppose that all the dimensions
of His Being-Becoming have no similarity (e.g., functional equivalence) at all to ours is simply inconsistent with the lines of reasoning that normally
guide us in understanding what is beyond ourselves.
Indeed, even to suggest that the unifying Ground is
"nothing at all" like anything we know is, once we
think out what this would mean, to say that we
should remain silent and not even consider it One,
or Ground. We cannot, even as a confessional gesture
to remind us of the limits of our understanding,
empty out of the One everything that, determinate in
its own way, is inadequate to characterize the One.
For in so doing we would cut all the ties that link
our lives with It. I submit that the notion of a
Ground or One as nonpersonal, if taken seriously,
cannot take on the qualities it requires to be contemporaneously related to persons-in-environment.
Put more positively, my contention is that in essence
the Realm is self-conscious Being-Becoming whose
quality, far from being 'beyond' the orderly sequences
that make it possible to speak of a universe, far
from being 'beyond' the purposeful action that characterizes finite persons, does in fact act, at 'His'
level of being-becoming, in concurrence with these
ways of being.

(e) In this context, and to anticipate our next
proposal, I restate the essential reason for conceiving that the purposeful Person is a Creator-
Person. It centers, to be sure, in the arrival and
survival of wanting-knowing persons, in persons who
cannot arrive or survive without the physical and
biological orders, yet persons who cannot be reduced
to the "ways of things" or the "ways of organisms."
But it is in persons who are free within limits to
choose the values by which their lives will be
nourished that we find the essential reason for
holding that persons are, as such, not the ways of
God either. They are created to participate in
further developments of themselves and the world.
The purposeful Person--whatever His relations to
other beings dependent on Him--is the Creator-Person,

at least insofar as personal agents themselves interact with His Being-Becoming and with each other as
they forge the realms of value. These realms are,
and will be, joint-products of their own natures in
interaction with ambients never of their own making
entirely. Persons, created ex nihilo, are co-creators.
It is the consequences of their co-creation, including the conditions for the value-qualities that
they co-create, that are most important considerations
in our deciding whether the Creator-Person is good.

4. The Goodness of the Person and the Cosmic Drama

(a) I have purposely re-viewed this gist of the ground
we have covered in the cosmo-teleological argument so
that the distinction and connection between these
links and the specifically ethical link might become
explicit. I have emphasized the procedural point
that God's attributes should not be deduced from each
other, and certainly not without being confirmed by
the evidence in human experience. The cosmo-teleological argument becomes the cosmo-teleological-
ethical argument as we turn to the evidence that
justifies the attribution of goodness to God and
helps to define it.

     I have more than hinted that God is good insofar
as he created wanting-knowing persons, granted them
freedom to make choices, and did so in a context of
physical, organic, and psychological laws. These
underlying structures agent-persons can use but not
change as they venture in knowing and acting according to the best they know. Thus persons' moral-
ethical agency, in realizing value and disvalues, is
set within the general providence of a cosmo-teleological order that the achievements of persons help
us to define more adequately. Whether the pattern
of values, presented as the 'unfinished symphony,'
is a fully adequate clue to what God's goodness
"should" mean will have to await our evaluation of
evil in the human-cosmic situation.

(b) However, there would be no concrete, experiential
way of defining evil except in the context of the
patterns of value that persons do find in the life
good to live. And these, I have contended, take root
not only in the interplay of man's value-potentials
and the value-possibilities beyond his control. They
also reroot themselves in a continuing interplay,
as persons give vent to their creativity in institutions and social-political ideals. The quality of
'creative insecurity' that persons experience as they
dedicate themselves to their ideals, is, consequently,
the result neither of inflexible patterns nor of
casual happenstance within themselves and their environments.

(c) It is not unimportant, then, that we articulate
the essential range of the ethical horizon in man's
moral imperative as he criticizes himself and his
environment-Environment. My earlier analysis has led
me to submit that the ideals of responsive-respon-
sible-justice-and-love are not accidents "whose time
has come" in a neutral or indifferent world. For these
ideals do appear, they do become eligible, for persons
in a process in which they, as persons, have responsibly selected basic value-patterns. And, as it
turns out, these value-patterns are patterns of
positive creativity because they conserve value-
experiences even as they increase them. They also
witness to a catholicity that neither runs roughshod
over individual differences nor minimizes the import
of the sacrifices that moral choice often demands.

(d) It is these basic factors that give us our clue
to what we mean more fully by God's goodness. God
is good essentially because persons and the Person
together co-create in transforming value-possibilities
into individual patterns and cultural trends, and because the actual, ideal pattern of values as discovered
in value <u>experiences</u> are mutually sustaining in a way
that discourages fruitless conflict and encourages
promising risks for all persons.

The Creator-Person may have other purposes:
those involving persons, as the history of man's

227

personal, social, and political ideals shows, were
not written across a sky for all to see once and
for all. Every stage of development is so complex
in its interweaving of persons as they interact with
each other in varied environments that the awareness
and realization of their ideals is uneven, to put it
mildly. But such unevenness must not obscure the
undergirding development that seems more promising.
Was there a time in history when persons, who committed
themselves to justice and love for all persons, did
not, in fact, take steps that more creatively expressed
their own natures and the potential of persons within
the developing orders of being? If some such tale
has no truth, we shall not know how to assess evil
and its place in a cosmic teleology which we call
good. Having indicated the human-cosmic drift, we
may rest our case, until we confront the problem of
evil.

5. The Aesthetic-Artistic Dimension of Personal
    Being-Becoming

     What is the import of the aesthetic experience
in this cosmo-teleological-ethical argument? I hardly
need to stress the evocative potency of the structures
in Nature to produce aesthetic responses. Persons
do respond to these structures in non-aesthetic ways,
but when persons do respond to them aesthetically it
is not surprising that they often claim to be in
the grip of what is <u>there</u>, as if their own aesthetic
and artistic creativity were not involved. But,
while we remind ourselves that Nature, presumably,
does not <u>depend</u> upon such aesthetic responses (the
topic is too large for us here), the aesthetic and
artistic response does depend on textures beyond those
within the aesthetically active person. I have already
referred to the suggestiveness of the aesthetic experience and the artistic symbol in the attempt to
express the divine; we shall return to this (chapters
thirteen and fourteen).

     But I expressly stop to note that an aesthetic

experience and artistic expression can challenge, threaten, and enhance the impact of other value-and-disvalue experiences by appealing to a fresh awareness of what has become routine and to dimensions that every other value can have _within_ the aesthetic response. The aesthetic and artistic responses take their places within the teleological pattern that places Nature, persons, and the divine within the pattern of moral creativity that is never merely moralistic.

The failure to discipline oneself aesthetically inevitably means at least a loss of specific value-growth in personality. No less a person than Charles Darwin wrote that he feared his mind had become "a kind of machine for grinding out general laws," and that if he had his life to live over again "I would make it a rule to read some poetry and listen to some music at least once every week."[5] And he added, the loss of "happiness" aside, that both the intellect and the moral part of his nature might have been weakened.

It is so easy to overlook the way in which a person, as aesthetic experient and artist, must struggle, even as he labors to express his vision, and also to find the medium that will aesthetically enhance the value he is experiencing. When we speak seriously of the culinary arts, or the art of dancing, or the aesthetic appreciation of the tragic, the comic, the sublime, we are speaking not of some extrinsic adornment but of a quality intrinsic to a situation and objective experienced--a quality we "enjoy" the more for its being aesthetically appropriate.

The aesthetic-artistic dimension of experience is so intimately bound up in the person's _total_ creative expression that--I would wish to argue further--one's aesthetic creativity does not simply seek out the expressive object but is itself caught up and shaped in different degrees by the way in which the situation-objective "captivates" the experient. To "personalize" aesthetically is not to relativize;

it is to discover-create oneself in the warp and
woof of the total aesthetic medium that develops
the quality of the person (for good or ill).

Again, in aesthetic experience--and again
differently in each "artistic situation"--persons
demand that their situations in experience and in
Nature give themselves even as they resist mere
manipulation. In artistic creation, persons, in
short, create in a way that does not destroy but
expresses more appropriately the difference the
situations make in their lives. No one can listen
sensitively to an accomplished violinist, for example, without experiencing the creative way in
which the violinist at once conforms to the work
that he is playing and transforms it to fit his
"arrangement" artistically. What cannot be stressed
enough, I would argue, is that the evaluation of any
aesthetic or artistic achievement--including the
judgment of it within the aesthetic dimension--must
find its fullest evaluation in the life good to
live most symphonically.

To apply this line of reasoning to man's relation to this universe: in one sense the dependable
sequences upon which persons depend for survival can,
as we have seen, be experienced and interpreted in
different contexts. But these sequences or "structures" cannot be neglected beyond a certain point.
The knowing-agent who sees them aesthetically relates
them to himself in some stage of his total development
so that they change from one context of appreciation-
interpretation to another. The aesthetic-artistic
response is not so much concerned to "violate" the
initial situation as it is to be creatively sensitive
to aesthetic value-possibilities in them. The artist's
aim in creating aesthetically is to bring these possibilities into his own experience and into that of
others who can enter into his fulfillment with a
fuller aesthetic awareness of what his world and his
own value-reaches can be.

For example, say that persons survive, act
forcefully and cooperatively, with grim, dutiful ef-
ficiency. Even the art of friendship, the gracious

and grateful acting out of the "duty," does not necessarily violate or go "beyond duty." However, the
artist, also a moral agent with his own aesthetic
responsiveness, may still set that duty into an
aesthetic context that enhances both the aesthetic
and the moral depth of the essential human situation
confronted and reconstructed. It is in this context
that I, for one, can see what W. Macneile Dixon meant
when he said:..."what has been the most powerful
force in the making of history...is metaphor, figura-
tive expression. It is by imagination$_4$that men have
lived; imagination rules their lives." [4]   The total
aesthetic-artistic, symbolic responses of persons are
no "merely convenient" adaptations to human situations.
They are the Person, Nature, and persons reaching for
new measures of value-creativity in being-becoming.

6. Reflective Overview

(a) Thus to emphasize as I have, with each basic
value-dimension, both the autonomy of each that resists arbitrary dictation and also any interpenetration that may converge, challenge, and threaten its
vitality and fruition, is to express once more a basic
theme. In placing persons in the context of Nature
and in the telic framework of the Creator-Person, we
are not merely screaming 'person' at the mystery of
being. We are anthropically conceiving of that Realm
as a self-conscious Unity, working out, contemporaneously and temporally, a plan, central to which is
shared responsibility for what can be further actualized in that Realm.

As the artist appreciates and recreates with a
purpose that is neither completely exhausted in the
medium nor is able to express himself fully and adequately apart from this medium, so the Creator-Person,
in the orders of the inorganic, the organic, and the
human, expresses in different dimensions His own creativity. There is no working from nothing; nor is
there any completed union of this Being with all there
is. What He does in history is a drama whose plot

231

cannot be appreciated, understood, or evaluated without realizing that He, the Creator-Person, expresses
and shares His creativity in ways that will not allow change of essential themes despite manifold ways
of co-creativity.

(b) If we adapt a conception of the relation between
composer, conductor, and orchestra, we may analogize
the kind of creative teleology that a personalistic,
temporalistic theist has in mind. The Composer, The
Creator-Person, in accordance with comprehensive
ideals intrinsic to His nature (the rational Given),
envisages a tremendous symphony whose movements and
motifs will be such that many orders of instrumentation will be required. The Composer, let us say,
has selected the compatible orders without which
finite composers and musicians cannot function (the
varied spatio-temporal, microscopic-macroscopic, inorganic and organic orders); and these orders require
His, the Composer-Conductor's, contemporaneous attention as the basis for continuity and for further
creativity. His attention turns to the kinds of musical possibilities that can be within the activity-
potentials of persons at different stages of development.

There will be those persons in the history of
mankind who are by endowment and discipline able to
understand, within limits, the Composer's main scores.
These persons translate the Creator-Composer's scores
into works that can be played by other persons, who,
in turn, join their aesthetic-artistic responses to
the disciplines of that score as interpreted by their
conductor. The human conductor--like the Composer--
will not allow any interpretation by members of the
orchestra, but he realizes that, even if it were possible, his own renditions must not be exacted in a
way that does violence to the creativity of individual
artists and their musical instruments.

There will be conductors who find good reason
to think that other conductors have simply not grasped
the Composer's genius and intent, conductors who see
that new instrumentation can enlarge and enhance the
received renditions. The conductor who is himself a

genius dedicates his creative insights to conducting
in accordance with the purpose of the Score(s). But
he, too, conducts in such a way that the members of
his particular orchestra can become co-creators--in
the harmony that is never mere peace but co-creativity. The 'world of persons,'--each person creative, each as creative as he can be, each, therefore, co-creative--this orchestrated whole of co-
creative persons--is the essential, purposeful, uniting,
and continuing goodness of God.

Since I have not so far included in the exposition
of the cosmo-teleological-ethical argument the place
of religious experience, I may anticipate here and
say that what is at issue is the relation of the experience of the holy, or the religious witness, to
the unfinished symphony. The last paragraph suggests that a different conception of the 'union' of
persons, Nature, and God is being suggested. My
concern is not to de-emphasize, let alone de-sacralize,
the essential religious thrust of those who claim
direct awareness of the divine. Whether this concern
is appropriately expressed may come out as I evaluate
the experiences of those evils especially that have
forced sensitive and acute minds away from any teleological views of the universe and the place of persons
in it.

Notes

1   Other somewhat opposing arguments include:
N. Berdyaev, <u>Spirit and Reality</u>, Scribner's Sons, 1939;
B. Blanshard, RAB; Erich Frank, <u>Philosophical Under-
standing and Religious Truth</u>, Oxford Press, 1945, 1966;
J. Hick, FAK; R. Kroner, <u>The Primacy of Faith</u>,
Macmillan, 1943; Robert C. Neville, <u>Creativity and
God</u>, Fortress, 1980; Ian Ramsey, <u>Models and Mystery</u>,
Oxford University Press, 1963; J. E. Smith, RG, AOG;
W. T. Stace, MAP; W. Temple, <u>Nature, Man and God</u>,1934;
Macmillan, 1964; and see Jack Padgett, <u>The Christian
Philosophy of William Temple</u>, M. Nijhoff, 1974; Paul
Tillich, vol. 1, ST, and my evaluation in PGI; Paul
Weiss, GWS.

2   Dag Hammarskjöld, <u>Markings</u>, trans. Leif Sjöberg &
W.H. Auden, copyright 1964 by Alfred A. Knopf, Inc.
and Faber and Faber, Ltd., p. 110; quoted with permission. I owe this reference to E.A. Burtt.

3   Charles Darwin, <u>Life and Letters</u>, D. Appleton,
1891; vol. 1, pp. 81, 82.

4   W. Macneile Dixon, <u>The Human Situation</u>, Longmans,
Green and Co., 1937, p. 65. See also Charles
Sherrington, <u>Man On His Nature</u>, Cambridge University
Press, 1940.

PART III

THE "TRAGIC" GOODNESS OF GOD

Chapter Eleven

THE MORAL PERFECTION OF GOD

1. The Constraints of a Reasonable Approach

The power and the goodness of God have meanings that reflect a controlling conception of a perfect Being or Perfection. I have been laboring the view that neither 'God' nor God's attributes, including the perfection of this or that attribute, can be defined independently of the total experiential situation of persons. I have already indicated that "perfect" power (omnipotence) cannot be defined independently of some designated objective. I now propose to pursue the question: Can God's power be considered morally perfect?[1] Again, a swift review of the whole argument now will also set the context for more specific considerations in the remainder of this book about the nature of God's goodness.

(a) In the foregoing chapters, our fundamental question has been: How shall we conceive of the Environment that we all grant nourishes, challenges, and threatens our being as persons? Our first response was to realize that persons approach the answer to this question with psychological certitudes that are neither consistent with each other in the course of their own lives nor with the psychological certitudes of other equally sincere persons. Without denying for a moment that 'lived-through' experiences count, we agreed to see how far we could get if we took the dimensions of experience seriously and turned to reason as our criterion for judging the claims made in the name of experience. Why trust reasoning? Because reasoning, once we examine it at work, grants arbitrary priority to no one dimension of human experience, as it seeks to weave different dimensions of experience together as coherently as possible. Reason, so to say, performs the role not of a dictator but of a sympathetic teacher who learns both from his subject-matter and his students, but is firm in demanding that the quest for truth be responsive and hospitable, without allowing claims of 'authenticity,' or of 'psychological certitude,' to become authoritarian.

(b) Reasoning persons, living within the mystery of Environment, realize that their own most disciplined efforts will not readily or fully comprehend that Environment. So, even if Environment announced itself as like-this or like-that, persons would still have to understand-interpret what that announcement could mean in terms of their own varied experiences. They cannot expect one-to-one correspondence (in any strict sense) between their experiencing and what is announced. Again, nowhere, either with nearby objects, or on the frontiers of knowing and acting, can we take photographic slides of the Environment.

This kind of constraint increases when we approach knowledge of values, where the difficulties of our complex experiences of feeling, emotion, and desiring make the task of arriving at reasonable value-norms even more venturesome. In the value-experiences of persons we can recognize similarity, but even here there is no one-to-one correspondence between norms and actual life-situations.

I have fallen back, consequently, on the conception of coherent relevance as the test of our truth-claims about our values, knowing that experiential relevance and coherence defy a neat definition in every area of human experience. I have tried to liken our human situation in 'knowing reality' to that of the player who finds that the piano keys he plays on, and with, do not copy the soundboard. It is the pianist's self-disciplined awareness and practice that issue in the realization of what the soundboard (the Realm of Eligibility) makes possible as he at once seeks to express his musical meanings and to learn what does and does not seem to be allowed by the soundboard. All such learning, all fact-value

learning, I have called _anthropic_, since between any
knower-actor and the Realm there is the mediation of
the "experience of the race" and the life-history of
the knower-actor.

(c) Neither by statistical chance nor by certainties,
then, have persons learned the pathways that express
their natures in interaction with the Realm. At no
one point of their involvement in environment(s)-
Environment do persons know with logical certainty
what further may be vouchsafed them, what will enhance, what will discourage and destroy, or what is
more eligible in the Realm. But their discovery of
themselves-in-and-through-their-anthropically-con-
structed-environmental-orders has called for examination of different dimensions of experience and has
led to pressing for the most probable account of persons and their values in the Realm.

(d) The "most probable" account offered suggests ultimately the central thesis: persons, as self-identifying unities-in-continuity, are constantly interacting with a Realm that, responding as it does to
their disciplined, cognitive, and practical efforts,
may now be interpreted to be a unified, telic, cosmic
Person. Details aside, the interrelation of persons
with "levels" of nonhuman order suggests that an immanent purpose is being realized with the arrival
and survival of co-creative persons. The very co-creativity of these persons depends on their appreciation
of patterns of value for which they alone are not
responsible.

(e) This cosmic Person, I have submitted, by exercising His activity in what persons interpret as the
physical and biological orders, gives witness to
power that is _contemporaneous_ with all that depends
upon Him as the Ground of these interrelated kinds of
order. The collocations of "ultimates" at every "level"
of order, requisite as they are for the appearance and
survival of self-conscious-knowing-agents, strengthen
the contention that the cosmic Person is aware of all
that must be known if this universe is to be what it
is. Hence, the quality of power of the Creator-Person

237

is to be understood in and through the qualities of His creativity manifest to us and that we can comprehend and appreciate in terms of our relevant, discriminating interaction with them.

(f) Accordingly, when we speak of the Person's _willing_, we are referring to His activity expressly involved in, and related to, the fulfillment of His purposes. When we speak of the Person's _reasoning_, we are referring to the organization of His activity as inclusively as possible in accordance with His purposes. Hence, we can say that the contemporaneous, active, self-sufficient Creator-Person gives ongoing expression to His reason and will--as far as we can know in the related orders of being-becoming available to our own being-becoming.

(g) In trying to depict the nature of the Creator-Person, I have been urging that we cannot become timid about characterizing Him in the light of all known manifestations. If the terms 'infinite' and 'absolute' are applied to His attributes in order to remind us that we are referring to a self-sufficient Ultimate, I welcome their use. But when 'absolute' and 'infinite' are used to suggest conceptual discontinuity with what we do know reasonably and relevantly, then we give way to the arbitrary. What is worse, we are tempted, in the name of mystery, to smuggle in characterizations of God and His will that we have no adequate grounds for assuming. The same _caveat_ applies to the terms 'perfect' and 'perfection.'

(h) I have, accordingly, suggested that the classical theistic conception of Perfection or of a perfect Being as the self-sufficient, nontemporal, unchanging Person be rejected, but only insofar as it requires us to renounce coherent comprehension. This happens when we interpret God's self-sufficiency as foreclosing the very possibility that as Creator-Person He is affected in any way by the changing order in which He is immanent.

Our constant task is to try to understand not

what it "must mean" for a perfect Being (in the classical sense) to be related to finite-persons-in-the-
finite-world, but to ascertain what kind of Being
is required if we are to have as coherent an idea as
possible of what it means for finite persons to be-
become-in-the-finite-world-of-being-becoming. We
have found reason to suppose that an ontically self-
sufficient Person, fully aware of Himself and His
purposes, and of all that can be known as He contemporaneously creates the different orders of
being, will not be less than a person in His creativity. Yet He will be affected in the quality of
His ongoing experiences by the consequences of His
creation and especially by the influence of created
persons who are by His permission co-creators.

    I submit that once we take the idea of creation
and creativity as expressive of the essential nature
of the self-identifying Person, there is no way back
to an 'absolute perfection' that knows no 'increase'
and 'decrease' in the quality of the experience of
the Creator. To be perfectly creative is, I suggest,
to be the kind of Being-Becoming who consistently
conforms His own creative activity to the nurture
of the quality of creativity within the capacity of
the created beings He Himself purposes in the scheme
of creation. This means that we do not understand
God's willing by His 'perfection' but by what we
may reasonably infer about that willing in relation
to what is actual and reasonably possible for the
varied "levels" of His creations. It is in this
broad context that we have sought, and now must further
elaborate, what it means to attribute goodness to the
Creator-Person.

2. Attributing Goodness to God

(a) It follows from what has already been emphasized
in our thinking about God's attributes that in referring
to the goodness of God I am not referring primarily
to what it means for God to experience psychologically
the goodness of His own being. Whatever may be vouchsafed us of such "psychological" quality must be re-

239

lated to our understanding of what it means to affirm
God's goodness in relation to the beings who depend
upon His activity for their goodness. Classical
theists, dominated by the classical view of perfection, will, understandably, ask: But is it not the
very nature of God to be good? Yes, insofar as this
means that His activities in all the dimensions of
being-becoming make for goodness as we know it in
our experience.

Still, what in principle is good for man is no
firsthand reading of commandments as principles in
God's nature, any more than the laws of natural environment as we understand them are exact reproduc-
tions of God's activity. Earlier we claimed equivalence and relevance of personal experience to the
divine; here we also claim equivalence, relevance in
the sense of compatibility. This is not to deny that
God has the equivalents in His experience of what we
call primary principles and values in ours. Positively, I am affirming that what we know as the
conditions of goodness in God are ultimately rooted
in the activities of the goodness in His nature that
make the goodness we experience possible.

(b) Can God's activity--whatever the actual psychological quality of His value-experience--be judged
good in relation to our experience of value and of
standards of goodness we derive therefrom? So far
our discussion of God's goodness has been guided by
two decisions into what is essential to the life good
to live for persons. First, the 'symphony of values'
is a joint-product at least of the nature of basic
human wants and abilities interacting with each other
in this physical and organic world. Second, persons,
free (within limits) to choose their world of values,
enhance, by their mutually supportive creativity,
the quality of their personal and social lives.

From these two decisions we came to a third.
Such a community of persons, respecting each other
and their values within a deliberately chosen horizon
of ideals, is our clue to the purpose of the Creator.
To summarize this basis for further discussion of the

meaning of God's goodness: since the responsive-responsible community and the values that make it possible are rooted in value-possibilities that are not created by persons in this kind of universe, we have reasonable warrant for concluding: the Creator is good. And this, whatever the total quality of His own experiences of Himself as the active Ground of all orders of being that express His purposes.

(c) Once more I am unapologetically anthropic. It is tempting to say: "God is good in this sense, and 'more'!" But, since we live in the mystery of being, I take our limitations for granted and will not add 'more' until I can be reasonably clear about what that 'more' would be. When we say that we are good to each other, when we say, that is, that we create and support conditions and relationships that increase co-creativity, we are defining the essence of goodness. We do so, realizing that ours is the unending task of continuing to appreciate and encourage individual and mutual values that give concrete meaning to co-creativity. Insofar, then, as persons do all they can (i) to participate creatively in each other's growth in value, and (ii) to extend the horizons of their value-experience expressive of the value-possibilities open to them (but not unilaterally created by them), we can infer that the Person's contemporaneous, purposeful activities include such goodness.

(d) I am purposely laboring this theme in order to oppose the contention, hidden in the classical theist's assumption, that to be God is to be perfect and, therefore, all-good; that goodness is whatever God does. But since we are reasoning to a conception of God, we can only set forth our grounds for the conception that seems best to fit evidence available to us. Even if it were possible to define the power of God independently of what that power affects, I would assert, in agreement with a host of persons, that since power, as such, never makes anything right or good, neither does God's power, as such, make anything good or right.

It simply is not the case that whatever God does
is not open to question on moral grounds, simply because He does it, quite independently of all that
persons deem good or evil--such as commanding the
death of an innocent child. Power as power, be it
that of the most powerful juxtaposition of mindless
events in a materialist's universe, or power as
power in a Person who simply uses it without any
intent to make the goodness that persons experience
possible--such power is not power for goodness. At
every point in our inquiry we have been trying to
understand 'power,' not only as power to act and to
be acted upon, but power as specified by the particular consequences. Hence, we cannot speak about
perfect power without introducing a standard or norm
that is not power as power. In asking about God's
goodness we are asking about the purpose of His
power and what it achieves. The answer given here
has been guided: (i) by such understanding as is
available to us of the natural world, and (ii) by
such goodness as is related to the natural world and
yet expressive of man's own participation in creating
a co-creative community. However, this general, if
basic, line or argument requires more analytic elaboration in anticipation of a more adequate treatment
of the problem of good-and-evil.

3. The Moral Perfection of God's Power

(a) Right away it is crucial to recall the distinction already made between _moral_ goodness (character,
virtues) and _the_ good, that is, complete good (_the
summum bonum_) inclusive of moral goodness. A person
may be morally good without being completely good.
(I shall use the term "ethically good" for the _summum
bonum_ or the actual realization of _the_ _good_.) A person is to be judged perfectly good _morally_ if he
consistently wills the good, as he sees it, to the
best of his ability. God is to be judged perfectly
good _morally_ if he wills the good as He sees it, to
the best of His ability, and perfectly good _ethically_
if, having consistently willed the good as He sees it,

He achieves it. I have in our earlier discussion advanced the view, largely adopted from Kant, that the good will (the moral good) in human experience is the jewel that shines by its own light. Persons, even if they, in their actual realization of value, are the victims of a stepmotherly Nature, are morally perfect provided they consistently choose the good to the best of their ability.

Persons who are not morally perfect are to that extent not ethically perfect. But even if they were morally perfect, there are factors in their own natures and in the environment that keep them from ethical perfection. In view of the range of good and evil, moral and ethical, in the kind of world that is ours, the questions that we must face from the point of view of a temporalistic, teleological personalism are: First, is God morally perfect? Second, granted God's moral perfection, can we attribute to Him ethical perfection? The remainder of this chapter I shall devote chiefly to the first question.

(b) In asking whether God is morally perfect, I bear in mind that He is a Person immanent in Nature and the Creator of finite persons who are free to choose, within the limits of their own changing being and of Nature, value-possibilities available to them. Persons fail to will consistently the good they acknowledge, both because they are free to do so, and also because their complex, developing, affective-conative dispositions can lure them, with their limited cognitive capacities, to be less than assured about means and ends in value-realization.

I am not asserting that knowledge is virtue, for virtue requires the willingness to adopt the best one knows. Persons who rationalize use their reason and knowledge to justify their doing what they (in some degree) take to be less than the best. Once more, then, a morally perfect person is one who consistently wills what he considers best, but his will and his reason are so welded together that to know the good is to will it. Consequently, persons are seduced into thinking that a given end is good and attainable

243

because their affective-conative dispositions are so allured, and because their inexperience with their developing natures leads to the premature conclusion that "this is the best I know," or "this is the best I can do."

In claiming, as I now shall, that God consistently wills the best He knows, I am not holding that His will is welded to His intellect, but that the Creator, in facing uncertainties, is not subject to the seduction of supposing the lesser to be the greater good. The Creator who knows all there is to know about the effects of good and evil, both on the perpetrator and on the victim(s), will surely, knowing what evil can be and do, not purposely choose evil for Himself or others. In short, the Creator who can will the best He knows will not adopt what will not be for the best. This consideration is supported by a related one that we tend to forget but is crucial in this context.

(c) If my analysis of value and disvalue is correct, evil in our experience has no independent agency. Evil "succeeds" only as a parasite upon the good in every dimension of our experience. As Plato long ago (Republic, I, 350) reminded us--and there is no more telling argument against the 'autonomy' of evil-- robbers can succeed in their plundering only if they are loyal to each other, and, of course, can depend on the goods that other persons have created and pre- served. If evil could have independent agency, were it not parasitic on goodness, we might postulate the existence of a cosmic Devil. As it is, a Devil could not survive without nourishment by the very values "He" destroys. (This is not to say that evil is it- self only the absence of good, for evil, of the non- disciplinary character I have especially in mind here, is the destruction of value and value-possibilities.) For example, cancerous cells themselves die when there is nothing left to nourish them. The ethically evil deed is evil to the extent that it obstructs the ex- istence and further actualization of the values it depends on.

Hence, to know evil for what it is, as essentially

244

unstable, as dependent on values not of its own making, has a basic consequence for the question: Would the Creator purposely will evil? I conclude: the Creator-Person, who knows all there is to know about values and their consequences, about evils and their con-sequences, is hardly open to the self-deception and ignorance to which finite persons are vulnerable. For anyone to suggest that the Creator could find it desirable to will evil purposely in order to bring about good is to suggest that He, knowingly, yields in His creative activity to what, by nature, is destructive of good in Himself and in His creations. I submit that the Creator-Person does not <u>choose</u> evil, <u>never chooses evil</u>--that He is morally perfect. But this conclusion does not rule out His choice of the lesser good (that involves as much good as possible) in the interests of a larger good.

(d) This discussion and decision will be recalled when we turn to the interpreting of nondisciplinary evils, but in their light I re-view what is involved in the positing of free persons. God, in creating persons free within limits, chose the good through which all other goods open to persons are enhanced. But such co-creators need not do the best they know (or obey God's will, however they conceive it). Thus, in creating free persons, He would be accepting the consequences of their evil choices, choices that, depending as all operations of choice do, on God's own commitment to orderly action, involve God's co-operation but not necessarily His approval. But to propose that the cosmic Person purposely <u>chooses</u> evil that is inconsistent with His goals (for a community of responsive-responsible persons) is to suppose that the Creator does not know what is best or the best way to achieve His purpose.

From this point on, then, I am assuming that we can reasonably affirm that God is morally perfect, and that His activity in creating, preserving, and increasing order-and-value, and in minimizing the value-possibilities and the actualities of evil, is the goal of His morally perfect willing. It is such <u>moral perfection</u> that I take to be the constitutive fact about the Creator-Person.

I am aware, however, that this is not the summum bonum involved in the classical theistic notion of God's perfection. The classical theist would reply that, on the view just advanced, moral perfection cannot be attributed to a Creator who, for all His consistently valiant effort, cannot achieve enough good or prevent enough evil from occurring as to justify ethical perfection. The question remains, therefore, whether, in view of the actual evil in God's world, we can consider the Creator-Person ethically perfect, granting His moral perfection. The question presses especially because of those evils that seem to serve no moral or ethical purpose.

4. Moral Perfection and Nondisciplinary Natural Evil

(a) The overwhelming majority of classical theists, in attributing goodness to God, have stressed the ethical perfection of God (with or without the moral perfection, depending on the exponent's view of human freedom). These theists have granted that they cannot understand why some excruciating evils should be so destructive despite every responsible human effort to redeem them and to quarantine their effects.

One can grant the validity of the classical theist's argument that, if there is to be an orderly world within which free persons can come to learn what is valuable as the outcome of their own actions, in the final analysis the Creator cannot be blamed for the ethical system that integrates human freedom with order. What follows is much less cogent.

For now the classical theists add that even un-merited, excruciating suffering, in quality and quantity, should be finally judged a disvalue only if we are wise enough to know what acknowledged goods will give the optimum quality to our lives. Are we sure we have such wisdom, and can we know that the present system, everything considered, is inferior to some other system? Indeed, classical theists persist, this world--the one that has led us to hold that an all-good, all-powerful, all-wise Purposer is at the helm--is no abstract 'best possible world.' It is the best compossible world, the one chosen in order that the perfection of the Creator-Person might be expressed in myriad ways and forms of being. In this best compossible world the goals of the morally and ethically perfect Creator, consistent with the goal of a community of responsive-responsible persons loyal to their continuant Creator, _is_ achieved, albeit in ways beyond our understanding. Moreover, could we know, for example, the kind of divine order that is consistent with the quality of personal immortality and creativity after death, we would know more adequately that this ethically compossible world justifies even the present undeserved and completely unrewarding evils so prevalent in history.

This classical thesis is inspired by the conception of God's Perfection we have already met-- of 'the only Being worthy of worship.' At its core is the self-sufficiency of God (_causa sui_). This self-sufficiency is taken to _imply_ that there are no restraints upon God other than those self-imposed, and, therefore, purposed in infinite wisdom and power. It is this same conception of self-sufficiency, as requiring no addition and no subtraction, that underlies the denial that God, although immanent in world history, can in any way be affected by what goes on therein. Even _creatio ex nihilo_ must somehow be so interpreted as not to imply that, in creating, God "at any time" is adding to His perfection.

(b) It is this view of perfection that is qualified in the counterproposal to be advanced. Even could this theistic view of 'absolute Perfection' be related to the changing, finite world in any illuminating way, the time has come to challenge this whole view of perfection. I would not minimize the various motifs that have inspired this absolutistic view of perfection. Yet, I now ask myself: Why, if 'perfection' is to express the best in all else as related to the best in persons, why should I deny perfection to a self-sufficient Person who _as_ omnitemporal and contemporaneous _is_ immanent in time and change? What is so "imperfect" about Being-Becoming as _causa_ _sui_ if no restrictions are imposed upon Him by any being beyond Himself, and if the quality of His own experience is affected by the working out of His own creative purposes? Why, in the name of perfection, should we find fault with creative alteration and _creatio_ _ex_ _nihilo_ in accordance with the best compossible goals? Granted, to be self-sufficient does entail that God's essential nature _depends_ upon no being beyond Himself. But why should _it_ entail that there be no factors, _given within His nature_, that can be altered in harmony with purposes He sets Himself to actualize as far as compossible?

Let us be guided by what characterizes our own experience as persons. My counterproposal is guided by the realization that complex, self-identifying, unity-in-continuity is heightened _in quality_ whenever purposeful creativity is expressed in the tensive and growing harmony of one's own potential. Creative orchestration of values, consonant with one's own activity-potentials and with the total environment open to one--this is _the creative insecurity that gives meaning to perfection in human experience_. If our analysis of self-identifying being-becoming is at all accurate, if it can be analogized with appropriate allowance for a cosmic Being-Becoming, there is no good reason for setting aside such creative insecurity as "after all, not really perfection." In any case, to conceive of a self-sufficient Creator-Person who enhances the quality of His own being by what He generates, Who is subject to the influences of creatures He Himself has created to be co-creators and not robots, is hardly to "finitize" the Almighty. And, especially, if this conception opens up new vistas of what 'creative perfection' itself may involve.

(c) I close this chapter with a suggestion of what this creative perfection involves _if we remain at the nonhuman level of creation_, reserving the human level for special consideration in the next chapter. Let us reflect upon our teleological interpretation

of physical, biological, and human history with the
problem of good-and-evil in mind.

Experts tell us that it took billions of years
for the physical world to become so organized that
an astronomical speck, our planet Earth, appeared.
On this Earth vast stretches of time elapsed before that ultimate collocation of being-events
occurred which made it possible for living things to
arrive and survive. The myriad species of cells and
their organization, at once taking advantage of their
habitats but also being destroyed by competing species,
unfavorable mutations, and by environmental changes,
witness to a new kind of being-becoming--in telling
contrast to the many changes known to us in the
physico-chemical world. Living creatures came into
being, though not in every earthly climate, and
found that they could, within broad physico-chemical
limits, adapt and survive.

As we move from the simplest forms of botanical
life to the more complex forms of animal existence,
adaptability increases. What is spread before us is
a stupendous chain of organic beings--each with its
individual qualitative demand for survival, each with
its patterns of "adaptive response" largely pre-fitted
from birth to survive in some, but not other, ambients,
each pre-fitted and (we may infer) capable of experiencing its own level of pleasantness and unpleasantness as intrinsic to its self-being, responsiveness,
and vulnerability to environment. I speak with no
special competence as I build on the reported in-
tricacies of mutual dependence among living beings
and on their ways of maintaining their own quality
of "enjoyment" as they arrive, survive, and make way
for their progeny. But even before the arrival of
the human species, a reflective Spectator, seeing
the mutual challenge and support among the living
species, must be impressed by the biological advance
toward complexity and flexibility that enabled organisms to adjust themselves to their spread-out
variety of habitats. At the same time, observing also
the kinds of unpleasantness and pain experienced by
the very creatures who "enjoy" more quality by virtue

249

of their complexity and adaptability, our Spectator
might well be tempted to speak of "Nature red in
tooth and claw."

(d) Can we draw any reasonable inference from the
fact that those organic beings are in general favored
who must rely less on sheer strength and procreation
to survive and more, relatively, on "intelligent"
adaptability? The inference I have drawn is that the
Collocator of physical-chemical events, the Creator
of living beings, has concerned Himself with the
qualities of organisms for their own sakes as well
as for their interdependence. Such interdependence
does not justify ethical descriptions such as "brute
selfishness" or "sacrificial altruism." But, keeping
in mind the grand scale of evolution, and noting that
in the grand biological march forward, the lower species
did not depend for their arrival on higher ones, we
may hazard a judgment. While the trend favors biological advance in terms of survival-value alone,
evolution is no mere matter of ups-and-downs. There
can be, and there has been, the outright loss of
species. In view of such losses, in view of the
uneven struggle, in view of the painful suffering in
the animal world, can we infer a Collocator-Creator
who is ethically perfect and in complete control of
all that has happened and still occurs in relation
to evolutionary change?

It is not a jaundiced eye that records the dis-
appearance of whole species whose endowments did not
allow them either to defend themselves against competing species, or to adapt to cataclysmic changes
in natural habitats. We may accept, with natural or
with religious piety, the struggle for survival in
living beings as part of the mystery of ultimate
being. But that miscollocations exist within the
context of more wholesome collocations--this suggests that the Creator has not and does not always
succeed in doing all that is mutually compatible,
either within the framework of a biological system
itself, or in its relation to the physical-chemical
order of things. The power of the Creator, if we
intend to take these failures seriously, is not om-

nipotent if measured by the best of compossible worlds for living creatures. These natural evils, biologically speaking, do not witness to the sway of an omnipotent Creator able to harmonize physical and biological orders in a way that justifies the verdict: compossible best.

If, then, creatures were brought into being and then were snuffed out because of some built-in-deficiency in themselves, or because of impossible conditions created by changes in their physical habitat, something is obstructing the Power at work in creation. We cannot reasonably postulate a Creator Who can look upon these dislocations and failures, with their attendant suffering, and majestically pronounce: "It is good!" Not, at any rate, if 'good' means an overall network in which the support system for living beings can be depended on to make their existence (granted the necessity of some pain and of death) such that there is a tolerable and wholesome relation between the pleasant and unpleasant for beings at such levels of organic survival. (I am assuming a minimum of debilitating pain and unpleasantness as a lower limit, to be a reasonable expectation for subhuman beings; see further comment in a moment.)

(e) Accordingly, staying at the subhuman level of evolution, and taking into account the factors that seem clearly to impede the fullest development, I shall postulate an Impediment, refractory to the Creator's will, yet not able to thwart completely the stupendous sweep of biological evolution in relation to the physical order. That billions of years passed before organisms appeared is witness to the persistent thrust toward as much creativity-in-order as possible in the supporting physico-chemical system, despite failures that might occur in the total process.

The Impediment requires further analysis, but, for the moment, let us build on a very suggestive concept of Plato, developed when he faced a problem similar to ours. For the One Absolute Perfection that is the source of all being in the Republic,

Plato substitutes (in the _Timaeus_, 30) a creative
(not Creator) Demiurge. This God, with His eyes
fixed upon eternal ideals, indomitably "persuades"
the relatively inchoate and resistant ananke (necessity) to conform as far as possible to the best--
here is a pregnant suggestion which we shall adapt
to our own purpose. For the stress remains on the
Demiurge's delight in seeing to it that everything
worth doing be done as well as possible, despite a
co-eternal recalcitrant factor, not of His making.
God's delight in the best--"that all things should
be good and nothing bad, so far as this was attainable"--this fits our interpretation that the essential
development of physical and biological evolution is
an essential victory of the "love of the good" over
intransigent but not intrinsic resistance. (I shall
argue later that the Impediment is eternally within
the complex Unity of the Creator-Person.)

(f) I have been arguing that "Nature red in tooth
and claw" cannot be reasonably assimilated to the
concept of an invincible Creator in the classical
sense of Perfection. But in arguing for a Creator-
Person, persuading (on the view to be developed) a
co-eternal refractory aspect in His own nature, I
am, hopefully, not over-influenced by an unrealistic
interpretation of suffering at the subhuman levels.
Not for a moment will I condone any pain and suffering
that is needless, at any level of being. But the more
a creature's consciousness is confined to momentary
existence, the less memory, anticipation, and imagination can that creature bring to a painful experience.
The less, then, is the toll of its suffering.

The problem of evaluating animal suffering is
exceedingly difficult, and our judgments must be
sobered by the ignorance that engulfs us in this
area. But to cite the monstrous pain and killing required all along the evolutionary scale as, in itself,
adequate evidence against the existence of a morally
perfect Creator, requires a confidence about the function of pleasantness and unpleasantness and suffering
in the subhuman orders that, as I see it, is all but
impossible to substantiate. Yet, I hazard a judgment

in favor of a morally perfect God, not an omnipotent Creator-Person, with the consideration in mind that the quality of suffering is not at the subhuman level in the same class as suffering at the human level where meaning plays so much a part.

Accordingly, were I asked whether a Creator should be held back in creating the system of subhuman living beings on account of the suffering they encounter, I, for one, would urge their creation if the alternative is their nonexistence. For, still mindful of ignorance that in this area must cut in all directions, I would assume that in the subhuman levels (and the more so the lower we go), to exist at all is to endure less "suffering" than pleasantness (at each level). Here, we need to remind ourselves that all experiencing of suffering and experiencing of pleasantness is in the individual. So we do not pile "monstrous suffering among animals" over against piles of pleasures. Each being appears, lives, and dies only _once_, and _counts for one_. In the last analysis then, though the number of deaths totalled must be deplored, there are not "many deaths" but one death for each living being, the death that each individual actually experiences (and, at the subhuman level, meaningless suffering).

I would not, therefore, consider a Creator morally perfect and ethically good, if, in view of the suffering and failures that might take place owing to the Impediment, He had decided not to create the vast scale of living creatures whose very existence is intended to involve a modicum of pleasant experience at their respective, qualitative levels. The world with living beings in it is worth what each may suffer in the course of making his contribution to the system as a whole. And I remind myself that the quality in survival (enjoyed for itself by each kind of subhuman organism despite its use also as a means of survival for organisms) might well be chosen, if the alternative were to be its sheer nonexistence.

I have been pleading for, and building on, an

appropriate conception of the nature and "quantity" of "enjoyment" and "suffering" that is part of the lot of subhuman beings. An adequate human ethic must not be casual about the killing of subhuman lives, but neither can it refrain from establishing priorities among living things that depend upon each other for such quality of existence as is open to them. But realizing the precarious bases of my judgment at this point, I have tried to indicate the grounds for the main thrust of this phase of my argument. The Creator is most intelligibly seen as working, within constraints, to increase the variety and quality of organic beings, and as doing so even at the cost of being less successful than He prefers in order that new kinds of self-existence be realized.

(g) It is at the classical, theistic claim that an omniscient, all-powerful God (with no constraints but His own upon His will-to-goodness) purposely wills interrelations between natural phenomena and living phenomena that enable organisms to destroy, without consideration of any sort for beings helpless to help themselves--it is at that claim that I recoil. It does little good to assure me that, were I to know the whole story, the belief in both all-powerful and all-good power would be made reasonable. If the evil we see in some situations is the best that an omniscient, all-powerful God can bring about, what grounds have we for the belief that this particular kind of situation would be improved if we knew the whole--even a whole completed in some future existence? The conclusion seems never more justifiable than at this point--only a Creator can be called morally perfect Who, working against some Impediment within His nature, does not purposely produce pain or suffering, but (even on such evidence as we have) accepts it as the costly, yet worthwhile, consequence of what this unfolding drama warrants.

I am purposely delaying the discussion of good-and-evil at the human level. In our transition to that level we must recognize the phenomena in the

subhuman realm that are sources of nondisciplinary
evil in the lives of persons. There are ways in
which the survival-attempts of cells in the body-
brain produce such pain, so destroy organic functions and undermine values, that persons are left
broken, incapable of quarantining, let alone transforming, these disvalues into values. To be sure,
there are the handicaps owing to bodily disease that
need not necessarily cripple the spirit, owing to
the compensatory and creative responses of the person;
but there are bodily diseases--not to speak here of
the psychic--that are so damaging to health and so
resistant to reconstruction that were any person to
will these for another we should judge him morally
perverse.

The questions, then, keep haunting us: If God
is omniscient and omnipotent in the classical sense,
must those orders of organic life be so germane to
such omnipotence and omniscience that, when they
break down utterly, the bodily and psychic consequences are so serious that no informed, sensitive
judgment can reasonably justify them as possible
disciplinary means to a larger good? Would an omniscient, omnipotent, and all-good God, in the
interests, say, of the richest variety of living
beings, knowing that some of these subhuman beings
could so interfere with a higher order of value by
creating nondisciplinary evils, ordain _that_ variety
of quality, with its accompaniment of nondisciplinary
evil? Persons who behaved in this fashion, when they
could have behaved otherwise, would hardly be considered
both morally and ethically good.

We are human and not God. Yet, can we avoid at
this point what we reasonably attribute to the Person-
God on such evidence as we have, and on the ethical
criteria we espouse? So, to put the conclusion
sharply: An omnipotent Creator Who has so many irons
in the fire that He knowingly endangers the compos-
sibility of values for persons, and this by way of
"unknowing" subhuman beings--can this Creator be considered morally perfect and ethically good? Our tentative conclusion is that if goodness is _not_ to be

assigned to <u>anything</u> God does, "since He is perfection," then we must indeed keep the meaning of "omnipotence" within the constraints of the <u>moral perfection</u> that encounters not self-imposed difficulty alone as He creates the best of compossible worlds. All the more must we consider the problem of good-and-evil at the level of persons as we attempt a further character- ization of Creator and Impediment.

5. Reflective Overview

Classical theists and nontemporalistic person- alists, wedded to the concept of perfection[2] that by definition cannot be measured by anything in the cre- ated orders of being, have resorted to the same defense whenever the attempt is made to relate the nontemporal, unchanging Transcendent to the orders of temporal change. They continue to charge human reason with arrogance at every point where relating such Perfection to a particular imperfection runs into difficulties that cast doubt on the premise. The majesty of such Perfection, for all the protective coloration that helped it pass unperceived, has had to yield to the persistent scrutiny of minds dedicated to the problem of relating the Transcendent to the changes that characterize an immanent order.

This chapter is part of the attempt to see what can be said when reason as experiential coherence is applied without "forcing" the evidence at hand. Our attempt to move from the variety of human experience toward the attributes of God has been sustained by the clues in Nature and man that allow both to be seen within a more reasonably comprehensible system than the naturalistic-humanistic interpretation. In the notion of Agency that is self-sufficient and self-conscious as it creatively works out its purposes, an hypothesis is at hand that does not do violence either to logic, to scientifically guided reason, or to the fundamental values that guide the very persons whose reason is ever saturated by hopeful, but never blind, faith. The law of growth in persons dedicated

to truth and value (and w-holiness) is not of their
own making alone. "I was made for fellowship in love,"
said the Antigone of Sophocles, and "not fellowship
in hate." Love of one's fellows within the fellowship
of God, that is a perfection, as we shall see, that
renders the "tragedy" of divine and of human existence
co-creative.

Notes

1   While I must accept responsibility for the views
presented in this and the next chapters, I suggest
that my readers look to Edgar S. Brightman in POR,
chapters 7 and 10, and in: The Problem of God, 1930,
The Finding of God, 1931, and chapter 17 in PAR, which
also provides a succinct, historical background and
exposition of the grounds for limiting the power of
God. See also R.A. Tsanoff, Nature of Evil, 1931,
and especially S. Paul Schilling, God and Human
Anguish, 1977, part II, for a sympathetic, recent
evaluation of basic theories of God and anguish.
The writings of E.H. Madden and Peter H. Hare, see
Evil and the Concept of God, 1968, are also helpful
appraisals of recent literature on the problem of
evil. The works of Hastings Rashall, McTaggart, or
William Pepperell Montague should not be neglected.
     In this and the next two chapters, I am devel-
oping views presented in my Introduction to Philoso-
phy of Religion, especially chapters 12 - 18. I am
indebted to the criticism of persons, pupils, and
colleagues who knew Brightman well. Perhaps the
best "internal" critique is to be found in Albert C.
Knudson, The Doctrine of God; L. Harold De Wolf,
The Religious Revolt Against Reason, 1949; A
Theology of the Living Church, 1968; and Andrew
Banning, "Professor Brightman's Theory of a Limited
God," Harvard Theological Review, 27, 1934, 145-168.

2   Again, my reflections on the doctrine of perfection
are much influenced by the work of my teacher and colleague, Edgar Brightman, and, along a partly common
track, by A.N. Whitehead's writings--drawn further
into the theological area by his creative disciple,
Charles Hartshorne.

Chapter Twelve

THE MORAL PERFECTION OF GOD
AND NONDISCIPLINARY EVIL

1. The Meaning and Import of Nondisciplinary Evil

Nondisciplinary evils are those that enter the experience of persons from any source with such destructive power that they cannot be transformed into any good; or their instrumentality for goodness is unreasonably incommensurate with the unwilled, devastating evils that ensue. My teacher and colleague, Edgar S. Brightman, at first called such evil 'surd.' But later, sensitive to the criticism that to call any evil 'surd' was to limit God's power to transform evil to any extent, he refined his intent to avoid so extreme an interpretation. In a letter (August 26, 1949) answering L. Harold De Wolf's criticism, he said: "My statement on page 246 of A Philosophy of Religion, 1940, that 'if there be any truly surd evil, then it is not in any sense an instrumental good' was unfortunate, although I intended the context to show that I was not committing myself to belief in that extreme type of surd evil. I should have written something like this: If there be any truly surd evil, then it is not in any sense an intrinsic good, and it can be an instrumental good only in a very imperfect sense."

I am using 'nondisciplinary evil,' or 'irreducible evil,' in the sense denoted in my first sentence and consistent with Brightman's last statement.

I am aware that this definition takes in a good deal in its sweep, but the theoretical situation we confront is not one that is significantly changed if it should turn out that an evil deemed irreducible could be reinterpreted to be "imperfectly" instrumental. Our judgments of value and disvalue are always open to further evaluation, but is there any real basis for denying the existence of a situation in which, no matter how hard we try to find the saving loophole, the evil experienced is such that the minimal good that might be achieved by all those affected cannot be seen as worthwhile? For example, there are natural evils--cyclones, earthquakes--whose fury sweeps away so much of value and of value-possibility, whose fury includes nothing of merited, let alone unmerited, suffering, as far as we can tell. Is it, in fact, reasonable to be "assured" that <u>the whole system somehow justifies such evil</u>? Can they indeed, "upon reconsideration," be reckoned as part of a larger good, and thus as instruments of an all-good, all-wise and also absolutely omnipotent God? My own hesitant answer must be negative; nor can I change it when I contemplate also those <u>moral</u> evils (owing to human choice) whose evil consequences are nondisciplinary since they are such that whatever redemption might be possible still leaves spirits broken beyond healing?

Given nondisciplinary evils, then, moral and natural (nonmoral) in origin, we must re-examine the claim that this world, with its value-possibilities and its actualized values, is ultimately the ideal realm for co-creators. How shall we conceive of God's goodness and power once we have cautiously considered what the existence of nondisciplinary evil involves for the Creator-Person and His co-creators? I shall undertake these considerations in order to show why the interpretation of evil advanced by classical thinkers, though not misleading in general scope, falls short at certain critical junctions. However, my main concern is to present the grounds for a view of God that coheres with the argument already advanced and that helps us to "corner the mystery" a little better. Far from conceding that only a certain kind of Being is perfect or worthy of worship, I shall suggest that the Creator-Person we know at work in natural and human history, accepting the slag of nondisciplinary evil in the course of furthering His aims in creating, is indeed worthy of the worship of co-creators.

2. Nondisciplinary Evil and the Power of God

(a) In the last chapter we noted that human beings are often afflicted by unmerited (natural) evils that are consequences of the fact that subhuman organisms are simply gratifying their survival needs. Assuming that value-experience can be extended to the awareness even of subhuman beings, I would grant once more the difficulty of assessing any situation as being devoid of value. Whether the value gained is significant, however, compared to the overwhelming evidence of disvalue in some situations--that is the question. If we declare in principle that no situation is devoid of value, will this help to define the quality of the Creator's power and goodness rather than defend a preconceived view of His perfection? It is an ill wind, they say, that blows nobody good, but shall we say this of a whirlwind and a hurricane? A morally perfect God, and persons seeking to improve every situation, will do all in their power to reduce and keep possible evil under quarantine. Granted that a particular instance of evil, claimed to be nondisciplinary, may even in the foreseeable future possibly contribute to some good, does this situation do more than encourage caution in declaring particular evils irreducible and nondisciplinary? Hence, while I join in providing a list of evils for which persons can in no way be held responsible, evils that snuff out values and value-possibilities with no regard for merit and for foreseeable disvalue, I prefer to avoid judging any particular evil--schizophrenia, for example--as necessary and in every case 'nondisciplinary' in the sense defined.

But such caution should not, I believe, absolve us of the intellectual responsibility of pointing to evils that, so far as we can see, bear little or no increment of value. They inflict such injury upon human lives that we have to resort to a strained, patch-up interpretation about their possible value in a larger-context-we-know-not-what. Which of us does not know some moral giant who, persistently was constructive in the face of constant unmerited evils, and was able, like a great oak, to sink his roots

261

deeper as he stood tall despite unmerited suffering, has not been uprooted by a final blow?

(b) I am not assuming that excruciating evils can be avoided in a world deservedly called 'good' (much as I shall not easily give way to the claim that they may do some good in a context described in traditional fashion as 'perfect'). For, as the classical theist properly reminds us, in a world of interpenetrating orders of being, and especially where freedom among the created is meaningless without supportive order, there is bound to be the possibility of major evil. I am not second-guessing a natural order in which the water that quenches thirst is also the water that drowns, to use F. R. Tennant's example. Nor do I depreciate a psycho-spiritual order in which persons who live sensitive to the highest concerns, moral and aesthetic, will also be the ones who may suffer most keenly when they are afflicted by evil to themselves and to others. No complaint is filed against the orders in Nature and man, for so much in our study so far is unified by the twin theses that the freedom of persons does not and cannot exist either in a vacuum or in chaos, and that persons are the kinds of being-becoming who, as they influence each other, require a nonhuman order that challenges and threatens even as it nourishes them and their values.

(c) But the very attempt to study the intricate and sometimes seemingly paradoxical relation between what we call "good" and "evil" brings into view harsh particulars very difficult to harmonize with a view of the universe as somehow unchangingly complete, or as governed by a transcendent Person whose con-temporaneous immanence faces none but self-imposed limitations in actualizing the best of compossible worlds. Nondisciplinary evils require more than a piety which waives further reasoning in the face of the stubborn remainder, even though we have tried to see every possibility in it of good in evil.

Hence, having argued for the <u>moral</u> perfection of God, I have not assumed that this entails <u>ethical</u>

perfection in teleology--which would mean that the best of compossible worlds is at hand or forthcoming (as defined by classical theists). The problem of evil has been argued so often, alas, in a classical context that defended both a moral and ethical perfection. This has led, I maintain, to forcing the negative evidence into a system that was held to be the only one worth defending. Rather than argue (or cease arguing) from a fixed conception of what God must be, I start off with the experience of good-and-evil and allow myself to be guided by reasonable inferences. My underlying contention is that reason can take us to a morally perfect Creator Who, engaged in bringing about and sustaining the interpenetrating and compossible orders, has not, in fact, produced the best compossible teleological order--the high mark of which must be <u>not</u> the absence of evil but the absence of nondisciplinary evil. In what follows I shall try to present an interpretation of data without assuming that the classical view has priority, and still relate my interpretation to understandable objections from classical theists and others.

(d) Some irreducible evils result from man's limitations as an agent-knower. We cannot, given the broad lines of our teleological argument, assume that more cognitive ability would, as is possible, be used to create more havoc. Accordingly, I cannot grant that an omniscient, morally perfect Creator Who had the power to create higher levels of basic cognition--levels better able, for example, to deal with the exigencies of Nature--would not have done so.

As we know, the development of <u>homo sapiens</u> was preceded by other species of "men" who were less capable of dealing with their ambient; theirs were the goods and evils related to their stages in development. But these species disappeared, along with the vast variety of organisms in their environment. The evolutionary process as a whole suggests no smooth and steady escalation "upwards" in which the simpler organisms develop step by step into the more complex-- as, for example, the seed of a plant matures into a flower. Each species, each individual, needs its own

environment as it thrives, and then dies. The lack
of a neat, continuous escalation--granted we can
even surmise what that might mean--offers in itself
no particular problem except as whole species dis-
appear owing to some drastic change in supporting
conditions. Such failure hardly confirms the concept
of Creator Who faced no obstacles that His power could
not overcome.

(e) I have cautioned against supposing that the lower
organism, as such, produces the higher. The higher,
once it appears, suggests, as we look back, that a
Creator having arrived at one stage in creation moves
on to another that can be related to the earlier, yet
is not reducible to it. Each species, each individual,
has its level of enjoyment, danger, suffering, and
death, and all are dependent on other living beings
and on their relation to a common physical environment
for the quality of their survival.

Homo sapiens appeared, but not in a cosmic setting
in which all was ready even for his biological health.
His was the uniquely creative task of establishing
his own environments among the physico-chemical orders
and among the species that responded in various ways
to his existence. By analogy with human struggles
for survival and fulfillment, we interpret observations about the myriad forms of subhuman beings-for-
self as limited to their own sensitivities and ability
to survive. On reflection we cannot but be impressed
by our dependence upon these living beings who make
such a difference to the quality of our survival within what we may call the nurturant energies of Nature.

But, again, this tremendous zest for living, so
profligate in some ways, so stingy in others, hardly
suggests the work of an omnipotent Architect, Engineer,
or Artist who builds in the sure confidence that His
materials will pose no problems as He seeks to create
lives compossible with each other and with an equit-
able balance of enjoyment and suffering. Awesome
harmonies do pervade the orders of subhuman adjustment, and the growth as these organisms interact
with each other and their common nonorganic environ-

264

ment; and the scale of living beings suggests that complex organizations of life were not simply a means to <u>homo</u> <u>sapiens</u>. But so uneven is the development on the whole that the quality of perfection is surely not that of an Alpha who is Omega either in time or in completeness that has no place for change. Once more, what suggests itself is a quality of perfection in which Alpha is omnitemporal and contemporaneous with every new level and pattern of creation; as for Omega, its time, at least, has not yet come. These levels of creation bring with them new contexts for good-and-evil as their members persist in pursuing their own forms of being-be-coming-for-self. Creator, yes; Creator <u>simply</u> <u>at</u> <u>will</u>, hardly. And here a further comment is in order.

(f) So dependent are persons on the orders mentioned that it is tempting to say that persons are 'organic to Nature.' In the position here suggested, 'organic' must not be interpreted to mean that a union exists in which free persons are lost as modes of the One, or to mean that the creative responsibility of persons is, in fact, annulled. For the exercise of the ac-tivity-potentials of persons, responding to the chal-lenge of nonhuman and human orders, produces selective meaning--value-patterns that at once reflect and add their own realms of order, especially by way of the personal, social, and political patterns of value. All along I have contended that, within the value-possibilities and eligibilities of the Realm, per-sons gradually carve out (again under the influence of their own interplay with each other as part of their varied responses to the Realm) the environ-ments and horizons they live by. I need not re-emphasize that the history of the human species is the tale of activity-potentials that did not work smoothly either within the person or within the species, let alone among the species. The value-patterns that developed reflect ignorance, stupidity, constraints placed upon persons with which they could hardly cope since the odds did not favor them.

Persons are not organic, then, to Nature, in the

sense that Nature itself reflects their struggle for meaning and value. Nevertheless, they are agents whose mutual nurture, however fumbling and tortuous, has become increasingly and sufficiently prudent, and also sufficiently in accord with nonhuman givens that Nature "participates" in their total mode of survival. From their beginning and through the ages of their evolution, persons have been in process of strengthening their inner and outer resources, individually and socially. Despite even serious reversals and upheavals, what stands out is the contribution made by their mutual challenge, by their criticism of the fabric of values that keeps them together. In this context the verdict suggested is that human history is not the story of <u>either</u> finite <u>or</u> infinite power to achieve the best of compossible worlds. Rather, it is the story of the persistent organization, in accordance with a comprehensive purpose, that is delayed, stopped, hindered, but committed to produce and preserve whatever is worthwhile, within its determinate power, and consistent with the best possible.

(g) The pattern of the best for persons is the symphony of values, to be orchestrated individually in harmony with the purpose of sharing both values and disvalues as justly and mercifully as possible in community. In achieving this ethical norm, persons in this world cannot live by "a balance of pleasure over pain," but only by the quality of creative insecurity that characterizes the ideal of actualizing and orchestrating symphonies of values in persons and social life. This ideal of moral-ethical order makes the most of the kind of conditions adduced in my cosmo-teleological considerations, including what was adduced about the nature of persons.

The best of compossible worlds, accordingly, is not one without varied suffering, or one with the neat distribution of good and evil, especially if we include the scope of beings-for-self. Insecurity is not only intrinsic to being finite, in conditions beyond one's control; insecurity inheres in the very nature of being a person whose

actual freedom of personal choice is involved in the
pursuit of truth and goodness. Intrinsic to the good
for persons is the insecurity that can become creative, because values are compenetrating, and because
persons themselves can choose orchestration-within-
pattern as they change and grow.

In this <u>creative insecurity</u>[1] persons at their
best are confronted, some more than others, by the
nondisciplinary evils arising from their physical
surroundings or from their bodily deficiencies and
diseases. Their trials and tribulations, evaluated
in their total environmental situation, are such
that we cannot reasonably say that a Creator-Person,
Who is morally good, purposes them <u>as</u> <u>part</u> of any
plan, or allows them to occur if He has the power
to avoid them.

The drama of history, then, is what it is because the Creator-Person, with His eyes fixed upon
the goals of a qualitative creative insecurity that
results in and from a responsive-responsible community, faces a recalcitrant factor, an Impediment,
the nonrational Given, within His nature. It is
this nonrational Given whose resistance keeps the
Creator from achieving His goals without the in-
cidence of nondisciplinary evil. In this grappling
with the nonrational Given, however, there is the
peculiar <u>blessedness</u> of creative insecurity (such as
that tensive, creative effort which we know in love
committed to co-creative forgiveness--see later).
The resultant, actual, evolutionary cosmos, with
the creation of persons who can know the creative
insecurity involved in realizing the symphony of
values, is still the pearl of great price. But
that price must be recognized as playing its part
in the dramatic development of natural and human
history, the drama that expresses the blessed goodness within the Creator's own being-becoming. Such
blessed creative insecurity I would call "tragic"
goodness, if every element of inner flaw can be dissociated from the word, and if the quality for accepting suffering within the blessedness of creative
insecurity is accepted as intrinsic to value-in-
creasing creativity.

3. Moral Perfection, the Recalcitrant Given, and God's "Tragic" Goodness

(a) There are difficulties which persist in the view just presented, and they will not be evaded. Those we shall consider right away seem to spring from the assumption that our intent is largely to modify classical theism by introducing into the otherwise perfect divine nature an Impediment that presumably enables us to explain nondisciplinary evil. This is a mistaken view of our purpose. The intent in this book is <u>not to modify a preexisting view but to reinterpret</u>, if you will, data and considerations upon which theistic and nontheistic views build competing, alternative interpretations. The concept of the nonrational Given, a response especially to the problem of nondisciplinary evil, is to be seen as part of a more comprehensive, <u>temporalistic</u> theism and personalism. But appreciation of contrast with nontemporalistic theism may clarify both text and significant debate.

(b) Let us return again to the conception of perfection dominating classical theism.

(i) A self-sufficient, nontemporal Mind creates, aware of all possibilities, all actualities, and all probabilities, impeded by no factor inconsistent with His purposes or imposed in any way upon Him; (ii) a morally perfect and ethically fulfilled Creator directly supports both moral and natural evil as essential to the best of compossible worlds, namely, one in which the moral freedom and ethical development of persons are supported and challenged by the dependable orders in relation to which they have their being; (iii) God's purposes for persons are not restricted to, or confined by, this present "vale of soul-making." God assures personal immortality for all--not as the way of rewarding and punishing persons, but as expressing His continuing concern for the moral-spiritual growth already expressed in this life. "Heaven" is no hedonistic paradise; it allows for the growth of potential consistent with the constant, divine care for the highest possible fellowship between God and His co-creators.

268

For years I lived and thought in the grip of this classical vision. A certain spiritual dynamics accompanies this faith in a divine purpose in accordance with which each believer "knows" that nothing can ever separate him from his Creator's care. It is not that such believers take either good or evil for granted, or, in calculating spirit, add up deserts. They give themselves to mitigating evil wherever possible and to keeping it within bounds. "Though he slay me, yet will I trust him!"--theirs is a hope-full resignation. Even their incomprehensible and unmerited suffering, they trust, must find its place and meaning within the total pattern of His will.

The inspiring and liberating power in this belief that even unmerited (and what I have called nondisciplinary) suffering is never the last word, in this belief that there is victory over every kind of evil and death, that every "cross" can be shared and every joy deepened by a humble gratitude--all this, and much more, cannot be ruled out in the evaluation of classical theism at its best. Any alternative must recognize <u>this</u> quality of creativity <u>without</u> ultimate insecurity--a faith that removes mountains that by itself it cannot climb.

(c) All the more, then, must I almost hesitantly enter a <u>caveat</u>. <u>Is</u> this spiritual dynamics actually riveted to the conviction that God is both morally perfect and ethically perfect? At any rate, whether the alternative conception of God I shall present is true or not, the time has long since arrived to question the view that consummate Being, consummate happiness, consummate significance depend on the conviction that whatever occurs and has occurred are, despite our frailties, ignorance, and moral failures, part of a majestic plan or pattern that, could we understand it, contains no real puzzle, no real insecurity, no "tragic" blessedness, within its all-embracing, creative Purpose.

Did the prophetic moralists and spiritual seers over the ages, the beacon lights for so many who in

their own way caught the vision, did these prophets
require that every step should be ultimately assured
in what they considered, after all, a venturesome
dedication to God's will for His people? Is the
venture of faith really an investment in gilt-edged
bonds backed by an omniscient, omnipotent Deity?
For such faith, is it not "the good" that is loved,
not the guarantee of its success? Must we, and I say
it advisedly, fuse the psychology of heroic living
exclusively with the conviction that the good, including creativity, cannot be the good, unless it is
successful, whatever the changes and the difficulties
in history? May we not affirm, as at least equally
profound and moving, the conviction, itself born in,
and of, venturesomeness, that what gives peak-and-
plane significance to the being-becoming of persons
is their dedication to creating as far as possible
that range and quality of value that keeps persons
creative at each stage in history? Can it be that
the self-giving, dedicated persons, with their in-
domitable conception that "what is good" cannot
really fail, have so resolutely been pointing to
only such an interpretation?

There are no easy answers here, and visions of
the good that inspires persons beyond all else must
not be dogmatic. There is always the pathos of
failing, despite one's very best effort, to overcome completely the obstacles in the way of actualizing ideals that could further enliven existence.
On either view, there is drama in existence because
creativity is of the essence. But I am suggesting
that the taproot of drama is a self-dedication that,
in history and in personal existence, counts the
possible costs but commits itself to a new form
of creativity in the face of "tragic" suffering. We
must return to this matter, but my caveat will continue to be: Does religious reverence at its best
require Perfection with creativity as its handmaid,
or does it define itself by the awesome experience,
human and divine, of accepting the agony that is
the unique ecstasy, the "blessedness" of becoming-in-
creativity? At least, the attempt I shall make to
justify and clarify the particular view of the

270

Creator and the nonrational Given will not be stopped
dead in its tracks by the assumption that the classical view of Perfection and creativity alone meets
the requirements of inspiration at its best.

(d) I move, then, to a presentation of God as the
Person-Creator whose cosmic purpose includes the
creating of limitedly free agents who can dedicate
their creativity as far as possible to values that
at once are novel and supportive of further ventures
in value. This conception takes root in several
theses, the review of which is to help clarify the
finite personal situation as a basis of appropriate
analogy for what is involved in referring to the
Creator-Person and the nonrational Given.

First, forsaking the view that only an Alpha
and Omega that transcends succession and change can
make either possible or intelligible, I have appealed
to what each of us experiences himself to be even in
any undeniable, momentary time-span. It is the very
being of this datum-person to become, and never to be
simply a succession. This complex, erlebt datum-
person establishes its continuity not by "emerging"
from its past as if it were a sheer product of that
past. The datum-person is self-identifying as it
changes in the course of its interaction with its
contemporaneous ambient. Thus, within any telic
datum-moment, it is a self-identifying being-becoming
that, in "ingesting" and "digesting" selectively what
is consistent with its complex aim, "concresces" without losing its identity. In essence, then, to be a
person is to be-become, as acting and being acted
upon, and yet to remain self-identifying within the
final bounds of one's activity-potentials.

Second, within the self-identifying unity of the
person can be distinguished his nonrational given (at
least sensory, feeling, wanting, emoting) and a rational given (at least the norms of logic and coherence). No one, in discriminating the rational and
nonrational givens within a person's unitary being-
becoming, should suppose that there is a bifurcation,
or an inner ontic dualism. For the person is con-

271

stantly involved <u>as a whole</u> in organizing and giving
further meaning to inner life, even as interaction
with the ambient is going on. (We could speak of a
person's experiencing "form" and "content," rational
and nonrational, or of the person's active and passive poles, if we resist the temptation to reify
"parts," and if we bear in mind that, as persons, we
are never sheerly passive.)

Accordingly, in the course of organizing and
creating, the person deals with his nonrational given,
within which he often confronts nonrational factors
<u>resistant to, refractory to, the particular aim that
he prefers</u>. But his experiencing is never a collection of happenings completely beyond any meaning.
Nevertheless, the person's never-ending task is to
weave, as it were, his nonrational givens, including
the given factors that would be fruitlessly conflicting,
into the patterns consistent with his varying aims.
Organize he must, and, in selecting, he evaluates
the "demands" inherent to, and latent in, his givens.
He cannot be-become without conflict, but he can be-
become creatively-in-conflict in every situation
(except when nondisciplinary evil prevails). A person will grow toward <u>moral</u> perfection only as he consistently wills the courage to conserve, as he orches-
trates the factors within his active, telic control,
as creatively as possible in situation after situation.

In the human situation as we know it, neither
<u>moral</u> nor <u>ethical</u> perfection is a final state for
either an individual or for society. My thesis is
that ethical perfection does not denote an ultimate
state from which insecurity and frustration have been
excluded, but one in which frustration and disappointment are kept from paralyzing effort to improve the
situation. And this, again, is possible not because
a person's increasing cognitive and moral-valuational
control begins with some sheer chaos of sense, feelings,
and desires. Will and reason, in my view, are always
present in the dynamic ferment confronting the tasks
of discovering and developing what can become in interaction with environments.

Third, in this total situation, at the human level there is no <u>given</u> fatal disease (no absolute original sin, no absolute death-urge) that gnaws away parasitically at the vitality of the person. But concrescence and rigidity can always come into being, themselves illustrating laws of growth and decay. The diseases that, like a cancer, can come into being, themselves illustrating laws of growth, indicate that there are factors within the person's different dimensions that require control in the person's interests, although their own telic trend is toward fulfillment at the person's expense. Yet, once "cancers" can maintain themselves, as it were, against the body's trend, in their very "success" they destroy the suffering person--only, in the end, to die with him. To the extent that they exist, they are disvalue-possibilities in the unified matrix of the person. The destructive, impeding, nonrational in the person, accordingly, has no independence; it "lives" within the relatively raw material for growth. Nor is the disciplined individual on the whole unable to achieve any degree of growth as the factors that I am calling nondisciplinary resist his rational will to the best he knows.

(e) In using the finite person's confrontation with his nonrational given as a possible source of insight into that of the Creator-Person, the dominant emphasis must remain on the fact that the Creator-Person's own being-becoming is characterized by the persuasion of the nonrational Given <u>within</u> the unity of His nature, in accordance with His rational Given. What, in the complex unity of the Creator-God, constitutes the nonrational Given is a question we shall have to face later. But even a possible failure to characterize it adequately should not keep us from realizing at present, to the full, that "a factor" within God's experience is recalcitrant to God's own choosing. This factor is compatible with, but not reducible to, the insecurity He invited into the quality of His experience when He delegated autonomy to persons. Even this creation invited insecurity into the quality of His experience. <u>His form of ethical perfection</u> will, therefore, include <u>creative insecurity</u>. <u>But the quality of that ethical perfection will be con-</u>

273

sistent with the fact that, as Creator-Ground, He
participates contemporaneously in all the various
ways of supporting whatever makes for mutuality in
the actualization of value.

(f) From the outset I have affirmed that our task
in philosophy and, I now add, especially in the
philosophy of religion, is to "corner the mystery,"
as Whitehead put it one day in class. This is no
place to give up the ghost and desist from rendering
the most probable account in terms of a fuller
theory of reality (although one is not advanced here).
But keeping in mind the theistic, personalistic
idealism already referred to, we can ask how an
Impediment within God's being may be conceived in
harmony with the relation of God's being-becoming
in the physical and organic realms of Nature and
in man.

(i) Natural nondisciplinary evils, on this view,
are not the result of purposing evil as an instrument
to good. They are the cost paid for the kinds of
orders of being that we have seen in relation to each
other with their value-and-disvalue possibilities,
with their "inducements" to good and evil. The
Creator-Person in working out His purposes has not
always been able to persuade obstacles, co-eternal
within His own complex unity, to take on the form
that would avoid nondisciplinary evil. But neither
did they prevent Him from creating the best possible
(not the best compossible in the classical, perfectionist sense). Such evidence as we have justifies
reasonable confidence that the Creator can continue
to create realms with their value-possibilities in
support of human creativity. The Creator Who has
come this far in His persuasion of the nonrational
Given will in all likelihood continue to maintain
His purposes.

(ii) But the perfection of God we now envision
is not that of an abstractly omnipotent Being whose
I am is I am, removed beyond any conflict from within. Neither is God a Being chained to an impenetrable,
nonrational Given "in a lump" that has its own unity.

274

For the awe-inspiring richness of the Person as manifest in the movement of cosmic history and in the constant, if uneven, evolutionary advance (with its interpenetrations of elements) suggests not an unchanging, omnipotent Power, but a Creator intent on so organizing the orders of being that they will undergird the advance in value-possibility and in value-experience to which history witnesses.

(iii)To envision change in God is not to invite cosmic chaos, if only we persist on throwing as much light as possible on the course our Universe has already traversed. As <u>causa</u> <u>sui</u>, the Creator, of course, will never be less than the ontic Being-Becoming He is as the unified Ground of all there is and will be. And in pursuance of His purposes there will be for Him satisfactions and disappointments as He experiences the actual course of natural and human history. For He knows better than anyone can know the general nature, though not the detail and the letter, of the consequences of good and evil, at least as deriving from His delegation of responsibility to persons for what persons can make of persons and of their environments. For example, surely there is in God's experience the quality of joy that results from satisfaction that persons can learn, as it were, to "think His thoughts after Him," as they discipline themselves to learn the ways of "physical" energy; but He knows also the quality of suffering when persons use that energy as if it were theirs alone, and to hurt each other, while He cannot morally withhold His cooperation from such use.

In a forceful and illuminating presentation, <u>God and Human Anguish</u>, 1977, one of Brightman's sensitive disciples, S. Paul Schilling, finds it reasonable to appeal to no more than the temporality of God to explain what I refer to as nondisciplinary evil. He consequently acknowledges a unique quality of "joy" and "anguish" in a God Who is responsibly related to a changing, orderly world and the reality of human freedom. I suggest, in addition, that a different quality of joy and anguish characterizes the experience of a temporalist God <u>Who creates</u>

despite the realization of the possible consequences of His dealing with the nonrational Given. I know not how to characterize this venturesome, creative, and fateful persuasion of the nonrational Given. The consequent nondisciplinary evil involves for Him truly the "agony" that is "ecstasy." His is a goodness that inflicts upon itself the inevitable pain of the creature that goes beyond "compassionate sorrow" and "creative love," to self-involvement in the perpetual, redemptive facing of evil that must be accepted but never "accepted."

It is such a "tragic" goodness of God, I submit, as a conception of the Person who takes us out of ourselves to the creativity of "sharing" joy and suffering. It is this quality of goodness that brings us to our knees in adoration, that is indeed worthy of worship. Indeed, to experience this co-creative tie as completely as possible at every stage of history, it is this "sharing" in "tragic" goodness that marks the hope-full, faith-full inspiration of religion. The majesty of God is not His omnipotence, or His omniscience, or His creativity. It is His constant dedication of Himself to the creation of the most compossible conditions for co-responsible creativity that constitutes His inspiring and humbling power over us.

4.   The Nonrational Given in God

(a)   What is the nonrational Given in God's experience? In my discussion so far my main concern is to make clear why some recalcitrant factor needs to be attributed to the experience of God in order to make more intelligible the course of all historical development. Keeping in mind the cautions we have noted in analogous reason from the finite to the cosmic Person, the basic suggestion now is that the nonrational Given in God's complex, active unity is relatively "raw material" that the Creator's reason and will co-eternally experience as He organizes His purposeful responses--raw material that, not chaotic, includes recalcitrant factors in relation to His ideals. In persons the affective-conative givens within their lives, the brute, sensory qualities and their obstinate regularities given to their thinking and wanting and will--from these, with these, resisting these, conforming to, or reforming these--this is the concrete becoming of persons insofar as they critically develop as personalities.

(b) What I wish to insist upon is that the non-rational in God is not given to Him, imposed upon Him, as our basic sensory "patterns" are upon us. What should be clear in what follows is that we must avoid, as beyond intelligibility, namely, a co-eternal, nonrational Recalcitrant Factor or Impediment whose being is in no way part of the complex unity of God. The major point of the analogy with the complex, active-passive "poles" of personal experience is to indicate that in our experience the factors that are given, for all their refractoriness, remain even in their recalcitrance within the matrix of our being, and are eligible within limits to the varied influences within the scope of our capacities. As long as we survive, they do not destroy our ontic unity-continuity, but they do "demand," "constrain," as would any relatively raw materials, and thus influence our expressive and adaptive powers, especially as we seek to organize our "symphonic" values more creatively. As in the lives of persons, "raw material" in God is not necessarily "of one kind," and not evil as such; it confronts the Creator-Organizer with its "grain(s)" and "strain(s)" that will not accept, at least without resistance, formative influences brought to bear upon them for purposes not intrinsic to them.

Having set this theoretical boundary on what the nonrational Given can intelligibly be, I purpose to follow largely in the steps of my teacher, Edgar S. Brightman, the very influential exponent of person-alistic, theistic idealism, especially from 1920 to 1953. He died before he could give the fullest expression to his conception of the relation of God to the physical world and to the biological realm, although I find in Person and Reality, 1958, artic-ulations that are at least compatible with the

277

selective account I shall give as my own to facili-
tate matters at this point.

(c) Earlier I indicated that the wider teleological
argument did not presuppose any particular ontolog-
ical view of the space-time realm, once it could be
seen as at least instrumental within a teleological-
ethical framework. According to classical theistic
realists (Thomistic or otherwise; see J. B. Pratt,
for example), the components of Nature are non-
mental "entities" that in their orderly course conform to God's purposes. The dysteleology of natural
processes is to be seen within the larger, presently
unknown pattern of the working of God's will. As
the realist sees it, the steady, impersonal, providential working of Nature must be protected against
idealistic versions that regard it as mind in some
form. Nature is that created witness to, and medi-
ator of, God's comprehensive purpose; at no point
does it have agency of its own. The cyclone and
the starry heavens above ultimately express no agency
but that of Him who is Alpha and Omega in spirit,
word, and deed.

It should be clear that an idealistic view of
Nature, such as Berkeley's, would not, in fact,
actually differ from the realistic account insofar as the explanation of moral and nonmoral evil
is concerned. Berkeley held that to think of Nature
as a material or non-mental realm independent of God
and man is, to say the least, an unnecessary inference
from what is perceived. Nevertheless, Nature, as
the immaterial or mental pattern of God's impersonal
interaction with human minds, still expresses the
ultimate purposes of an all-wise, all-powerful, and
ethically perfect God.

(d) But suppose that, taking important clues from
Berkeley, Kant, Schopenhauer, and Hegel, one sees
in Nature not the orderly network of non-mental events
independent of God, but the actual, predictable, energizing of God's will in accordance with His reason--
as did Borden Parker Bowne (1847-1910), the founder
of Personalistic Theistic Idealism. Suppose further

that we disabuse ourselves of the widespread fear that, if Nature is Mind at work, somehow we cannot expect the steadiness and order that is so critical to scientific endeavor, let alone "instinctive" common sense. (After all, as just suggested on realistic or idealistic views of Nature, it is the rational, providential will of Mind that is the ultimate source of confidence in Nature's lawful behavior.) Finally, suppose that, as Brightman, the temporalist would have it (at odds with Bowne, his teacher, at this point and in the interpretation of nondisciplinary evil), the history of Nature is the actual, standard development of God's immanence. Nature, accordingly, is God; but God is not confined to His activity in Nature (as is evident in His creation of persons who exist in partial dependence on Nature).

Moreover, Nature, for Brightman, is not "idea," or "thought," in any sense that separates willing from reason. Nature, to put it summarily, is at its core God expressing Himself impartially, impersonally (not non-personally); it is God's standard willing, the common ground for all interaction among persons, the arena by which the concrete creativity of all persons is conditioned, challenged, maintained, and elaborated. Again, Nature in human experience and knowing is also the shared vitality and (at least) the ground-condition for the creativity that can occur in moral, aesthetic, and religious dimensions of the divine-human relation.

Brightman--and here he differed from many with generally similar views--with natural, nondisciplinary evils in mind, looked into this natural aspect of God's total activity and saw in it the influence of God's creative "persuasion" of the recalcitrant, nonrational Given thus far. God has throughout His own history been persuading this Given to express purposes that comprise the best of compossible arenas for His co-creators.

Again, I must emphasize, the nonrational Given is not a "lump-Given" in Nature or in God, to be molded and conformed to His will, or a something "cancerous," somehow independent of His unity, that must be healed.

Brightman defines the nonrational Given by saying that in God there is "in addition to His reason and His active, creative will, a passive element which enters into everyone of His conscious states, as sensation, instinct, and impulse enters into ours, and constitutes a problem for Him."[4] What should be noted carefully is the "as..." clause here, for we shall return to it. Yet the nonrational "passivity" is not sheer passivity; it is to be conceived as relatively resistant to the aims of the Creator-Person whose own Being-Becoming is guided by His rational Given also. The Creator, as history indicates, is not satisfied with the harmonies that become rigidity; He takes the kinds of risks that result in nondisciplinary evil but also in advancing the aims that, as I have contended, include the possibility of the moral-ethical development of persons.

(e) I have, taking my lead from Brightman's own analogy, likened the Impediment to the nonrational varied, sensory, affective-conative tendencies in our own experience. Brightman's intent, as I see it, is to emphasize the relatively inchoate, the relatively unorganized and resistant from the point of view of purposes and norms expressive of activity in relation to His rational Given. There would be none of the purposive and purposeful orders in our world had the nonrational Given been unyielding to persuasion in the total process of God's reasoned creativity. If the nonrational Given were sheer formless, sensory or nonsensory "material," if it were "blind will," or sheer chaos in God's being, there would be no grounding of the kind of control over the nonrational Given that makes for the modicum of order we know in human experience and that we know in the orderly operations of Nature.

The Creator-Person, I accordingly suggest, cannot do all that is worthwhile in the natural, biological, and in the psychic realms because, contending as creatively as possible with the "brute factors" that are present in His unified Being-Becoming, God's creativity is not powerful enough to accomplish all that would be worthwhile. However, were there no divine control of the nonrational Given, there would not be the steady groundwork for creative advance that forms my basis for belief in the Creator-Person. What the future holds may be more in the hands of God's co-creators than we know, but, given the course of history insofar as it depends only on God, there is ground for confidence that He Who has continued in control of recalcitrant factors will not arbitrarily discontinue His creative activity.

5. Is a Panpsychistic Explanation of Nondisciplinary Evil Tenable?

(a) Some philosophers, influenced especially by Whitehead and Hartshorne, think that the explanation of evil suggested above would profit from a philosophical move not inconsistent with personalistic idealism, namely, panpsychism (or, as David R. Griffin prefers to call it in <u>God, Power, and Evil: A Process Theodicy</u>, "panexperientialism").[5] Griffin, unfortunately, in referring to Brightman's view, seems to think of the nonrational Given as an "internal flaw in God's nature." (He, therefore, himself falls temporarily into a classical, perfectionist ideal that he thinks mars Brightman's vision at some points.) I hope the above discussion shows that the underlying intent in Brightman's temporalistic personalism--and, in any case, in mine--is to reject the view that the nonrational Given is a flaw in perfection as conceived in this personalistic concept of dramatically creative, "tragic" goodness. Any polarity within Deity that is creative at every level is no "drag," except as these words are seen in the (false) context of classical perfection.[6] But were these difficulties as unanswerable (as I think they are misconstrued), I would then turn to Griffin's panexperiential alternative (that follows Hartshorne's "correction" of Whitehead's at relevant points).

281

According to this panexperiential view, we should envision physical, organic, and human worlds as ultimately interacting telic agents, all self-determining to some degree. They range from the simplest being-becoming unities in the "physical" realm, through the more spontaneous species of subhuman beings in the organic scale, to the quality of self-determination that persons exhibit. On this world-view, God seeks to persuade and not "dictate"; His ongoing purpose is to relate Himself to this immense variety of individual, self-determining but never isolated, beings, so that there may be the richest fulfillment of each in the creative advance for all concerned.

Griffin, presumably, needs no coeternal, nonrational Given to account for nondisciplinary evils, since on his view God does, and has always had to, deal with creatures whose limited self-determination He never creates outright. I have some difficulty with this aspect of panexperientialism, but, disregarding that, let me join forces with Griffin's view that God is the most unifying persistent source of creative advance and productive harmony. I agree also that God cannot (morally) overcome by power; He persuades in all the ways open to Him as He experiences in Himself the confluence of the agencies in the world.

(b) On this view it is understandable that aggregates of these partially self-determining (subhuman) agents might well resist God's own aims for them. On this panpsychistic view, therefore, nondisciplinary evils (again, like cyclones, cancer, and schizophrenia) are not traceable to a "drag," or nonrational Given, coeternal with God. They are to be traced finally to failures in God's persuasion of creatures He never created ab initio anyway.

As I see it, such an initial, coeternal situation leaves much to be desired theoretically. But stress must be placed on the fact that, in this view, without God's telic agency, there would not be the kind of world history, including the human, that we have. Hence, as Griffin puts it:

There still might be tension in God's experience, in the following sense: Through
love for the creatures God would empathize
with each of their individual desires for
fulfillment. Many of these desires would
not be compatible with each other and with
the good of the whole. Accordingly, God's
will and resulting influence would run
counter to many things which God in one
sense desired....But this type of tension
should not be seen as reflecting any imperfection in God's nature, since empathic
love for others should (at least by a
Christian) be regarded as a perfection, not
a flaw.

What, then, does Griffin substitute for what he
(in part wrongly) perceives as a passive, unwilled
element in God's experience--comparable to the
passive pole in human sense-experience that Brightman suggests? His basic contention, I take it,
is that any creative being would experience tension
once he limits himself to persuasion and not control
of all ranges of self-determining beings.

(c) This seems to be a very promising insight at
first. But should we not expect on this world-view
that, given the degree of order we do find in the
low-grade, self-determining beings at the "physical"
level, God's persuasion could have been more effective? I take it that the degree of self-determination
in the varieties of feeling-unities, since God re-
fuses to do anything but persuade, results in the
fact that an exceedingly simple order of momentary
self-existents do resist Him with very unfortunate
consequences (natural nondisciplinary evil). The
same considerations apply to the hideous, nondisci-

283

plinary damage affecting the organic level. For here, too, elementary self-determining beings can resist God's persuasion as He works, presumably, for more compossible ranges of value in the lives of animals and also of persons.

(d) I come, then, to my greatest difficulty. I assume that, on this view, God in His creativity resists, or does not encourage, the "trivialities" of becoming at any point in the history of His persuasive activity. Then why would such a God, whose own creative response is never simply limited by what this subhuman range of creatures can do, not be able to persuade such creatures to become more conforming to His purposes at "higher" levels of self-determination? Since God has, indeed, established the degree of dependable conformity we witness, why allow such trivialities of becoming to take their course in view of the risks involved at higher levels where the consequences are so horrendous? To account for this "failure," must we not return, I ask, to something within God (a nonrational Given) that prevents Him from doing what we would expect in view of the fact that, by persuasion, He has already been able to create the conditions for the higher forms of creativity we observe?

I would go farther: Does the panpsychist or panexperientialist himself not require a nonrational Given to explain why his persuasive God seems to have more irons in the fires of creativity than can effect the best of compossible co-creative worlds? Positively stated: Given the quality of beings to be persuaded at different levels in the hierarchical, interrelated orders (or, better, given the fact that so much is achieved by the governance of persuasion), could it be that the loving, persuading God is kept, by a coeternal Impediment within Him, from that quality and kind of persuasion (not power qua power) that would not allow nondisciplinary evil?

There are other issues (including the nature of personal identity) between panpsychism and idealistic, temporalistic personalism. In any case, I fail to see,

in the various forms of panpsychism, as I understand
them, how panpsychists themselves escape what they
regard as a drag-nonrational-Given. So I set this
general alternative aside and add several comments
that may clarify more completely the temporalistic,
theistic, personalistic view.

(e) To repeat, it would be a misguided interpretation of this idealistic view of Nature to think of
Nature itself as being the nonrational Given that
has so far been persuaded to take on the teleological
order we observe. The analogy of our sensory experience (that grounds our interpretation of Nature)
should not be allowed to mislead us at this point.
For the dysteleological events in Nature, like
cyclones, that do keep Nature as we know it from
being the adequately benign support of living beings
and of human creativity, are the products of the
Creator's struggle with the nonrational Given in His
 very nature. The Nature that human beings now interpret in certain ways is indeed, on its nonhuman
side, that universal energizing of God's will that
makes possible, as we have said, the systematic
support of living beings and of persons at their
respective levels of being-becoming.

    To resort to picture-thinking for a moment: a
cyclone is not one of those impediments of God-in-
Nature that are outside the complete control of God.
The nonrational Given, within the unity of God's own
complex nature (including His will-reason), is the
pole that (like our sensory and conative activities)
resists God's full-some expression of Himself in the
eligible ways that we call 'Nature.' Moreover, the
same nonrational Given in God's being-becoming is
recalcitrant to God's will as He creates the levels
of living beings. That recalcitrance is inferred by
us to be the source of what we judge to be the unnecessary suffering of living beings, owing both to
dysteleology in 'Nature' and to dysteleology in the
various levels of organic life.

    Again, the same nonrational Given is at the root
of human suffering caused by the kinds of survival

subhuman living beings require and that result in
the disease and suffering that are humanly unman-
ageable and destructive beyond reasonable justification. And the same nonrational Given it is whose
resistance keeps God from creating human psychic
life that can resist nondisciplinary mental ills.
The advance of cosmic teleology, toward persons
sensitive to their horizons of value, does not
bespeak a Sisyphus condemned forever to have his
efforts undone. But that advance does, in its vast,
orderly spread and tremendous, interrelated multi-
plicity of living forms, suggest a Creator reckoning
with, but never simply yielding to, whatever in His
being-becoming resists His creative striving in
favor of the qualities of value-possibilities that
would undergird the most co-creative of possible
worlds.

6. Reflective Overview

(a) In trying to interpret the presence of nondisciplinary evil in a world whose very existence, as
we know it, witnesses to prevailing teleological
order (moral goodness, and growing vision and achievement of value by persons), I referred first in
general terms to an Impediment to God's creative
goodness. I then availed myself of Brightman's term,
the nonrational Given, in order to relate the recalcitrant Impediment to a promising analogy within
personal experience. But I have tried to avoid
identifying, or confining, the nonrational in God's
experience with the realm of Nature, or the universal, orderly energizing of the divine Will.
For, as I have indicated, the evidence suggests a
recalcitrant, nonrational factor that is resistant
both to the best compossible order in the subhuman
living world and also in the psychic personal order.
"Nonrational given," then, is to be understood as
active energizing within the unity of the divine
(and of finite persons) that stands in contrast to,
in resistance to, but not completely alien to, personal activity as reasonable or reason-generated.

Once this is said, I know not how to characterize further the nonrational Given in God beyond saying that there is that in His being-becoming that resists, but is not completely alien to, either His nature or purposes.

(b) And this is the time to emphasize that, having focused on the obstacle to the best compossible creation, we must not for a moment overlook the supreme fact that the Creator is _as_ Creator neither chained to, nor riveted at every point in His creativity to the problems of resistance. Were that so, we should not be here to talk about this stupendous universe with its far-flung value-possibilities and with its myriad possible and actual accomplishments. The baby may be born to the mother in pain, and there may always be some sadness and sorrow in the relationship that develops, but the mother has plans for her offspring and dreams of mutually enriching ministrations.

Notes

1 Apart from discussion in ch. 3, my RCI expands the ideal suggested here, in the context of other psychoreligious considerations. See also Norman Pittenger: _God and Man in Process_, 1976.

2 J.B. Pratt, _Personal Realism_, 1937. In addition to notes referred to in ch. 11, see B.P. Bowne's works (especially _Philosophy of Theism_, 1887) and those of Teilhard de Chardin (especially _The Phenomenon of Man_, trans. Sir Julian Huxley, 1957).

3 See also B.P. Bowne, _Theory of Thought and Knowledge_, 1897; _Metaphysics_, 1882, rev. 1898; and _Personalism_, 1908. See also note 4 in ch. 9.

4 E.S. Brightman, _The Problem of God_, Abingdon, 1930, p. 113, italics added.

5 David R. Griffin, _God, Power, and Evil: A Process Theology_, Westminster Press, 1976, p. 248.

6 Ibid., p. 249.

7 Ibid. [The same page as the preceding note.]

Chapter Thirteen

RELIGIOUS EXPERIENCE IN CONTEXT

1. The Context of Religious Experience

In Chapter One we found sufficient ground for
deferring decision about even our most convincing
experiences, be they of Nature, man, or God, until
claims based upon them could be brought before the
court of reason as experiential coherence. Far-
reaching claims like the following by Seyyed
Hassein Nasr deserve scholarly respect; they are
conclusions from experiences of disciplined spirits
who assure us of a Realm accessible to persons who
become fully aware of what and who they are. "The
Ultimate Self in its inner infinitude is beyond all
determination and cosmic polarization....The human
self, as usually experienced by men who have become
separated from their archetypal reality, is itself
a faint echo upon the cosmic plane of the Spirit
and ultimately of the Self..."[1] But we have been
exploring alternative routes that by comparison are
homely and workaday; their greatest virtue is the
broader experientialism of a zigzag path hugging
the geography of an oftentimes troublesome terrain.
As I now return to the interpretation of religious
experience, my major concern is to avoid assuming
that such experiences add no knowledge or that they
may be treated as addenda to more reliable knowledge.[2] I shall suggest that they help in further
decisions about the suggestions now before us.

(a) We have been interpreting what we take to be
the teleological drift in a universe within which
persons--knowers, evaluators, actors--appear and
survive. We have persistently refused to separate
the person's quest for the life-good-to-live from
his search for truth-as-information; they are mutually dependent aspects of wholesome wisdom. The
person's values are subject to great caution in interpretation, but a lasting separation between value-
experience and their interpretations, and sensory

experiences and their interpretations, is simply not open to actor-knower-evaluators who live by the truths and the values that enter into their constructions of environments-within-Environment. Granted human obfuscations that sometimes arbitrarily block theoretical exploration, granted the elemental cruelty and pain along the route of natural and human development that forbid our regarding the historic process as an escalator, the actual values and the undergirding value-possibilities open to persons sustain our melioristic outlook.

(b) Indeed, the notion of a neutral world, impervious to all value-patterns realized by persons, is at best no more than a temporary stop on the way to a more challenging option. True, our 'will to believe' cannot opt for a cozier world in which cherished fancies and symbols gratify inexperienced, infantile wishes. Rather does it opt for a way of understanding the ventures of persons as they discover that their orchestrations of patterns of value, calling for increase in value-experience, are not their own doing alone. Hence, even if we could conceive of a universe as a rational Web of Being and yet neutral to persons and their ideals, experiential coherence itself would naturally raise a further question. Why should we have confidence in such a Web, if it is indeed neutral to the courage and honesty of persons who faithfully pursue the evidence, as they see it, to such a conclusion? Why, in the midst of such cosmic neutrality should we even trust our value-judgment that the good and evil in history are such in their proportions and relations that the Web must indeed be impervious to it?

(c) If, then, our "wider" temporalistic and personalistic teleology holds, we might approach our evaluation of the place of "the religious witness" in this argument by adapting a suggestive metaphor of Arthur Koestler's[3] as he tries to evaluate the difference that the religious experience can make to the human pilgrimage. Assume that we, like the captain of a ship, set out with sealed orders, not to be opened until we are on the high seas. On our way we often confront odds so great that we wonder what good can come from such a voyage on such seas. The time to open the sealed envelope arrives. The captain finds an invisible text. It will yield its secret to no chemical treatment, even though a word here and a phrase there become visible and then fade. Thus, the captain still has no assurance that he is complying with his instructions.

Nevertheless, does the fact that there are orders, even though they resist clear deciphering, not make his situation as a captain different from what it would be if, "thrown" on those seas, he had no sealed envelope and all-but-blind orders? If he had no cryptic orders at all, if only his acquired acumen in dealing with the ways of the seas seemed to be his sources and resources, he would still, I have argued, not be warranted in concluding that the seas are ultimately indifferent to his own deepest concerns.

To return to the underlying themes in the light of this image, I still submit that we know <u>with no finality</u> whether our most promising value-dimensions are the most reasonable interpretations of the Realm. However, there is ground for reason to grow courageous and to interpret the different signs, some more ambiguous than others, as clues to the Mystery whose detail must forever elude us. And the substantial hope that our lives are not afloat in an indifferent Universe permits us, nay encourages us, so to live that we become more sensitive to the Creator-Person and the ways in which He makes both His ways and our own lives more creative.

(d) At this point, bearing in mind the varieties of religious responses to the Realm, we cannot disregard the different levels of intellectual, moral, and aesthetic development that must lie behind the way in which "the invisible text" is interpreted. At the same time, we cannot be so critical of the bewildering variety of responses to the text that we can conclude, almost naively sometimes, that it is better to treat them simply as "psychological" symptoms outright. My contention is that, though we cannot accept these messages from on high as codes

with final authority, this way of 'direct' experiencing
deserves a fairer interpretation. For, on the whole,
it has inspired the experients to link the good and
the evil at different stages in their lives with the
conviction that they, far from being simply adrift,
are in the currents of an inner purpose in the Realm.
Accordingly, even without evaluating the "witness"
of the religious experts, the mystics, it becomes our
theoretico-ethical duty to review this basic conviction and to see whether our teleological, melioristic
conclusions need revision.

I add one last reminder to fill in the background
we need here. I reject the final neutrality of elec-
trons, agitated forever in ways partly discernible--
and this not solely because they are non-mental and,
therefore, impenetrable to any reasonable linkage with
the theorizing of persons. I reject it also because
that neutrality is neither self-evident nor the likely
outcome of the interest and activity of the very persons who, in every dimension of human experience, have
trusted 'invincible surmises' that kept them exploring
their imperatives, as hopeful links to realm(s) that
gripped their attention. On the other hand, one motive for my protest against one notion of perfection,
spelled out as 'infinite' goodness and power, is
opposition to the view of a God who so transcends
time, change, and the actual strivings of persons
that, in the end, the quality of His own experience
remains untouched and impervious to what persons
think and do.

The linkage I have found more forthcoming
theoretically is with a God whose creative, general
providence nourishes uniquely the lives of persons
who commit themselves to conscious seeking and
searching for ways in which they may contribute
to His total creativity. Such creativity, as I
have urged, means the "blessedness" of creative insecurity in co-creativity. Is this the ultimate
meaning of the goodness of God and man? My answer
so far is "yes." But I hope that a closer examination of issues involving religious experience, and
especially its cognitive and moral-ethical imports,

will also eventuate in a broader base for judging
trunk-and-branch theological systems the world over.

2.   The Life Good to Live--in Religious Context

(a)   Summarily, the doubt among earnest believers
and the disbelief among concerned humanists center
around the variety of religious experience and the
conflicting cognitive$_4$and ethical claims drawn from
religious experience.[4]   Often believers save the day
by holding that human standards of goodness cannot
be applied to the divine; while humanists fervently
contend that "the will of God" becomes an opiate of
the people that enslaves every dimension of the human
spirit in the name of divine mystery.   However, many
believers and disbelievers recognize, but weigh
differently, the fact that sincere belief has often
encouraged mortification of the flesh, resignation
to oppressive poverty, condemnation of psychological
deviation and illness as deserved depravity, and
censorship of much in the realm of art and in the
organization of family, social, and political life
that would improve the human situation now.   The
general condemnation of these evils and other forms
of obscurantism must stand despite the allowances
we should make for sheer ignorance and understandable
doubts about the impact of presumed reforms by
mortals vulnerable to the vanity of power.

(b)   But there would be no history of religion, if
this dismal version were the whole story.   I must
say that some critics of religion display percep-
tive powers much more acute in tracking down the
worst in religious history than in observing positive influences of religious dedication on cultural
values.   A scrupulous reading of the record shows
important credits as well as debits.   Without religious yearning and commitment--"Here am I, Lord,
send me!"--there is no adequate accounting for the
utter dedication of persons who, inspired by their
vision of God's will, have found no place, no animals,
and no persons, so unclean, so perverse, so cruel,

so unworthy that they have been unwilling to endure
every hardship and make every sacrifice in order to
alleviate suffering and to establish higher norms
of thought and action. Without such "seers," such
"saints," there is no understanding the growth of
human dignity. Much more needs to be done, of
course, but religious dedication will continue to
contribute its share. Men have always built, or
sculpted, or painted, or danced best for their God--
and this is true even when the God is 'unknown' or
has become the art itself.

The religious songs and music that are human
ways of coping both with the humdrum and misery of
life, as well as human ways of symbolizing the sense
of mystery and of expressing hungers and hopes that
will not die--these, not "arguments" for religion,
should be thrown into a fair-minded critic's scale.
The birth of a child, the confirmation of the individual's own promise at adolescence, the glad acceptance of solemn responsibilities for sharing in
the continuation of the human family, these are
"dates" in any spiritual calendar. Again, the deep-
ening awareness of dependence on powers beyond human
control is so often accompanied by a "miraculous"
renewal of hope, and of trust in one's capacity for
self-discipline. Is it surprising that all these
fill mind and heart with awe? It is impossible to
exaggerate the ways in which "the mystery of things"
has fired rich imagination, powers not to be dis-
sipated like so much smoke by the winds of skepticism.

Moreover, persons stand in awe of even themselves
and what can happen to them, deserved and undeserved,
during their pilgrimage on earth. Responsible for
evil and also beset by evil, they, nevertheless, try
to express appropriately their sense that they do
not deserve either a certain quality of joy or of
sorrow that overtakes them on their journey. "What
is man, that thou art mindful of him?" cries the
psalmist in grateful awe, though, at another time,
Shakespeare's Gloucester will bitterly propose that
we are "as flies to wanton gods; they kill us for
their sport." Such vivid moments of 'disclosure'
come to believers and unbelievers alike.

On the whole, then, if we make allowance for
stages of development and symbolic modes of expression that often are "the realities themselves" to
the experients, such vivid moments bring to believers convictions of epiphany, standpoints from
which it becomes their duty to see themselves in
some native relation to mother-earth and far-flung
skies. And with the privilege goes a sense of responsibility. Even bitter denial gains its pathos
in the very rejection of a God who "ought to be."

(c) I have actually been approaching my thesis:
it is one thing to call in question the cognitive
and evaluative _independence_ of religious experience,
another to separate the whole-seeking religious
dimension from the other dimensions. Though we
may try to enthrone in splendor of its own any
dimension of our being-becoming from any other, as
"lived-through" the religious response heightened
by 'the holy' or 'the sacred' grows from humble
roots in so many nooks and crannies of experience.
No, basically, I am not referring to "an" experience
that is simply "added" to our other streams of
thought and value. It is this widespread embedded-
ness of religious response that does not make
easier the task of evaluating those more _specific_
knowledge-claims about our relation to Nature and
God that so persistently emerge even from religious
experiences presumably 'ineffable' and 'unutterable.'

Thus, as I ask _now_ what religious experience
adds distinctively, I do so in the context of a
conception of the good that does not _depend_ upon
any religious norm as such, either of truth, goodness,
or holiness. However, I can assert now with greater
assurance that persons, whom we have found to be
supported in the range of their values by the Realm,
may trust their conviction of "direct union" with
the Realm that they refer to as holy _but_ should interpret it in relation to--not dictation to--the
other dimensions in the life good to live.

3. The Cognitive Import of Religious Experience

Agreeing with William James that religious experience is not as much married to any particular metaphysics or theology, I propose to set out a basic conclusion, and then assemble the major reasons for it.

(a) The claim of religious experience almost universally is that the world, though often defined in relation to our senses and to our nonreligious values alone, is in fact related to an Ultimate (Realm) whose activity is not confined to "the world." Emphatically, in religious response the experient is aware of a Presence--not necessarily <u>an</u> entity among others--that is Other than himself and all-important to him, even though he cannot articulate in any precise, and certainly in no final, way what that importance is.

I would not expect any experient to be satisfied with this abstract formulation of his awareness of the all-important Other. But this formulation allows him and others to articulate, at particular phases and stages of life, the meaning of this Presence to their ongoing experience. It is for this reason[5] that I borrow and adapt William James's term, '<u>More</u>,' to emphasize that the experiences of the holy are unique, irreducible root-responses that enlarge "the world." Indeed, they underlie the experient's realization that all else he undergoes and knows needs to be seen within the context of this penetrating 'revelation.'

(b) The experience of 'More,' I am affirming, inspires and evokes a new way of regarding all there is in the experient's way of thinking of himself and his environment(s). Some readers may object to "inspires and evokes" for fear that this way of speaking does not grasp the 'union' of experient and 'More.' I shall need to return to this point. What I wish to emphasize first is that the experient, be he Everyman or Mystic, does not experience 'More' in abstraction from the stage of affective-conative, intellectual, moral, and aesthetic development at the time that he is "overcome," "grasped," "renewed," or "liberated" by the experience.

Throughout I have stressed that a knower-evaluator-actor does not simply mirror his ambient; and I still see no reason for supposing that the person's experience of the holy at any stage in his development mirrors (the) 'More.' Accordingly, we need to be more appreciative of, and interpret more adequately, the varieties of description-interpretation of 'the One' in human history and in the experience of individuals. The experients themselves witness that their unique response forever goes a-begging for articulation; the more self-critical realize that over-awing experience is embedded in their own stage of spiritual development.

Let me restate this first suggestion. A fair-minded survey of the total, varied, and developmental experience of the race will find good reason to trust as valid the pervasive conviction that arises in and from the experience of the holy. It is the conviction of 'More,' within and beyond persons, a conviction that would not have the awesome quality it has were its roots only in the experient and his past learning. The experience is often so challenging that in its light all else he values loses its finality. If we can hold to this root-experience and its "intrinsic" conviction, we can then go on to judge which is the more reasonable of the many accounts of what that 'More' is, and what Its import ought to be. And we can afford to review the witness of the mystics, or of any "messengers" of God who proclaim that their experience of God itself warrants this or that revelation no matter what other meanings and values make up "established" values and horizons.

(c) The second suggestion builds upon the first. We must constantly remind ourselves that the experience of the holy comes into a life not as "an" addition, as though it were some spice that must be mixed with what is already in ferment. It comes to the person who is engaged in living on various fronts.

297

He now sees himself and his experience suffused by the More that transports him and all else; his experience-interpretation of himself _as he is_--in gladness, in sorrow, in frustration, in hope--is moved to another qualitative dimension that calls for revaluing priorities and meanings. From such contexts he emerges with a sense that all is new, without being simply novel. What he is, believes, values, he is now convinced is grounded in that More at once within and yet beyond his grasp, at once inspiring and challenging. It has always been _there_, but awaiting his appropriate response to Its varied dimensions of creativity.

It is _in this religious situation_ that the problem of interpretation, or of the specific cognitive value, of religious experience now arises. This kind of renewing experience resists reduction to other qualities and values. Nevertheless, despite the experient's "psychological certitude," the nature of the connection between the experient, "his worlds," and the More is open to multiple interpretations. We can understand the hesitancy to break the momentum, to question the union, lest one overreach himself and be dislodged. But, as we have seen, the change and growth in the individual's responses require the inclusion of his total thought, valuing, and action in any assessment of its scope. Such loyalty will be rewarded also by the aid it provides for those who "share" his stance _up to a point_ short of his own, more confident commitment.

(d) It is here that the impact of much in the foregoing argument makes itself felt. If I am at all correct, this account of religious experience as description-interpretation of the More, confirms our basic affirmation _via_ cosmo-teleological-ethical argument, that man and his values are bound up with, tied to, the nature of the Realm or Environment. Throughout I have resisted claims, so often "grounded' in psychological certitude, that cognitive conclusions about man, Nature, and the Realm are _independently true_. The same judgment about direct religious _cognition_ as _independently_ _true_ must stand. This does

not entail skepticism, but only the conclusion that
what the nature of man's linkage is with the Ultimate
cannot be accepted without further examination, despite
the protestations of even those religious witnesses
that we find more attractive and compelling.

I, myself, am more than impressed by those who articulate their experience, as does Rudolf Otto, in terms
of the kind of holy expressed as numinous in the
quality of the experient's 'absolute dependence.'
But, appealing as it sometimes is, I finally turn
away from any interpretation of the ec-static holy
as 'union' with the Unconditioned that, as I see it,
ultimately loses the individuality and freedom of
the person, or establishes a hierarchy of values in
which all other dimensions of value are subject to
claims made in the name of such union. My past experience leads me to repeat that I am rejecting the
claim to the strict cognitive independence, to the
strict evidential autonomy, and not to the importance
of religious experience in more adequately interpreting any of the characteristics of the Realm, or
the More, or God, or the One.

(e) However, having reached this point in an argument seeking coherence on a comprehensive basis, I
must equally emphasize another theme. Granting that
the experience of the holy involves different needs
and abilities in the matrix of lives seeking further
value and meaning, the fundamental import of religious experience fits reasonably into the drift
of other evidence for belief in the conservation
and increase of value.

I can now, for example, see at least two affirmations, buried in larger psychological certitudes, that may not be ignored or simplistically
impugned. First, all else man is and knows and hopes
is related to the More that is already there and "at
work" in all of his undergoings. And the More can
be increasingly effective in persons who, once they
become aware of Presence, indeed see all things new.
I can suggest with reasonable confidence and trust
that the experience of the holy, with its varied

imports for the affective-conative, moral, and aesthetic phases of persons' experience, with its manifold, theoretical suggestions to the experients, becomes a source for further quality in value-creation. Second, and at the same time, we must remember that persons who experience the holy are in this respect also different in their ability to grow, and thus may be expected to develop different levels of meaning and value, given their gripping religious experience, as they seek to express the meaning of the More. We should expect the very variety that confronts us in religious witness and creed. And we experience anew the imperative to <u>understand contexts</u> as we insist also that difficult, "uprooting" changes may be in order, and that our value-appreciation, actions, and "invincible surmises" move toward a tensive but more creative harmony.

(f) So much more should be added that I must leave unsaid. But I will reaffirm my objection, in the light of our inquiry into the grounds and interpretation of relevant evidence, against dismissing or minimizing traces of the roots of religious experience in the <u>wholistic cognitive matrix</u> of the believer's life. The claim that religious experience and appreciating must be, or more probably is, illusory is plausible only when (on grounds that need much more explicit articulation and defense) it is assumed that intellectual strivings, ideals, and achievements must remain extrinsic to the drift of the ec-static experiences of persons.

On the other hand, the protest of some believers against "reason" in the area of religious experience turns out invariably to be, in essence, like the protest against reason in the areas of sensory, moral, and aesthetic experience. When reason-as-logic imposes its norms, as if logic could by itself yield what <u>must be there</u> without confronting the structure-and-content of the experiences being interpreted, believers may rightly rebel against this intellectual pontificating. But by now we should realize that reason's weaving of experiences uses logical rules as an indispensable tool while the whole person

seeks truth. For the experience of logic is one
thing, and a so-called logic of experience another.
Reason needs and seeks a faith that often outruns
evidence at hand, but in so doing it neither can
dismiss logic nor distrust the evidence. At the
same time, faith, grounded in reason, is courageous
and not merely prudential; it leads the person to
plan further experience, further thought, and action
that spurns self-righteousness.

(g) All the more, then, must we realize that theoretical and creedal formulation of religious experience
as such, or aesthetic principles, styles, and rituals
as such, are no direct and independent deliverances
of "authentic" ethical values. But neither are they
external, cultural additions with no inspiration in
the varied dimensions of our human outreach, however inarticulate they often may be. To repeat an
earlier figure, the creeds, rules, rituals, are
branches that manifest in an 'objective' form the
root and trunk in our given personal-institutional-
social history. We must be ready to prune them when
such branches threaten the very life of the tree.
But here, too, we must also be ready to admit that
variety and proliferation themselves witness to some
rich sources of interaction in the common soil between ourselves and the More.

(h) We may remind ourselves all the more that we are
in a realm where the humdrum "practicalities" of
life are seen as products of our own "necessities."
These "practicalities" can always stand being re-
viewed in terms of possibilities that are latent in
other dimensions of our experience. To use word-
balloons that, fortunately, have not been deflated
yet: There is an aesthetic grandeur about so much that
the senses yield, a nobility in moral demands, a
sublimity in aesthetic expression. Nevertheless,
each of these is not so cut away from our other feelings, desires, and emotions that we cannot recognize
the distinctive way in which each enhances particular, if often neglected, dimensions of experience.
Take now the experience of the holy that, if I may
put it thus, can yield a "wholly-experience." Such

301

an experience at once makes everything else seem more meaningful; yet it must be hospitable to, without being "indulgent" of, meanings and values that seem intrinsic to other dimensions. It is along this path that I suggest we approach the balancing-off-effect of religious experience. Such "balance" must be live, alert, and tense to the imbalance of growth that gives it its <u>raison d'être</u> and its grace.

Perhaps a homely illustration can suggest, negatively, what makes the elusive, yet so eloquent, religious difference in human existence.

Two persons, having built their marriage and family and home, come to the point where, for whatever reason, their loving commitment to each other has died. The "furniture" of their lives is still there with its homely associations, and the separated partners remain humane and decent to each other, wishing that "separation" were not the actuality. But they know that something that had inspired their communion is gone. Their marriage and family, once a cathedral serving many functions, is no longer a place, a way of worshiping what would keep them "together," for better, for worse. A student, reflecting on the faith he had given up, said bitterly: "I'm just mad because I don't believe in God any more!"

How can this be put positively? He who sees a work of art, another person, not as simply "there" but as expressive of an overwhelming, over-awing, over-arching Concern, now sees him every day anew; and the newness is not an external addition but a renewal by virtue of the fact that, so to say, the work of art and the person are the labor of care by Another. When persons see the starry heavens above and the moral law within, in all their grandeur, nobility, and sublimity, both for what they are and also as partial expressions of a Realm to which their own responses give forth symbols of patient, creative Purpose--it is then that persons may well have confidence that their "sense of belonging" deserves their trust. However, this line of interpretation suggests a view that would not satisfy some experients of religious 'union.'

4. A Teleological Interpretation of Religious Union

(a) We return, then, to the watershed question:
What interpretation of 'union' is more reasonable?
We remind ourselves that to be "one with God" does
not have the same meaning even for those mystics who
speak of being 'truly united' with God. Teilhard
de Chardin thinks the aspiration of all mystics is
"to be united (that is, to become the other) while
remaining oneself."[6] In union the experient would
now seem not to be the Divine in the way in which the
Divine itself is. But there is no doubt that in
contrast to this view, the monistic or absolutistic
interpretation of mystical experience intends a
quality of togetherness that surrenders self, loses
self, in the blissful serenity of 'oneness' with the
One.

At this point, I have sided with the dominant
theistic tradition[7] and rejected the monistic interpretation of union, for I am convinced that the
monistic interpretation ultimately cannot consistently
affirm the individuality and free-willed autonomy that
is so essential to the being-becoming of a person.
But I must interpret Teilhard's "remaining oneself"
and "one with God" in accordance with the temporalistic, teleological view of God and man. Accordingly,
the experience of 'union' supports and sustains the
person's more deliberate effort to e-laborate and
liberate, so to speak, value-potentials that express
his being-becoming, both as a co-responsible member
of an actual "social" community and also as cen-
tering his will on bringing into being the universal
(not homogenous) community more fully sensitive to
God's will. As has been suggested, the person worships not an Absolute, Unchanging Unity. The person's
worship of God is his uniting himself in a more comprehensive, co-creative effort, one in which God can
all the more share His creativity with those who commit themselves to purposeful fellowship with Him in
the conserving and increasing of as much compossible
values as possible.

(b) This view of worship is in sharp contrast to a

very appealing view of Perfection and the worshipful.
The following passage, excerpted with permission, is
taken from a lecture on "The Myths of Plato" by John N.
Findlay, delivered to the Boston University Institute
for Philosophy of Religion in November 1977.

> I react worshipfully to something which is
>
> not an instance of perfection but Perfection
>
> itself, which embraces in itself all species
>
> of perfection and possible perfection com-
>
> pletely, and which in something analogous
>
> to   envious kindness has generated myself
>
> and the other imperfect beings around us....
>
> I am glad to think that my Creator transcends
>
> finite personality as He or It likewise
>
> transcends every form of finite thinghood.

In contrast to my respected colleague's vision,
I have been "glad to think" that the imperfect person
is "something analogous to" the Creator-Person, whose
transcendence cannot lose its links with, or remain
unaffected by, the imperfections of the "generated
world." Hence, I have eschewed the idea of a Perfection, an Absolute that transcends every form of
finitude, and have gone so far as to urge that we
may call God perfect in a sense that includes creativity in "kindness" that transforms the meaning of
"embracing" perfection. I have also submitted that
the being-becoming Creator "evokes" worship as He
expends His creativity--a creative insecurity at
that--in making possible, and enhancing at every op-
portunity, the fellowship of co-creators. Further
still, I have referred to His creativity as all the
more awe-inspiring because it involves a concrete
struggle with a nonrational Given in Himself.

Therefore, I say: "I react worshipfully to a
Creator whose very being it is so to create that
others, too, may enter into the dramatic goodness
of creativity that accepts but never condones needless forms of suffering. I can worship Him Who for-

ever stands ready to accept the small offering of
creativity in my life which He ultimately, and often
proximately, has made possible. I worship the forgiveness that is merciful, long-suffering creativity; I
worship the love without which power never can do anything lastingly."

(c) I continue an earlier theme when I add that in
religious experience of a "holy-wholly," the accent
is ultimately not on a 'deliverance' or on a 'message'
as such. Whatever the experience of 'the holy' as
transforming and creative, it is both a settling and
unsettling way of experiencing: "I am at home," and,
"It's not the home I know." Hence, I do not use
the word "creative" in a specific, honorific sense,
since the particular form of creativity will depend
on the quality and preparedness of the person experiencing and also on the quality of the worshiper's
total experience subsequent to his undergoing the
holy. The quality of creativity is related to the
person's initial and continuing transaction.

All the more would I stress that, even when the
experient is aware of the chasm between his own
quality and achievement and the More, even when he
is aware that he is "undone," "sick," "unclean,"
"sinful," "estranged," the very "heightening" in
such experiences of the More suggests a kind of
"victory" that yields hope of what he can still be
and become. There is an intimation that all is not
lost, that there are resources "available," "at hand,"
that will help him "right" himself. Here we must not
forget those gratifying experiences that we may liken
to pressing with one's burdens against a door and
finding that somebody on the other side is opening
it too. How the worshiper will express all this
cognitively, including theologically, remains his
problem, even as there also remains the problem of
how to act in reverent gratitude.

(d) Once more, then, we remind ourselves that the
"trunk" experiences can "grow" into branches that
flower or bear fruit (as minor and major religious
traditions) evident in terms of the symbolic ex-

pressions that are most "telling" for the experients.
I find especially meaningful Jesus' attempt to convey
his conviction about the relation of God to man in
the parable of the Prodigal Son. As I try to interpret this parable, I ask myself: Why does this freely
dissolute, repentant son, aware that he has wasted
his substance, decide to return to his father? Would
he have done so if he had thought that condemnation
and punishment were the last word? I doubt it.
Having returned, he finds a welcoming, concerned
father. But home is not "home, sweet home," as his
censorious brother, who feels ill-treated, makes
evident.

On the other hand, the father's reception is
loving but not sentimental. His forgiveness is not
tantamount to saying: "It does not matter that you
wasted your substance." Out of the depth of his
sorrow and joy, of his acute concern for both brothers,
he finally turns to the discontented brother and says:
"He who was dead is now alive!" I suggest that in
the father's experience there was a unique quality
of rejoicing but no unsullied happiness. Both sons
have fallen short, and both have new relationships
to work out with each other and with their father.
He relates himself to each son at the level each can
be dealt with at this point. Meanwhile, he lives in
the blessedness of a creative insecurity, hoping
against hope that each brother in his freedom will
join in a higher level of creative insecurity, in a
higher level of responsive-responsible community.
It is such a Father who keeps worship and action
most creative.

5. The Goodness of God and Religious Experience:
    Two Theistic Views

(a) When one explains nondisciplinary evil by reference to the nonrational Given, as I have, it is
tempting to refer all unusual hardship in human experience to the nonrational Given and to neglect
the more fundamental theme that we have been exploring.

306

So I must leave no doubt about the underlying fact without which I could not have even attempted a book entitled The Goodness of God.

Nondisciplinary evil is irreducible evil--I cannot paper over the difference it makes to experience and theory. But were it the final fact about persons-in-their-universe, there would be no telos, no structure of value, to give meaning to any evil.

If nondisciplinary evil, if the recalcitrant factor within the Creator-Person had independent agency, I should not know what power to assign it. "Recalcitrance," I repeat, is to be defined within a larger context of telic-unity: it is no coeternal lump-Given, no dissociated part of God that can thrive on its own accomplishments. Nor must it be taken to mean "an actively defiant, rebellious tendency," as S. Paul Schilling,[8] guided by linguistic meaning, does. Then it would indeed have the "dualistic overtones" I explicitly reject as I define the kind of unity and the quality that constitutes God the Creator He is.

My underlying theme is that within the Creator's experience, we must recognize more than "peace without conflict," or "triumph without some sorrow." There is also the creative agony in ecstasy. By referring to God's goodness as "tragic," I repeat, I point to no "fatal flaw"; but rather to God's unflinching creative insecurity as He labors to implement His own comprehensive purposes.

The final fact, then, about God, Nature, and persons is a comprehensive purpose, the actualization of which is the expression of God's will--not for the sake of "peace," "security," "success"--wherever the creative insecurity involved in worthwhile creation is "the cost." God, whatever else, persons, whatever else, do, and can, create the kind of structures and systems that we have seen to be the orderly groundwork for sustaining the horizons of value that are monuments to persons' creativity in the Creator-Person's realm.

307

Much in this central affirmation of the goodness and power of God articulates the essence of classical theism. It is fitting to reemphasize what I take to be the considerations that seem to the classical theist strong enough to justify his unwillingness to accept any recalcitrant factor in God other than "recalcitrance" intrinsic to free-will. For we must be sensitive to his most moving evidence, that of heroes of a faith who suffer agonies but can remain steadfast. He argues that such power over evil can derive only from belief that strength to endure comes from the "perfection" of his God.

(b) Who, indeed, can set aside the ineluctable witness of those who have undergone suffering beyond anything we could imagine endurable--evil that they in no way deserved, evil that, even if deserved, could bear no reasonable relation to the evil committed? In every age there stands before us that great host who creatively confronted monstrous, terrifying agonies that scarred and maimed the body but never conquered the spirit. It is these witnesses who defy us to make any sense at all of the kinds of bodily, psychological, and spiritual evils that they overcame--"not by our power alone," they say. Their victory was of the spirit, not of the flesh. They struggled unyieldingly and relentlessly, without shame or pride, even as they fell before the inevitable. Who can view such awe-inspiring actions, "death is not dying," without asking, "What is man? What is the source of the power that must make us mindful of Him in this universe?" All the more, then, must I respond to the question: Does not such self-creation in sacrificial love suggest in its very extreme that the good, despite all appearances, does reign in a perfect (all-powerful) God?

I shall not here retreat from my contention earlier that character is the moral crucible in which the person himself creates ex nihilo--without neglecting the fact that much in the unfinished symphony of values influences and is influenced by factors beyond himself. To choose, to shape and

308

reshape, I have suggested, never occurs in a vacuum; and the choosing person will live in the ethical structure that at once confines and liberates him as he moves from choice to choice.

In advancing this thesis of "self-creation," I would hope to strengthen the classical theist's faith in the 'redeeming power of evil' that handicaps, but does not cripple, human creativity. For, as I see it, there is a value-orientation, a life style, that frees one for the qualities and dispositions that quarantine evil and inspire the good. An interesting comment comes from an unlikely source, a recent study of the horrors undergone by human beings in concentration camps. In The Survivor, 1976, Terence Des Près, analyzing the anatomy of life in death camps, observes that the persons who seemed most able to survive were those who concerned themselves with helping others. They liberated themselves from themselves, to "radical selfhood."

No "happiness" in this value-orientation; rather the "blessedness" of those who live at the level of creativity that never cries out in self-defense alone, as they witness and undergo unforgettable horror. If there are indeed 'eternal' moments, among them we must include the kind issuing from this special sort of creativity that liberates rooted selfhood.

(c) Pressing such considerations, all the more can I see why the classical theists find in them the clue that must dominate our thinking about persons and God. The loving power of God, the power that knows nothing but short-range and long-range, self-imposed limitations--this power it is that rules the world and is at the heart of saving-and-serving religion. No wonder is it that classical theists declare that "my" conception of the nonrational Given in God destroys the foundation on which persons build their lives. That foundation is not simply the love that will not let them go, but the love that will finally overcome.

Accordingly, one must admit the force of the warning in a passage from the writings of a long-time colleague and friend, L. Harold De Wolf.[9]

> It is doubtful that it [belief in a finite-infinite God] would encourage the kind of absolute dependence or unconditional trust in the holy God which we have found--along with Augustine, Schleiermacher, Kierkegaard, Rudolf Otto and other penetrating observers-- to be characteristic of religious experience at its more profound and creative levels. Not only great Christians of famous names, but also millions of humble believers with great faith, have reached their depths of assurance and sense of the divine presence __precisely__ when they have accepted suffering or loss of God's holy will. The shrug of the shoulders which would follow logically from belief that God shares our partially ineffective struggle with evil He cannot prevent may be admirably courageous....[But] if Jesus had supposed that the Father could not save him from the cross...he would not have had to view it as the Father's will. If Paul had doubted that whatever pain and sorrow occurred were willed or permitted by God, he would not have found the cross at first a stumbling block and then a means of salvation. How much of the Bible would have been written if evil had been explained by

the ancient Hebrews in the finitistic
manner?

(d) In this last section I have gladly joined in
pointing to peaks of moral-spiritual creativity in
the lives of persons as basic data in our appraisal
of goodness in man and--I would insist--in God.
But De Wolf is asking us to affirm that such peaks
of moral-spiritual creativity could not have been
attained on the basis of the particular version of
creative insecurity I have been advancing. If, he
presses, nondisciplinary evil is the consequence of
God's inability to overcome recalcitrance in His
own nature, if nowhere in the universe is there final
relief from this partly uncertain struggle, then, he
is convinced, moral and spiritual creativity and the
assurance of the ultimacy of good over evil is un-
dermined. For once persons realize that there are
evils that never contribute to any good in human
or divine history, the hope central to religious
creativity loses its substance. As I have said,
it would be folly to minimize the possible impact of
those contentions against "my" particular view.

(e) We are again at a watershed of interpretation,
the more so because the interpretation of evil within
the religious experience is seriously divided. Be
it noted that great traditions, stressing the importance of solving the problem of evil by real-iza-
tion, by rising in spirit to the One, or losing self-
centeredness of every form, also emphasize that the
experient, returning to "self," does have new power
to overcome temptations of flesh and spirit. I cannot forget that the earnest religious seeker struggles
not only "morally" but that he also faces the spiritual
struggle inherent in his being faithful to the verities
of his religious experience and growth. Again, I also
gladly note a more recent emphasis (whatever the exact formulation), namely, the underlying moral-religious
confidence among most process philosophers as inspired by A. N. Whitehead's "image" of God, "the tender
case that nothing be lost,"--an almost succeeding sentence being, "A tenderness which loses nothing that
can be saved."[10]

311

In such inspired company, I remind myself of the whole drift of the analysis of value-experience advanced above. In that context, I dare to wonder whether the spiritual psychology to which De Wolf points really has grasped the dynamics of forgiving love. All theists, especially in the Judeo-Christian tradition, do hold that the experience of creative love, a love conserving and increasing value, is the spiritual law of Reality, is the most creative factor in the lives of all persons. But usually "creative love" means: rooted in the conviction of ultimate victory, <u>in the sense in which a loving, omnipotent God would assure such victory</u>.

(f) One can fall, I suggest, into the habit of attributing motives to actions that are morally more worthy and attractive than the alleged motives. Many have suffered heroically without faith in God or His omnipotence. Thinkers who lay stress on such evidence suggest that the motives of such sufferers are morally purer than those of believers, for they love the good because it is good, or they love love for love's sake, or they love humanity for its own sake. They give themselves without assurance of the reward that is an ultimate victory guaranteed.

The fact also seems to be, in the religious situation of our time, that such motives appeal to many as being more purely religious. It is such souls that reject classical theism because they think its proponents, while discussing the "problem" of evil in the light of "redeeming" experiences, still do not give deserved attention to the failures even of the most creative as they face what I have called nondisciplinary evil. Such spirits might well be attracted to a faith in God creative at times in an insecurity and agony that results from the failure of His "persuading," and find that such a view is in actuality closer to their moral practice and worship.

May it not be that the final temptation to be overcome by the classical theist himself is <u>the</u> temptation to place God's omnipotence (ultimate

312

assurance of victory) above God's suffering love?
It may be that the kind of creative insecurity we
have been affirming as ultimate is itself intrinsic
to the quality of victory that is the final lure of
the moral-religious person.

6. Reflective Overview

At this point it is my appeal to the criterion
of truth as growing, experiential coherence that
carries the day for me. For I reject not the appeal
to creative moral-religious heroism but only to one,
historic interpretation. For all the respect it deserves, it still does not allow experience as a whole
to be knitted together. This "absolutistic" view of
religious union, together with the absolutistic view
of perfection, if they are taken as final interpretations, distort individuality, freedom, being-becoming
as we persons undergo them; they do not render our
experience of moral-spiritual creativity adequately.

And here, of course, is where each of us must
fall back on his best reflective judgment about
value, and the value of creativity[11] in particular.
There is much talk about the importance of creativity,
but I confess that what seems to me never to be
faced squarely is that <u>to be creative is to be insecure, be it in God or persons</u>. As we have seen,
for the finite being insecurity is always rooted
in his contingency, be he creative or not. The
problem for the finite person, nevertheless, is to
decide whether the way to overcome insecurity is to
find security or to seek such creativity that intrinsically invites significant insecurity.

The contention that underlies all that has been
written in this book is that, for persons at least,
the great seduction is to think that we can escape
from insecurity to security as the full-some ideal
of completion. However, since 'creativity' can become a false idol, especially when it tends to take
on certain honorific (usually more "elite" hedon-

istic) connotations, I have tried to keep the phrase
'creative insecurity' qualitatively defined. I have
articulated it as an (unfinished) symphony of values
that requires constant (insecure) orchestration in
individual and social life. I have also pointed to
the qualitative difference that such creativity makes
to persons as they discriminate and relate their own
value-experience and ideals responsively and responsibly to the qualitative ventures of others, including God. In so doing they cannot escape that
quality-in-risk, that creative insecurity, which
makes them sensitive to what it means to be a being-
becoming person in this kind of universe.

But to this value-judgment, itself not necessarily dependent on belief in God, we must add the
fact of the variety of outreaching religious experience and the tendency to misconstrue its impact.
There is a unique, individual difference that is always qualified by the kind of discipline the individual
himself undertakes in response to God's world, God's
children, and to God for Himself. A person knows
not what the outcome of his religious pilgrimage
will be; his hope is his hope; in that hope, peculiarly his, he finds creative insecurity even at
his moments of profound "security." That hope,
respected opponents will say, is for the day when
God's final aim will be accomplished "somehow."
But, do we need to be sure of a final victory in
order to fight well? And is that final victory the
final test of love? Or, is it that in discovering
dimensions of our own responsiveness and responsibility we are sustained by the More that, in some
small measure, is enriched in the quality of His
being by our creative growth?

Such creative insecurity, I submit, often
strengthens a person beyond expectation. Itself a
joint-product, it brings with it not only the willingness and the power to overcome obstacles, but also
to see one's own struggle among men, and along with
God, as indeed a redeeming and renewing vision. I
am affirming that, whatever else, this quality of creative insecurity is characteristic of much vital religion. And, if so, we find confirmation and devel-

314

opment within the religious dimension of our lives
for what we have found in other dimensions of our
being-becoming. Religion is joining one's creative
insecurity to God's as a self-conscious discipline
and celebration.

Perhaps I may make a final comment relevant to
those persons who know creative insecurity but can
find neither in reason nor religious experience what
I have been pointing to. Such creative insecurity
as I have proposed is no flight from insecurity, no
return to the comfort of the womb; no more is it a
"raging" or a "serene" acceptance of the ultimate
indifference of the universe. Indeed, if anything,
such religion has added acceptance of responsibility
for creativity--not only with man but with God. It
is part of a comprehensive plan in which persons must
choose their share in cosmic-social creative insecurity. It has been, and can be, a sobering and inspiring conviction that in fulfilling one's own life
one is neither wandering in a vacuum of value nor
destroying opportunities for self and others need-
lessly. It has been, and can be, even more sobering
and inspiring to believe that one's own total creative
response links in with that of the Creator Who, in
part, also realizes Himself in creative insecurity.

Notes

1   Nasr, Seyyed Hassein, pp. 6-7 of a paper "Self-
Awareness and Ultimate Selfhood," delivered at
International Society for Metaphysics, New York, 1977.
See also his An Introduction to Cosmological Doctrines,
Cambridge University Press, 1974.

2   In addition to relevant references in ch. 1, such
as R. Otto, ION, see John E. Smith's "Religious Experience" in Encyclopedia Britannica, 1974, as well
as his Experience and God, Yale University Press,
1968, for comprehensive contrasting interpretations.
My "Psychological Interpretation of Religious Experience," in Research in Religious Development:

A Comprehensive Handbook, ed. Merton P. Strommen, Hawthorne Books, 1968, reviews basic issues in dominant psychological accounts. Also, for contrasting, suggestive accounts, see Louis Dupré: The Other Dimension: A Search for Meanings of Religious Attitudes, Doubleday, 1962, and Transcendent Selfhood, Seabury Press, 1976; and Raymond Van Over, Chinese Mystics, Harper, 1973.

3 I owe this reference to W.T. Stace, The Teachings of the Mystics, p. 233; its original is in the second volume of Arthur Koestler's autobiography, Arrow in Blue, Macmillan, 1977; I have made use of this passage in a similar connection in Is God For Real?, Thomas Nelson, 1971.

4 While I am basically influenced by F.R. Tennant's (see Bertocci, EAG, and PGI), and by Brightman's views of the essentially noncognitive value of religious experience, I must accept responsibility for the conception as here presented. The reader would do well to read the essays of John Lavely, "Faith and Knowledge: Is the Ineffable Intelligible?," and John Findlay, "The Rationality of Mysticism," in Howie and Buford, CSPI. See also H.D. Lewis, Our Experience of God (OEG), and the essays in Mysticism and Philosophical Analysis, ed. Steven T. Katz, Oxford University Press, 1978.

5 See W. James, VRE, Collier-Crowell, 1961, pp. 393-397. From the varied examinations of religious symbolism, apart from works already suggested, I call attention to the sensitive writings of Roger Hazelton, (see his Ascending Flame, Descending Dove [An Essay on Creative Transcendence]). See also Harry S. Broudy, Enlightened Cherishing: An Essay on Aesthetic Education, 1972; David Martin, Art and Religious Experience, Buckness University Press, 1972; Paul Ricoeur, The Symbolism of Evil, Harper and Row, 1954; and for even broader significance, the work of Michael Polanyi, Personal Knowledge, Univ. of Chicago Press, 1958; and G. Van der Leeuw, Sacred and Profane in The Holy in Art, Holt, Rinehart, Winston, 1963, let alone the

works of Nicolai Berdyaev, such as _Spirit and Reality_;
The Meaning of Creative Art, 1955; and _The Divine
and the Human_, 1961; Amos N. Wilder, _Theology and
Religious Imagination_, Fortress Press, 1976.

6 Teilhard de Chardin, _The Divine Milieu_, Harper
and Row, 1968, rev., p. 116.

7 See Langdon Gilkey, _Maker of Heaven and Earth_,
Doubleday, 1959, and Alvin Plantinga, _God, Freedom,
and Evil_, Harper, 1974.

8 S. Paul Schilling, _God and Human Anguish_,
Abingdon, 1977, p. 243.

9 L. Harold De Wolf, _A Theology of the Living
Church_, Harper, 1953, pp. 135-136 (italics added).

10 A.N. Whitehead, _Process and Reality_, Macmillan Co.,
1930, p. 525.

11 See my _Religion as Creative Insecurity_, 1958;
Greenwood, 1973, and "Creative Insecurity: A Style
of Being-Becoming," in _Humanitas_ 10, May 1974.

Chapter Fourteen

THE GOODNESS OF GOD AND THE CO-CREATIVE COMMUNITY

1. The Overriding Religious Concern

(a) Far from my intent is the view that religion is
essentially morality, or morality "tinged with
emotion." In the last chapter I submitted that religious experience, though unable to yield independent,
cognitive value, is no appendage to the values in the
life good to live. It inspires new levels of response
within the total personal experience of value, and
it confronts persons with tasks unique to religious
persons. For example, persons creative with God in
His world, among His children, experience unique
challenges in the attempt to "do justice, love mercy,
and walk humbly with thy God," and, consequently,
they are especially aware of their failure in humility, gratitude, compassion, and forgiveness. They
will grant that many unbelievers think, feel, and
live in a way that puts some believers to shame. Yet,
they strive to live up to their understanding of what
the world of persons can be once they can give cre-
dence to what, in the most general terms, I have
called their experience of the More. It remains for
me to bring together essentials of basic conclusions
reached,[1] and to make suggestions that will articulate
what is involved in the religious world-view here
presented.

(b) I begin by reaffirming that the quality of human
religious creativity represents the inner growing
edge of Person-to persons' interaction. It is in the
Creator-Person's universe that the believer conducts
his thought and expresses and adapts his affective-
conative tendencies in accordance with his limited
freedom to will at different stages of development
what he conceives to be the best. It might seem that
religious creativity always basks in the glory of
the signs of approval. But communion also knows its
'dark night'--with ingratitude, resentment, and despair.
The religious quality of life--never separated from

319

other dimensions--is no "yielding door" experience;
"doors of the spirit" do not open like electric-eye
doors. Earnest religious persons enter into the
fellowship of prayer and worship; they are aware
that the climb upward will depend not on auto-
matic escalation but on their willingness to face
new ills, perhaps, as they, in their "divinely inspired" visions, put one foot in front of the other
without looking back.

(c) Again, what I may call the religious person's
marriage to God--not a mere friendship be it "un-
calculating" or "calculating"--demands the total
refocusing of 'vocation.' Yet, it moves from day
to day in the trust-ful assurance that makes so
many details both more and less significant, but
never purposeless and boring. To repeat an earlier
figure, every nook and cranny of one's life must be
seen in divine perspective, each task carried out
with the right spirit. Of course, the "furniture
of life" is all "there," but the atmosphere of that
environment takes on the quality of hope and love
that goes with creative faith.

Such undertakings support and link much of the
"creativity of religious experience" with the insecurity that stems from an interchange with the More.
The assurance of victory is not the condition of
creativity. The commitment to creativity is not
the commitment to victory as the final test; it is
to co-creativity, be it in victory or defeat. This
is the implication of a view of God, man, and Nature
that makes the goodness, intrinsic to creativity, a
victory not dependent upon classically conceived
perfection.

Keeping in mind this quality of the life good
to live and of the goodness of God, we now can look
back on our reasoning as a whole and suggest several
other consequences coherent with meltoristic,
temporalistic, personalistic theism.

320

2. The Providence of God and Human Value-Realization

(a) Our pervasive theme has been that the patterns
of cardinal values persons build into their living
as relatively free persons belong not to them as
persons alone, nor to Nature alone, but also to the
Realm as Creator-Person-God. It is what we earlier
called the Eligibilities in God as Creator-Person,
undergirding the regularities and developments in
Nature as anthropically discerned, that give special
meaning to "the rain falls upon the just and the
unjust." For without the underlying, unlearned activity-potentials of persons, without Nature as
common ground for so much of persons' interaction
with each other, and without Nature's uniform,
omnipersonal laws, there would be no basis for that
sustaining guidance expressed in "as you sow, so shall
you reap." The free choice of persons is choice
within the limits of their given constitution and
within the constraints that their acquired personalities place upon their will-power. There would be
little to choose from without the variety of value-
experiences and without the increasing awareness of
both the range and the patterns of value eligible for
persons. To choose the greatest good steadily under
these conditions is to establish the foundations of
value-dependability amidst joy and sadness; it is
to choose the promise of further creativity--as
persons, both alone and in communion, center their
devotion on the God Who cares.

(b) Consequently, it is also plain that _much_ in the
orchestration of values within persons and their
communities _depends_ _on_ religious experience and the
interpretation of their God resulting therefrom.
The responsibility for the realization, organization, and the orchestration of values begins with
persons. For each person the good, insofar as he
can be responsible for it, is _his_ moral-ethical
good. But insofar as it is realized in and through
God's providence, it is also God's good, even though
a person can point to no one particular organization
of good as the sign of, or proof of, God's priorities.

The fact that God does not concur with any person's responsible choice does not mean that He withholds His cooperation insofar as it involves His commitment to the freedom-within-order in the realms pertinent to human choice. Part of God's "tragic" creativity consists in His working for the good at a level, not His specific choice, that is the consequence of persons' free use and abuse of each other and of natural resources. What intelligent, caring parent does not know what it means willingly to help his children, with all in one's power, consistent with other obligations, yet with sadness. For the predicaments that his children's actions have created often leave so much to be desired; they force such a gap between the parents' remedial creativity and what might have been accomplished under better conditions. Similarly, God's enlightened compassion perpetually confronts value-realization at a lower level than would have been possible had the persons involved chosen with greater appreciation for each other and of the fact that they and their fellows are in God's world.

(c) We are prone to make two mistakes in interpreting God's relation to individual persons, granted His creative care for them. The one is to assume that there is no other way but through general law that God can affect the person who needs and asks for the fellowship of forgiving help. The other is to suppose that God will suspend any psychic and physiological interconnections intrinsic to a person's nature or any learned formation that the person has allowed to become firmly established. Without claiming to know the ways and means by which God's grace in individual circumstances works its way, we may assume that God's very goodness would keep Him from nullifying the system of general providence by which we have learned to trust the regular sequences in the physical, physiological, and psychological realms. God's moral concern for the petitioner cannot extend to interfering with the system of law that undergirds the moral conditions for the growth of persons.

But all this must not be taken to mean that God is a prisoner of His own commitments to the system of general providence as we know it thus far. Outside the specifically religious realm we know that persons, without suspending moral commitments, can create a new "human" environment in which "impossible" value-realizations become possible. The Creator-Person is committed to persons and to laws insofar as they establish that trustworthy network which both He and persons require as common ground for basic community. But new creations are possible, we have reason to believe, without suspending laws. We have seen that much of the quality in the values that persons experience depends on mutual concern in affiliation and in creative, responsive-responsible risk. The religious life of prayer is the concern for responsive affiliation with God that, no doubt, has its own minimal requirements at the particular individual's level. But once these are met, renewal beyond all expectation is in order.

In short, through the ages the fundamental witness of religious experience in prayer and worship is that individual persons find themselves renewed to a degree that often exceeds even their own hopes. Such witness cannot be set aside as if we already knew God's ways with man or man's with God, or as the limits in an individual situation are fore-set. Whatever realms may be in God's making beyond our knowledge, the realms of personal fulfillment or of healing compensation in the patterns of value-orchestration—these are made possible in and through earnest and faithful communion which is still in the making.

3. Co-Creativity in the Religious Fellowship

(a) Our emphasis has allowed for the many facets of creativity issuing from the degree and quality of the compenetration of a person's religious vision in his unfinished symphony of values. Indeed, depth and

breadth in religious growth may be measured by the
nature of one's appreciation that he lives in God's
world along with all the other beings that express
God's creative concern. But in our exposition of
the pattern of cardinal values and of the constant
need for their orchestration in the learning and
maturing person, we did not overlook the relative
autonomy of the dimensions of value-experience.
The development of bodily health or intellectual
powers requires attention to their unique potentiality
in each person; aesthetic appreciation and artistic
creativity, while not fully expressing the contours
of the person's individuality, can here and there
contribute a rich accent. If autonomy is good, it
can sometimes stand in the way of a better. Because
God, like the air we breathe, is everywhere, it is
all too easy to take God's presence for granted and
to neglect the importance of specific attention to
the quality of our fellowship with God for its own
sake. For example, how easy it is to assume that if
one lives "a good life" there is no need for prayer
and worship, let alone one's participation in a church.
It is as though the successful routine of an even more
complicated housekeeping could make unnecessary the
more intimate fellowship of man and wife. Religion,
too, is a "marriage."

(b) If the accounts of our religious experts, the
mystics, teach us anything, they teach us that there
is a life of the religious spirit--"the flight of
the alone to the Alone," as Plotinus put it. Indeed,
so gripping, so fascinans, so tremendum (to use
Rudolf Otto's language), so fully satisfying may be
the steps and stages in finding and being found by
God that the temptation for many mystics is to dis-
count the importance of "the world" and "the goods
of the natural man." Readers of this book may well
wonder whether in my concern to evaluate the meaning
of conflicting reports about 'ecstatic union' with
God, in the light of moral freedom in particular, I
have done justice to the richness of the mystic witness. I mean to do full justice to the value of
the mystical experience and yet not underestimate
what William Ernest Hocking called the "principle

of alternation," of drawing close to God and also "returning" to our and His world.

(c) Hence, keeping before us the example of the mystics in and outside of every religious community, and without discounting what might be called the achievements of mystic discipline (since in unison they witness to the Realm afar and near, invisible but not inactive), I focus on the values of religious experience in value-contexts that will keep us from homogenizing it or the values with which it fuses. My concern in what follows is with a minimal interpretation of prayer and worship.

(d) In prayer, persons "tune in" on the God they worship. The meaning intended by this image is that God's response, related to the individual's sensitivity and preparedness, is _there_ for the asking, yet is still His. But the mechanical image must go no further. For the person's purpose essentially is the heightened awareness of himself in the 'presence' of _his_ Creator. In and through this heightened awareness, related to different dimensions, interests, and concerns in his own life as they relate to God's purposeful activity, there comes an enlivenment that is "empowering."

It is not only "the belief" that has an empowering effect, although this cannot be discounted as one step in the total experience. For, in his interaction with the God he worships, the person develops attitudes toward himself _in_ the situations that he brings to prayer--and these, of course, range from his cry for strength, to his grateful response, to his plea for insight. He may see himself in a way that would simply not have occurred had he not sought a 'closer' relation with God. A _religious co-creation_, as it were, takes place.

The ultimate _how_ of this interaction is no more within our comprehension than the how of _creatio_, or, for that matter, the _how_ of the growth of an acorn into an oak, or the _how_ of an artist so disciplining his vocal chords that the rest of us respond with trembling fascination. After any creative "leap,"

religious or otherwise, has taken place, we try to
trace what we can inspect and observe step by step.
Nevertheless, in the religious dimensions of creativity we have the right to consider the testimony
and "expositions" of those who have achieved more
than we have. Not for a moment, of course, especially at this stage in our argument, would I be
skeptical of religious witnesses whose integrity
I have no reasonable ground to doubt. Even so,
with no thought of describing _hows_, or of pre-
scribing limits to what is possible to the more
creative religious seers in our midst, I am concerned to keep the experts' witness relevant to
the drifts of creativity in every dimension of our
value-response without minimizing the variety of
the mystics' disciplines and visions. Accepting,
then, the actuality of religious interactions,
rooted in the caring fellowship between persons
and their Creator, and the sustaining power of religious experience for religious believers, some suggestions guiding the evaluation of claims made "in
the light of religious experience" may still be in
order.

(e) Responsive as the Creator is, He does not turn
a suppliant's will around mechanically, as it were,
any more than He provides messages that would be
meaningless to the experient. It is essential to
avoid "input" and "output" analogies for any relation between persons in which meaning and values are
involved. The person, responding in ways he and
others have found helpful, prepares his feelings,
wants, emotions, thoughts and actions so that God
can respond creatively to the praying-worshiping
person in a way not open to him morally if the person were not "ready" to receive in this situation.

It is difficult to avoid analyzing an "atmosphere" between persons into "if he does _this_, then
the response is _that_." But the following example may
be suggestive at least of what would still seem not
to violate the "intimacy" of religious searching
and response. As a teacher I find that some of my
students, having listened to what I have included

in my lecture to the class as a whole, find issues
that can surely stand further elaboration for their
unique situations. When such students, on their own,
come to my office and lay bare what concerns them,
they have already generated a unique, emotive-cog-
nitive atmosphere for the discussion that takes place.
They often leave both more encouraged and more enlightened because the inter-view seems to have become
more meaningful for them in a caring context. They
assign meanings to what goes on that, in fact, are
products of the co-creative situation we set up. This
"didactic" situation has overtones and undercurrents
on which we might base an analogy between listening
to a symphony on records as opposed to being caught
up in the different "climate" we are caught up in
when the conductor guides his orchestra in and before
an audience.

(f) God, then, is Creator and Co-creator, both in
His commitment to general providence and to individual inspiration under conditions that suit the
person with his particular problems of change and
growth. The growth in spiritual fellowship sought
for by individuals, in verbal and nonverbal symbols,
in rituals that express or celebrate a complex of
values-and-disvalues--this is the schooling, this
the creation of conditions in which God can be creative because concern must be responsive to the varied,
mutual appreciations established. Persons who "know"
this dimension of communion, who do not yield to the
temptation to isolate it from other values in life--
they, indeed, see themselves in His Presence in new
ways and are sustained in their hope.

Again, a parallel from our daily lives may be
helpful. Each of us responds to stormy weather, to
sunlit skies, twilight, and sunset with all we are
at the time. We respond with our affective-conative-
emotive, and with our conceptual and aesthetic awareness; and our moral and religious sensitivities are
not simply additions to these responses. We live in
the atmosphere we help to create within conditions we
discover, and within limits. Similarly, when we
respond to the More, "beginning" with our varied ways

of "drawing nigh unto Him," we do not necessarily
undergo experiences that draw us away "from the
daily routine," as such. We return rather to our
everyday perspectives and routines with a renewed
sense of their values in our lives, in terms of our
most comprehensive commitment.

To summarize this aspect of the co-creativity
of prayer-worship: the difference made by the human
experiences of prayer and worship--not to mention
mystical dimensions and progressions--nourishes and
"enlarges" persons' sense that the things that
matter most to them also matter to a Person whose
activities fertilize their roots, trunks, and branches.
At certain points their lives are pruned and ripened
by His general providence; in prayer and worship,
communally, they and their co-creators sustain each
other as they cooperate in growth and change. I have
already warned against picturing "the life of prayer"
in terms of spatial images of "input" and "outflow"
from communicating compartments. It is the dominant
experiential trend or drift at a given time in the
experient's "value-preparedness" that remains as the
matrix of fellowship--although this whole is always
in different stages of differentiation, of new living
and new dying.

(g) It goes almost without saying that in prayer a
particular, religious person may undergo moments of
deep 'absorption' into the More, another come away
morally inspired, another aesthetically enriched, and
so on, dependent on the regnant pattern of value-
disvalue "open-ness." There is no safe generalization
we can make. We cannot even affirm that one necessarily grows as a whole from some experience; nor can
we predict the experiences that will foster growth.
A man may experience himself as an "adopted child"
of Nature--even as a "step-child"--and still his
'encounter' may leave him 'regenerated' and 'reborn.'

Yet, generally speaking, that person who, in and
through prayer, becomes convinced that he is never
beyond God's care experiences a liberating gratitude
that keeps his own efforts, ideals, and failures in

better perspective. St. Paul's "hopeth all things" captures, I suggest, the spirit, if not the specific meaning, of transforming, prayerful dedication.

The undertone of this interpretation reflects the view of the transcendent Creator at the prayer-ful dimension of fellowship. Now the sustaining effort extends His general care to each suppliant; prayer becomes the occasion for God's creative response in ways, conscious and unconscious, relevant to the suppliant's preparation for change and growth. For, in this view, it is each person's life that is the crucible of creativity. The blessedness of creative insecurity remains integral to the religious honesty, courage, gratitude, meekness, humility, repentance, forgiveness, tolerance as the suppliant deepens his sense of what it means to be within the community of persons responsive to God above all. Neither growth nor "miracles" of achievement can be attributed to the goodness, power, and wisdom of God alone. He restrains an arbitrary favor out of moral respect for persons. Yet such restraint does not inhibit God's full response to the person who has met the conditions of growth.

4. The "Humility" of God's Love

In determining the nature of man's tie to a Creator-Person, I have placed power as power and all notions of sovereignty and majesty within the framework of a cosmic community of responsive-responsible Care. I do not minimize the power of God as Creator and Sustainer of all His creations, but I do make a value-judgment that is crucial to the moral-religious striving of persons. It is that power as power, be it in the Cosmos-Maker or in the tremendous energies at work in the firmament of galaxies, or in the sway that men can have over each other, and, at points, even over natural forces--all power as power is ethically neutral. Assuredly, power as power is not worthy of worship.

(a) If the argument of this book relies on any one value-judgment, it is simply this: our deepest admiration goes out to Power when He "humbles Himself" in love. Were the cosmic Power an architect rationally working His way in all the interconnections of being-becoming, or were the cosmic Power the indivisible One in whom all is united, there would be much to inspire our wonder and sense of dreadful sublimity. Were God the majestic, all-powerful Creator-King, He might well command unquestioning obedience, every kind of sacrifice, as proof of "loyalty." The history of religion, as well as the history of persons' relations to each other, is the story of mixtures of awe, dread, and different qualities of "serenity" of spirit.

Obedience to infinite, inscrutably wise divine Power, partly manifest and partly (perhaps, menacingly) hidden, has understandably controlled much human thinking and response. For persons, from early childhood aware that power can arbitrarily destroy, all too readily come to think that the human goal, to which even creative energies are geared, is the persistent search for power over whatever threatens danger. Creativity, consequently, is devoted to security. And this, I have submitted, may be the seductive goal, intrinsically impossible to attain. For security is always ready to settle for a minimum of what can be permanently assured. But creativity is always pushing off from the home base, like Dante's Ulysses, even to risk shipwreck in what turns out to be forbidden water. In the end, creativity passes through the Pillars of Hercules and makes a fortress of it. But this is to guarantee for the creative spirit an open sea for itself and for co-creators.

Am I minimizing the importance of power? Hardly! For to be without any power at all is to be nothing. And power, considered in the heavens ordaining the moon and the stars, can arouse the psalmist to a "What is man that thou art mindful of him?" But our admiration is shared between the divine power and the divine concern. Infinite space and infinite power terrify man, as Pascal knew, and he finds his God not in the wind and the storm but in the "still, small voice." In God's magnificent presence persons know

that they have grasped for lesser things, and many
have also seen the hubris of so many of their efforts
and demands. They have also come to worship the
beauty and sublimity of Holiness, and a new dimension
enters their lives that "holiness-of-beauty-and-
sublimity" may convey.

(b) Still, with all this, it is the power of His
patient Caring that ennobles and dignifies. Perhaps
God's deepest grip is on our gratitude, as we accept
the grace of shared creativity in being-becoming.
Our self-respect, our joy, are sobered by needless
suffering in which we have involved Him too. With
no self-pity we learn to mourn with those who mourn;
and being reviled, we are moved to suffer injustice
rather than do it. For our undergirding, if not always triumphant, faith in the Creator-Person stirs
our yearning to belong to that fellowship of loving
in which caring overcomes self-absorption and uproots
arrogance and self-righteousness.

It is this quality of Power, spread out in general providence and individualized in religious fellowship, that leaves so many persons accepting their
lot in the spirit of: "I put my life in His hands."
Their endurance of their crosses may not always
"save" them, but they do not feel betrayed as, with
Job, they cry: "Though He slay me, yet will I trust
Him." They cannot always feel that their crosses are
lighter, but their resignation is not in anger and
bitterness even in the face of unwelcome death. They
have a way of standing on their feet, especially
aware of the sorrow that cripples rather than handicaps, and yet still convinced that in their loyalty
they are not alone.

(c) Why is an elusive, yet unique, quality of gratitude, humility, courage, meekness, hope, trust, and
love so characteristic of the caring that is earnestly
religious? In our analysis they reflect our critical
awareness of value-possibilities realized and of the
possibilities in the future that are the promise of
the present. We keep on noting that values, expressing being-becoming persons, cannot stand still;

331

to conserve them is to increase their scope and
quality even as we outgrow some. Again, although
it sometimes seems so, we realize that this dynamics
of values is not of our own making alone, even as
we create, sustain, and sort out the values we cherish.
The world of persons is bitter chaos without compas-
sion--this we know. It is this world that expresses
the telic cosmos--"a vale of soul-making" of the
Creator-Person. Co-creation in a love that reaches
forgiveness and knows no indifference to suffering--
this is the norm of the moral-religious realm that
was so directly put in the prophetic plea: "...do
justice, love mercy, and walk humbly with thy God."
Our God is Himself humble as He fully accepts the
meanings of His creative being in moving as far as
possible beyond justice to loving mercy.

5.   The God Who Cares; The Persons Who Care
     Religiously

(a) "God loves us! God cares for us! God saves us!
The God to whom we belong!" In these exclamations
we draw near to the center of religious prayer, worship, and symbol. In these pages I have developed
the outlines of a teleological theistic personalism
that is consonant at least with the prophetic trend
in moral-religious outreach. The goal, the telos,
is not union with God as identity. It is a growing
awareness of another form of union that occurs as
persons discover the relation of their co-creativity
with the Creator-Person who cares. Their "union"
is with the God Who has aimed through the ages, Who
in every now dedicates His power in ways creative
beyond our most enlightened insight. Ours is the
goal of a "fellowship of love" that can be destroyed only by indifference.

     In this union there is no place for hybris or
for homogenization of differences among persons, or
among persons and their Creator. This union expresses
sensitive responsibility for respect of persons, without using "respect for persons" as an excuse for

failure to do what concretely needs to be done by responsible persons. Compassion must not give way to sentimentality, but reroot itself in what is and can become. Co-creation, faltering when the crowded and careless ways of life allow "love" to be used for self-advantage, will call for suffering <u>with</u>, and suffering <u>for</u>; it comes into its own when persons share strength and weaknesses for mutual renewal.

(b) We are not simply seeking a pathetic "something in common with God," but neither do we find it proclaimed in fact, logic, or reasonableness that the nature of God's beatific satisfaction is impervious to even the <u>minutiae</u> of unnecessary disorder, evil, and suffering in all that depends on His care. Surely, the Creator of co-creating purposers lives as creative persons must live--in a hopeful meliorism. Mutual weakness and suffering often do unite spirits. As persons in this cosmos we know much is still in the making, with all its risks.

Yet we may now propose more reasonably that the best in any situation cannot come into being unless persons join the God Who cares and accepts, as needs be, the full meaning of His co-creative caring and sustaining. For there are conflicts at every level of creativity. We come to know that creative orchestration reaches beyond mere harmony. Still, to yearn for the God of our salvation is to yield ourselves in trust; and in so doing often to find unknown resources. As caring persons, within the fellowship of love, we bear more--or less--of the burden; but supreme is our unflinching duty to be loyal to the foreseeable, promising, but not assured, growing fellowship of love.

(c) When we, as persons, see ourselves as His in this perspective, when we see each other never as belonging to each other alone, never as possessors of each other in any dimension, when, indeed, we do not use God but cooperate with Him as insightfully as we can, we are, ourselves, at the growing edge of God's will for each of us. For in His spirit we have joined in co-creating the community of responsive-responsible persons.

Such a religious community reaches valiantly through the ages, daring to reach beyond "this" world, "this stage" of human growth, toward some richer revision and renewal of life despite the often heartrending break with the cherished familiar. Spiritual heroes of every day and historical, spiritual prophets have died convinced that in living with the Unseen for the unseen they could die but pass on the inner flame. Such persons are willing to die, as they have lived, for the new order that may be only a candlelight in them, but a cleansing fire in the Realm.

(d) An emphasis that highlights this relation of God to men draws on a different conception of goodness and perfection than the one that captured Aristotle's imagination. Characterizing the great-souled man, Aristotle[2] says that he "is fond of conferring benefits but ashamed to receive them, because the former is a mark of superiority and the latter of inferiority. He returns a service done to him with interest, since this will put the original benefactor into his debt in turn, and make him the party benefited." At the same time, the great-souled man will face danger, even risk his life, "in a great cause," for he "holds that life is not worth having at every price." And here, I suspect, the cost is to the self-esteem of the great-souled man.

The dominant, theistic tradition, as I see it, never succeeded in making up its mind on what was to be the "mark of superiority" for the magnanimity of its God. Thus, in dominant forms of Judeo-Christian theism, God remains as the cosmic Great-souled Being. To be sure, the "great cause" to which the Creator would give His own creativity need not be the self-protective 'mark of superiority.' Yet, despite the emphasis on the historic necessity for the 'suffering servant,' or on the God that "so loved the world that He gave His only begotten Son," there persists as the mark of God's superiority His independence of all possible benefactors! Such Christians, like the Greeks in Athens at St. Paul's preaching, will not allow their God to be contaminated by an act consigned to "the Son."

334

Discontent--theoretical, moral, religious--with this view of the great-souled person as the model for God is the background of this book. In opposition to this aspect of the Graeco-Judeo-Christian conception of perfection, and taking courage from the conception of a self-sacrificing, yet self-active, perfection, I have found the 'mark of superiority' in a creativity that cannot be benefited by full independence. Indeed, I remind myself that while Aristotle knew of justice and friendship, while Plato knew of the overflowing Good expressive of Its infinite richness, neither knew of forgiving love that seeks to redeem the sinful. And I would argue that the redemptive side of Judeo-Christian thought cannot root salvation in the wiping away of sins any more than the Buddhist ideal can defend salvation as liberation from self-as-desires. Salvation, liberation, for great-souls, comes by making the great cause the renewal of human creativity by what I have called even a "tragic" creativity. Such self-giving does not fear to "lose face" from acceptance of unmerited, inglorious suffering. Again, the power of the good Creator-Person is saved only as the great cause is one in which all persons dedicate themselves to the best compossible community of responsive-responsible co-creators at every stage in history.

(e) The haunting question persists: Is such creativity really worth the price? We can direct the question to the Creator, since an Impediment lies deeper than the myopia of persons and even of their cruelty to their fellow-persons. Acknowledging mystery that is inevitably the background for any human questioning, I have tried to be theoretically responsible in suggesting a style of life that persons do experience as they live in and through the ranges of feeling and desire, as they face imperatives and pursue invincible surmises and hopes. Their way ends not in denial of an evil more radical than the classical theists will consent to; it sets evil in the perspective of creative insecurity--that paradoxical fusion of purpose, joy, and travail that many a person has known. Yet, even so, I repeat the question: If the Creator could do no better in providing a vale of soul-making, ought He to have tried?

335

My own answer has been given. It could not be
affirmative apart from the realization that evil has
no independent power. It could not be affirmative
without a verdict about the disproportionate, unmerited anguish and suffering that, seeing no good
in such evil, yet accepts it as the unwanted product
of a unique creativity in any creator-person. Creativity is always a victory, but it necessarily involves a cost often beyond our imagining. But when
the qualitative options are probed, when the actualities are balanced, I cannot but glory in a God Who,
caring for more than variety of sheer survival,
creates persons. The creation of persons is, indeed,
a test of creative caring. For with God-given intelligence and freedom, persons can, with deliberate
cunning and brutality, inflict so much agony on each
other, so much unnecessary pain on animals, and yet
continue in perpetual search for creativity in their
horizons of value and ideals.

(f) Sometimes I wish I could remain neutral, make
no judgment one way or another. I cannot, for the
vision persists: a Creator Who cares so much about
making value-possibilities and co-creators as comprehensively compatible as possible, a Creator whose
joy finds place for the sorrow that is part of the
near-tragedy inherent in His creativity. To suggest
that part of a creative person's sorrow is allied to
the "tragic" goodness of God is to say that sorrow
is part and parcel of the value of creativity that
must accept the risks of its very nature. But this
sorrow and disappointment, this suffering has
meaning in a symphony that, in remaining unfinished,
also retains novel, moral-artistic-religious orchestration.

In this melioristic personalistic perspective,
then, the religious venture is to know what it means
to live in community, and with a joy in creativity
that does not minimize the cost, that never resigns
itself to that cost. Since co-creation is never
between "equal" co-creators, the community of co-
creation, the orchestration of mutually enhancing
values in community, is the lure and task of every

336

creative factor in the Creator-Person's world. No greater love, then, have persons than this--a kind of caring that is never merely "happy" but always blessed. It is the blessed love that is made perfect in the creativity of the forgiving community. Such love alone is capable of a less than propri-etary vision of the realm of Nature, one in which persons realize that Nature is not only God's standard work of providence for human beings, but is also the habitat to be shared with Him and, as appreciatively and mercifully as possible, with the myriad forms of living creatures. In this vision of excellence, the goodness of God means: Thy creativity is our blessedness. Thy world is ours, to make it more fully Thine.

Notes

1 Since this chapter is a reflective overview of the basic interpretation of God, goodness, and re-ligious experience inherent in preceding chapters, earlier references will be pertinent, but this is an appropriate place to acknowledge other relevant writings: Austin Farrer, Love Almighty and It's Unlimited: An Essay on Providence and Evil, Doubleday, 1961; John B. Cobb, Jr., A Christian Natural Theology (Based on the Thought of Alfred North Whitehead), Westminster Press, 1965; The Structure of Christian Experience, Westminster Press, 1967; Anthony Flew, The Presumption of Theism and Other Essays, Barnes and Noble, 1976; Errol E. Harris, Atheism and Theism, Tulane University Press, 1977; Richard Swinburne, The Coherence of Theism, Clarendon Press, 1977; Lewis Ford, The Lure of God, Fortress Press, 1978.

2 Aristotle, Nicomachean Ethics, trans. H. Rackham, Book IV, iii, 23, 24, Harvard University Press, Loeb Classical Library, 1911.

SELECTED BIBLIOGRAPHY

This bibliography, all too restrictively, lists
works by which this book as a whole is influenced
and which also provide more complete, and contrasting,
treatment of the themes presented. When any of these
books is referred to in the text it will be denoted
by author and capital letters standing for that title
(for example, Brightman, PAR). References at the end
of each chapter, supplementing these, will include
only the author, title, and date; permission to quote
will be duly noted.

Allport, Gordon W. Becoming. Yale Univ. Press, 1955.
                   (BEC)
                   Pattern and Growth in Personality.
                   Holt, Rinehart, and Winston, 1961.
                   (PGP)
Bertocci, Peter A. The Empirical Argument for God in
                   Late British Thought. Harvard Univ.
                   Press, 1938; Kraus, 1970. (EAG)
                   Religion as Creative Insecurity.
                   1958. Greenwood, 1973. (RCI)
                   The Person God Is. Allen and Unwin,
                   1970. (PGI)
Bertocci, Peter A. and Millard, Richard M. Personality
                   and the Good. McKay, 1963. (PAG)
Blanshard, Brand   The Nature of Thought. 2 vols.
                   Allen and Unwin, 1939. (NOT)
                   Reason and Goodness. Allen and
                   Unwin, 1961. (RAG)
                   Reason and Belief. Allen and Unwin,
                   1974; Yale Univ. Press, 1974. (RAB)
Brightman, Edgar S. Moral Laws. 1933. Kraus, 1978. (ML)
                   A Philosophy of Religion. 1940.
                   Greenwood, 1969. (POR)
                   Person and Reality. Edited by
                   Peter A. Bertocci et al. Ronald
                   Press, 1958. (PAR)
Burtt, Edwin A.   Man Seeks the Divine (A study in
                   the History and Comparison of
                   Religions). Harper and Row, 1957.
                   (MSD)
                   In Search of Philosophic Under-
                   standing. 1956. Hackett, 1980.(SPU)

339

Ferré, Frederick   <u>Basic Modern Philosophy of Religion</u>.
C. Scribner's Sons, 1967. (BMPR)

Hartshorne, Charles <u>The Divine Relativity</u>. Yale Univ.
Press, 1948. (TDR)
<u>The Logic of Perfection</u>. Open
Court, 1962. (LOP)

Hick, John   <u>Faith and Knowledge</u>. Cornell Univ.
Press, 1957. (FAK)
<u>The Existence of God</u>. The Macmillan
Co., 1964. (EOG)
<u>Evil and the God of Love</u>. Harper
and Row, 1966. (EGL)

Hocking, William E. <u>The Meaning of God in Human Ex-
perience</u>. Yale Univ. Press, 1912.(MGH)
See also Leroy S. Rouner, <u>Within
Human Experience</u> (The Philosophy of
William Ernest Hocking). Harvard
Univ. Press, 1969.

Howie, John, and Buford, Thomas, eds. <u>Studies in
Contemporary Idealism</u>. Cape Cod:
Claude Alan Stark, 1973. (CSCI)

James, William   <u>The Varieties of Religious Experi-
ence</u>. (A Study in Human Nature).
1902. Doubleday, 1978. (VRE)
<u>The Will to Believe (and Other
Essays)</u>. Longmans, Green & Co., 1931.
(WTB)

Lewis, Clarence I. <u>Mind and the World-Order</u>. Scribner's
Sons, 1929. (MWO)

Lewis, H. D.   <u>Our Experience of God</u>. Allen and
Unwin, 1959. (OEG)
<u>The Elusive Mind</u>. Allen and Unwin,
1969. (TEM)
<u>The Self and Immortality</u>. Seabury
Press, 1973. (SAI)

Lovejoy, Arthur   <u>The Revolt Against Dualism</u>. Open
Court, 1960. (RAD)

Mitchell, Basil   <u>The Justification of Religious
Belief</u>. Seabury Press, 1973. (JRB)

Moore, John M.   <u>Theories of Religious Experience
(with Special Reference to James,
Otto, and Bergson)</u>. Round Table
Press, 1938. (TRE)

Otto, Rudolf   The Idea of the Holy. Translated
                      by John W. Harvey. Oxford Univ.
                      Press, 1958. (IOH)
Ross, James F.   Philosophical Theology. Bobbs-
                      Merrill Co., 1969. (PT)
Smith, John E.   Reason and God. Yale Univ. Press,
                      1961. (RG)
                      The Analogy of Experience: An Ap-
                      proach to Understanding Religious
                      Truth. Harper and Row, 1973. (AOE)
Stace, W. T.   Mysticism and Philosophy. Lippin-
                      cott Co., 1960. (MAP)
Tennant, Frederick R. Philosophical Theology. 2 vols.
                      Cambridge Univ. Press, 1969. (PT)
                      The Philosophy of the Sciences.
                      Cambridge Univ. Press; Greenwood,
                      1973. (POS)
Tillich, Paul   Dynamics of Faith. Harper, 1957.
                      (DOF)
                      Systemic Theology. 3 vols. Univ. of
                      Chicago Press, 1959-1963. (ST)
Werkmeister, W. H.   The Basis and Structure of Knowl-
                      edge. 1948. Greenwood, 1969. (BSK)
                      Man and His Values. Univ. of
                      Nebraska Press, 1967. (MHV)
Weiss, Paul W.   Nature and Man. 1947. So. Illinois
                      Univ. Press, 1965. (NAM)
                      The God We Seek. So. Illinois Univ.
                      Press, 1964. (GWS)